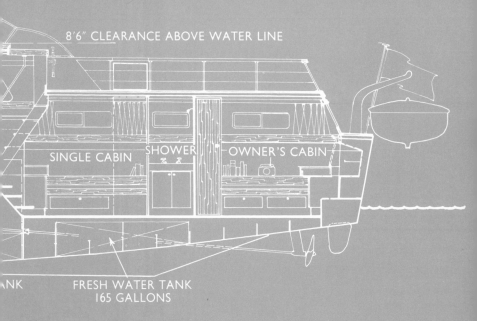

8'6" CLEARANCE ABOVE WATER LINE

SINGLE CABIN   SHOWER   OWNER'S CABIN

ANK   FRESH WATER TANK
165 GALLONS

SMALL BOAT TO ELSINORE

Some other books by Roger Pilkington

SMALL BOAT THROUGH BELGIUM
SMALL BOAT THROUGH HOLLAND
SMALL BOAT TO THE SKAGERRAK
SMALL BOAT THROUGH SWEDEN
SMALL BOAT TO ALSACE
SMALL BOAT TO BAVARIA
SMALL BOAT THROUGH GERMANY
SMALL BOAT THROUGH FRANCE
SMALL BOAT IN SOUTHERN FRANCE
SMALL BOAT ON THE MEUSE
SMALL BOAT ON THE THAMES
SMALL BOAT TO LUXEMBOURG
SMALL BOAT ON THE MOSELLE
WORLD WITHOUT END
HEAVEN'S ALIVE

For Younger Readers

Adventures in Boats
THE MISSING PANEL
THE DAHLIA'S CARGO
DON JOHN'S DUCATS
NEPOMUK OF THE RIVER
THE EISENBART MYSTERY
THE BOY FROM STINK ALLEY

Non-fiction
THE GREAT SOUTH SEA

SMALL BOAT
TO
ELSINORE

BY

ROGER PILKINGTON

Illustrated by David Knight

MACMILLAN
London . Melbourne . Toronto
ST MARTIN'S PRESS
New York
1 9 6 9

Published by
MACMILLAN AND CO LTD
Little Essex Street London WC2
and also at Bombay Calcutta and Madras
Macmillan South Africa (Publishers) Pty Ltd Johannesburg
The Macmillan Company of Australia Pty Ltd Melbourne
The Macmillan Company of Canada Ltd Toronto
St Martin's Press Inc New York

Library of Congress catalog card no. 69–14542

Printed in Great Britain by
ROBERT MACLEHOSE AND CO LTD
The University Press, Glasgow

*For Miriam, after her first
thirty years as mate*

MAPS

'Bad weather now and then makes the pleasant days all the more
enjoyable; besides, yachting would be no more exciting than a voyage
on a Thames penny steamer if the weather was always fine.'

E. F. KNIGHT: *The 'Falcon' on the Baltic* (1889)

FOREWORD

A FOREWORD is an introduction, and the character I wish to introduce is the *Thames Commodore*, 45 feet in length and just over 13 across the hips. She and her elder sister (now married off in middle age to a Frenchman) are already well known to many, and this is the fourteenth time that I have had to introduce one or the other with a few words so that those who stow away for the voyage, tucked safely in her bilge compartments, may know what sort of a ship it is whose pulse throbs through the steelwork at about 1600 a minute. For some it will be enough to say that she is just the same as she was when in Luxembourg or on the Moselle, except that two chests have been added on the deck to serve as seats and to store the hosepipes on the port side and the meat and fruit to starboard. Others will need to know that she is an efficient little ship of 23 tons register, comfortable and reliable and sufficiently inquisitive to have forced her bulk through London's Zoo and (in this present book) through the Hadelner Canal of northern Germany.

I could write passages about the *Thames Commodore*'s anatomy, her water-circulating system and plumbing, her forepeak and transom, bilge and beam, and the delicious smell of hot oil which one can scent by lifting a trap in the floor of her saloon, but for those who are not canal cranks or boating fanatics these details would be merely tedious. On the other hand there will be those who are anxious to know about her construction, and for them I have provided the handsome sketches which form the end-papers fore and aft, drawn by John Silvester Horne, who was the first apart from my wife and myself to step aboard and voyage with her in foreign waterways.

Aboard this ship we are soon to sail away for the Baltic, for the strange waters of the Little Belt and the Øresund, and to that Elsinore which Shakespeare placed on the map when he chose it for the setting of his tragedy of the Danish prince. On the way we shall dock in such obscure places as Dyvig and Onsevig, and try to do so in Norsminde. Indeed we shall not hurry over the journey, for this is to be the *Thames Commodore*'s first tour of the northern countries.

In the days of the Grand Tour it was fashionable to begin the journal of travels at London, or at least in Ramsgate harbour. The packet lay at her jetty, the captain stroked his beard, the steam-whistle sounded, and to a threshing of paddle-wheels the reader was swept away to the English Channel and the adventures which lay beyond. Soon the machinery was groaning, the beams and bulkheads creaking and shrieking, the wind howling and striking mercilessly at the vessel with the force of a battery of mighty sledge-hammers. That at least is how a certain Mr Hurton described it, adding that the only sensation he experienced was a decidedly pleasurable one – until he was awakened by a tremendous crash as a wave came in through the open porthole. Drying himself in the galley he pondered the mystery that there was on board 'something which rose superior to the grandeur and power of the elemental strife, the glorious Intellect of Man'.

Mr Stanfield was another who found the discomfort of the voyage stimulating. The very jolting of a journey opened his imagination, he wrote, and set the moral faculties craving as well as those of the body. Mr Michael Quin delighted in the departure from Tower Pier, followed so swiftly by a grounding in the endeavour to avoid running down some small craft which got in the way. But by reversing the paddles the *Phoenix* was drawn off the sandbank and soon she was moving at a brilliant pace past Greenwich Hospital and Gravesend and on toward the North Foreland and Ramsgate.

Mrs Trollope was naturally a very critical seafarer. She found her ship dirty, the food both bad and insufficient. Had any accident detained the *Liverpool*, even for a few hours, she wrote, the passengers must have suffered very seriously from want of provisions. Yet like the others she began her tale at home, and with a direct 'I left London for Ostend on the 1st of June' she was off to adventure.

Mrs Trollope searched for food and cleanliness. Mr Quin remained fascinated by the power of steam. Mr Stanfield found his imagination opened, Mr Hurton his philosophical musings stimulated. And all by the voyage itself, from the moment it began. It is easy to deride the nineteenth-century diary travellers, yet I am sure that they were right in following their instinct and beginning the tale on the dockside, for at that long-awaited moment when the paddles began to churn the silty water of an English port the exotic began. Ahead lay the Channel, and beyond it the extraordinary realms of foreigners, as different from the safe and familiar scenery of England as the lands of Kubla Khan.

Though modern inventions have made of one flesh all the nations of Europe and have reduced the travel time between London and Paris to such a short span that the air hostesses have no time even to hand out a sandwich, the magic of a voyage into the unknown still persists for anyone who sets out on a reasonably small ship, not at several hundred miles an hour but at knots counted in single figures, at a gentle pace which gives time for reflection and day-dream, and the chance to see the world of land and water slip by in slow undulation, each impression merging into the next – just as it did for the Grand Tourers.

Besides, afloat one ploughs a bow-wave through history, and through nature, too. I remember the enchantment of anchoring one night off the dismal Isle of Grain to wait for the tide and the dawn, and finding that the water surging into the lavatory basin through the Blake pump tingled and flashed with an unearthly green as the tiny micro-organisms of the summer sea were stirred into activity. Or, during the voyage described in this volume of the *Thames Commodore*'s travels, the sudden realisation that those delicate birds which stood in groups along the canal bank at Emden to turn up their noses at her passing were avocets, creatures few travellers by other means would ever see.

So this voyage begins in London, in the heart of Cockney Stepney where live some of the kindliest people on earth. We shall reach the Baltic all in good time, but aboard the *Thames Commodore* one cannot be in a hurry. Along the route there will be much to be seen, and smelled, and heard. And learned too, for neither the *Thames Commodore* nor her elder sister ever returned from a summer's voyage without having discovered something new in the behaviour of river or canal or sea.

Highgate, 1969   ROGER PILKINGTON

Regent's Canal Dock

I

By night to Ramsgate – canals of the French fens – Furnes
and Nieuport – Flushing – de Ruyter and Pepys – an admiral
in pickle – the song of the broom

'THE ship had on board it a jolly brave captain, master, gunner and his mate, boatswain, and pilot, besides the ship's crew, continually toping, bousing and carousing, who for joy of coming to England, having the pot or quarter-can continually at their noses, get merry with drinking their majesties and his lordship's health, discharging a cannon at every round, the boatswain giving the signal with his whistle. Three great huzzas are given, and the health is renewed with cannon, as before, and a bowl of punch.'

The vessel was the *Perseus and Andromeda,* inward bound from

the Levant, and she sailed the streets of London in 1689. The
streets, not the river, because she was in fact a tableau in the Lord
Mayor's show of Sir Thomas Pilkington. She was 'laden with
spices, silks, furs, sables, panthers and all manner of beasts' skins
hanging in the shrouds and rigging', and the people cheered as she
sailed bumping along Cheapside.

Compared with this scene of bousing and carousing the departure
of the *Thames Commodore* from London is quiet indeed. She has
aboard her myself as the jolly brave captain and my wife as mate,
boatswain and crew combined, and so one evening late in March
she takes her place in the exit lock of the Regent's Canal Dock
along with an empty lighter and a Dutch ship from Groningen
which is to move out into the Thames stern first. Ten minutes
to ten and the bell rings as the road bridge is swung aside. The
gates open, the Dutchman's stern shoves swiftly into the stream,
and the *Thames Commodore* follows. The coaster has the legs on
her by perhaps one knot, and by half past midnight her stern light
is out of sight in the wideness of the estuary.

By day the run from Limehouse to Ramsgate is scenically dull.
There are marshes, pylons and chimneys, and the jetties of
Beckton gasworks, Ford Motors, and the sewage outfalls. Briefly
the *Cutty Sark* and the hulk of H.M.S. *Worcester* add their
moments of romance, but otherwise there is little to see and much
to be smelt. Yet the same journey at night is a voyage of incredible
beauty. The most sordid unloading pier is ablaze with lights which
set aglow the smoke and steam of the ships like so many pillars of
fire by night. At Shell Haven the twisting pipes and tubes of the
refinery are lit like some gigantic Christmas tree, and the rippled
water to the shore is a pathway of quaking silver. One by one the
pairs of masthead lights soar higher above the red and green of the
port and starboard lamps as each upcoming ship bears towards us,
hidden in mystery. Is she a mere muck-boat, a German coaster, or
maybe a flat-iron collier? Or will it be a great liner, inward bound
for Tilbury? A tank-lighter such as the *Bold Knight* and *Black
Knight*, or a fruit-carrier of ten or fifteen thousand tons? Always
the oncoming ship is no more than a dim shadow tipped with lights
until she is running past us to leave smooth undulations over which

the *Thames Commodore* can gently surge as she keeps on her way. Then, and only then, can we see her profile against the slight pallor of the moonlit sky.

And all the way other lights are winking, the friendly buoys which edge the channel for the big ships, or mark the sands. Tilbury and Ovens, then a hammer strikes solemnly upon a bell like that of some cathedral sunk in the waves, echoing down the nave where ghostly monks summon to a requiem. The Sea Reach buoys blink in mid-channel, then comes the sparkle of Southend, still aglow long after midnight, and the constellations of flashers in the Edinburgh and Prince's channels. Close to a red flashing buoy we can see the silhouette of the thin legs which support a one-time gun-platform, and up in the air a light glows in the window of the hut where an unsleeping announcer works through his pile of records for a 'pirate' radio, still broadcasting in defiance of impotent governmental ragings. And at last to starboard the great red glow of the North Foreland, like a weird planet in some other universe. We are six hours out of Limehouse now, and I know we can turn down a little, clearing the banks to cut round towards the Downs.

Off Ramsgate the very faintest touch of dawn pales the horizon beyond the hidden Goodwin Sands. We put in between the moles to drop a friend on the ladder, and a voice hails us from the control tower. A sleepy official comes round the harbour on his cycle to collect the dues and he tries long and hard to copy the name of the boat on the receipt. He cannot spell the word fifteen, either. He is a simple soul and pleasant enough, but no great advertisement for free education.

A quick pot of tea and we are away again, out into that curious and capricious strait between England and France which has always been calm yesterday but is more likely to be tossed into foam-flecked heaps today. I have known the Channel as calm as a pond, but on this early morning in March it has decided to show what the equinox can do. Everything we have so tidily stowed in our galley is turned over and the floor is sticky with a paste of water, flour, coffee and macaroni before that glorious moment when the very last of the waves tips up the *Thames Commodore*'s

stern and she glides past the red light-tower on the tall-legged jetty
into water so calm that it seems as though the world has stopped.
A Frenchman is winding up his drop-net, and as it breaks surface
we can see some silvery little fish tossing and flapping in the
bottom. Somewhere ahead and to the left a locomotive gives a
steamy *foupe* to warn that it is about to steam away for Amiens and
the Paris line. This is France, and we need have no more rough
water for weeks to come.

When we left Limehouse I had intended if possible to make
Flushing in a single day's run, reckoning that we should be there
in time for dinner at the Old Bourse. Had we sailed one day earlier
we should have had a calm and easy voyage to that pleasant port,
but now the weather had suddenly worsened. By mid-Channel I
had decided that another hour of tossing was enough, and I shaped
up for Calais instead – for along the continental coast one may
enter the canal network at any port from Calais northwards.

We had run through to Holland by these waterways before. They are not spectacular, but even where the odour of pig manure is dominant they are much more pleasant than the outside route if the sea is tossing and turning. Besides, there is a strange restfulness about the French fens, where one may count a dozen great horses at one time, all plodding across the fields to turn damp and shining furrows of glistening black. There are few barges and fewer hamlets, and the clouds sail over a wide sky and a landscape broken only by a distant row of trees where a country road or a draining lode cuts across the country.

Two hours beyond Calais we hove to, so that I could lower the bucket and trap the nice new ball of a little boy who was crying disconsolate on the canal bank. Through the pretty lock of Hénuin we turned left for a few miles of the stately avenue of the river Aa, then right again to enter the Canal de Bourbourg through a stop-lock which could be closed when the river was in flood. A fine fat Union Normand tanker barge, shining in its coat of orange and blue and silver, sat squarely in the opening, its broad stern effectively barring our way. The skipper had been sure that no other craft was coming that way and he had conveniently hove to between the lock gates and had set off across the fields to a farm where he could buy a chicken for the evening meal. He had not reckoned with the arrival of a ship from London.

His wife explained that she could not move the barge, and she began instead to blow loud and long on the ship's powerful hooter. Yet if the skipper heard the sound at all he probably thought the children were amusing themselves with the hooter, and as the *Thames Commodore* happened to be hidden by the bridge he sat undisturbed with his farmer friend over a glass of wine.

Ah, said Madame, it was annoying, was it not, that we should be so obstructed. But I said no, we had all the time in the world, and if we had happened to want poultry for supper we would have surely gone to the farm ourselves. She should not distress herself. Eventually her husband would return, eggs and chicken and all.

At length somebody at the farm must have noticed the unusual sight of the aged and lame lock-keeper, his wife, the entire barge family and ourselves all standing on the bridge waving their arms, and told the skipper that he must be needed back aboard his ship,

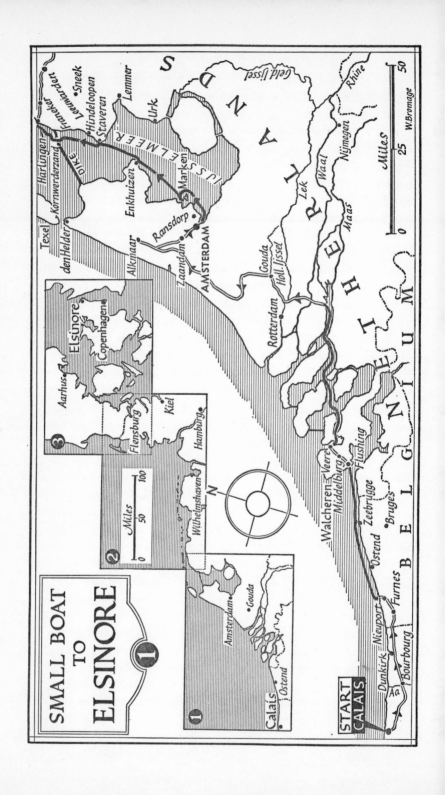

SMALL BOAT
TO
ELSINORE

W. Bromage

NETHERLANDS

BELGIUM

for at last we saw a figure in a dark blue jersey and nautical cap hurrying across the furrows of the dark peaty earth. He had a chicken, stuffed and dressed, and a slab of fine salty butter and some eggs as brown as teak – enough for a feast in honour of the birthday of the elder little girl, he explained.

By Bourbourg and Dunkirk the route led us to the familiar jetty by the Pont de Ghyvelde, where the Canal de Furnes leaves French territory and the customs men pause from checking the Whitbread bowsers and the cars of tourists from Britain to think what it is that they are supposed to do when a yacht arrives. In fact it is only a matter of a rubber stamp, a *bon voyage, monsieur et madame*, and a quick surreptitious glass of rum if the superior is not watching. Then Belgium, and across the fields over which the peewits twist and turn in the sheer joy of springtime sunshine the canal leads directly into Furnes.

Furnes is one of the most beautiful little towns of all Flanders, and always it seems to me to have a strangely brooding spirit. Perhaps it is because we have each time passed through the place at Eastertide, when in St Walburga's the statues are covered and cloaked in shrouds of ecclesiastical purple as though the world has died and patiently awaits the resurrection. As on earlier occasions the stark white crosses were standing at street corners with their Flemish legend 'Remember, O Man'. The roadways were silent. Rooks called to their fellows in the trees by the school, and the abbey ruins lay peaceful, undisturbed by any but the sparrows checking that nothing edible lay unregarded along the pathways.

The morning was fine and clear as we resumed our journey to Nieuport, a few miles along the cut. The crossing of its tidal roundabout of canals can only be done at half tide or more, but there is time enough for the boatman to leave the canal, turn down by the fishmarket and run the two or three miles down to the sea jetties and there have a look at the state of affairs in the Channel. If conditions are bad he can still turn back in time to catch the other lock on the farther side of the basin before the tide has fallen too far for the gates to be opened. As the previous day had been calm and sunny we thought there might be a chance of running up the coast instead of taking the canals inside, and the fact that a bank holiday was approaching made us realise that by following the canal route we were sure to be immobilised for at least a day, probably at some particularly featureless farming hamlet or perhaps in the dock area of the Bruges Ship Canal, or the extremely pungent waterway outside Bruges itself. To reach Flushing by the cuts would in any case take two and a half days, and the public holiday could conceivably spin it out to four, but the outside journey was a comparatively short one. In fact the sea proved so pleasantly calm that we had only to turn right, run past the fashionable resort coast of Belgium, glance at the fishermen on the jetties of Ostend and Zeebrugge, and the mouth of the Scheldt opened out before us. Flushing with its belfry sparkled nobly in the sun, and a little under three hours out of Nieuport the *Thames Commodore* blew a long blast and clipped reasonably close round the bullnose of Flushing's busy harbour.

Fishermen are the same the world over. The mere act of winding in a great length of line and then flinging it out again seems somehow to deaden the senses and make reactions slow. On the Meuse, Moselle and Lahn the *Thames Commodore* had already collected fishing lines flung across her path but it still surprised her when a holiday fisherman standing on the very tip of the harbour jetty at Flushing swung back his rod, and then with all the muscle in his two arms cast a leaden imitation fish straight across her path and only eight or ten feet ahead of her. The line had not even time to fall on the water before she took it on her stem and drew it tight.

The fisherman, like others before him, found it difficult to hold on the hook a steel ship with a deadweight of more than twenty tons and moving at a speed of eight knots. He shouted, as others had shouted, and we could hear the whine of the ratchet as his line ran out. After a while he decided to apply the brake, and bracing his feet against the rail he leaned back against the lighthouse, holding tightly the grip of his rod. It was a strong line and a stout rod, and I wondered which would break first, or whether perhaps the strength of the nylon was such that we should get ready an automatic lifebuoy to throw to the man when we had pulled him right off the jetty into the entrance. But at the last moment another and wiser angler intervened, and pulling the man's rod down behind the rail he held the line tight over the edge of the jetty. It broke, as he intended it to, and as we made up for the lock the fisherman was ruefully reeling such little of his line as remained to him.

Flushing was preparing for Easter, and there was a holiday mood in the air. The Breskens ferry was crowded with visitors, and even the customs officials seemed to be extra smart in their uniforms of black and blue. There were several small yachts tacking on the broad water of the Walcheren Canal, and they waved us a cheerful welcome. As always, they were proudly conscious of belonging to a club, an organisation which had its own yacht harbour with clubhouse and water and bar and baths laid on. We did not intend to make for this basin, for although such a place may be pleasant and friendly the *Thames Commodore* much prefers to find her way to an ordinary quayside as near as possible to the centre of the town or port, where the life of the place is in full swing and one need only walk a hundred yards to find a baker and a milk-shop.

Looking at the town plan of Flushing we saw that there was just such a reasonable inlet running up between some warehouses into the old part of the town itself, and we turned across towards it. Penetrating some way along it we drew in, and were just picking up the lines to heave them ashore at a handy if rather dilapidated quayside when we were hailed by a small Dutch sailing yacht which had pursued us into the town with no other purpose than to tell us that there was a yacht harbour, and that they would sail ahead of us and show us the way.

It is difficult to refuse the kind attentions of others, and more than once I have unwillingly taken the advice of local yachtsmen rather than offend them. On this occasion, too, I thought it would seem boorish to refuse, so we thanked the Dutch family and regretfully dropped our lines back on the deck to chug along in the wake of their sailing boat. Before very long we had reached the entrance and the little boat obligingly waved us inside the private water, then went on its way.

The yacht harbour was just as I had expected it to be, packed tightly with craft moored between stakes set too close together for

the *Thames Commodore* to have been able to insert her rump between them even if the berths had not already all been occupied.
It was also on the opposite side of the Walcheren Canal from the
town, so we should have to walk a mile further to reach the shops.
But by now others were giving us friendly nods and waves and it
seemed downright churlish to do the sensible thing and steam
quickly out again, so against our own judgment we drew in where
their waterman directed us, across the end of the yacht basin and
at the quay of a large shipbuilding enterprise which, because of the
public holiday, was deserted. Our berth was at the particular side
of the shipyard where shot-blasting was carried out, and the ground
looked very much as Pompeii must have appeared after the erup-
tion, everything being half buried in several inches of spent
blasting material, a nigger-brown deposit like a large-grained and
sharp sand. The only thing one could say in its favour was that even
if it filled one's shoes the material was at least not coal dust.

Flushing is not a very great port, but it is intimately concerned
with the sea, for it stands right at the entrance to the estuary which
leads to the Belgian ports of Ghent and Antwerp. It is a town of
pilotage and shipbuilding, and once it stood as a bastion to protect
the isles of Zeeland from cruel Spaniards and fickle French and
despicable English. The massive wall on which the hotels are
perched has long served to keep the sea from inundating the streets
below, and just at the boundary of estuary and open water stands
Admiral de Ruyter himself. At his back are the drifters, snugly
packed in the fishing harbour, and also the jetty from which every
few minutes a pilot cutter hung with tyres dashes out below the
red lantern tower which crowns the sea wall, to accost one of the
huge freighters clipping close round the beach, outward bound
from Antwerp. The Sardijngeul or Sardine Channel which many
of them will take cuts so near inshore that the giant vessels pass
within one hundred yards of the dining-room windows of the
hotels ranged along the Boulevard de Ruyter.

It was an evening of hot stillness when we walked along the top
of this great marine rampart, and as it was also a Saturday the
Hollanders were there in their hundreds, many of them visiting for
the first time an island only recently made accessible by direct road

from the north by way of the great bridge which leapt the water between Schouwen-Duiveland and Noord Beveland. They would drive slowly round the feet of de Ruyter, whose proud and defiant stance seemed to suggest that he did not think very much of small family cars. His heart was more in the stout ship of oak with a thousand men aboard, ready for a scrap with the English.

No great sailor could have a finer position from which to stare out in perpetuity to the sea which was the scene of his daring lifetime raids. Beyond the horizon lay England, the land of the inept Duke of Albemarle and an administration so stupid that had it not been for that curious naval secretary Samuel Pepys the English navy would long since have all rotted, or been burned, or broken up. That same civilian Mr Pepys was to make a note (now in the Bodleian) of the facts given out from the pulpit in Bow Church one morning in July of 1666; 'The Dutch Totally routed. 14 ships taken, 26 burnt and sunck. 2 Flagg ships taken, and out of them 1200 men, and what else they would, then sunck them. Taken in all 6000 men. Oure shipps have blockt up the Zealanders in Flushing, and ride before them top and gallant.' It all sounded very satisfactory, but Samuel Pepys was not particularly pleased at the news, for he thought it but a poor result after the fighting of two so great fleets. 'We keep the sea,' he noted in his diary, 'which denotes a victory, or at least that we are not beaten: but no great matters to brag of, God knows.'

But on the following day he was more elated, for now there was news that de Ruyter was in disgrace for the losses the Dutch had incurred. Indeed, it was reported that the population of Flushing was so enraged that de Ruyter dared not come ashore for fear of the people. Certainly this was a welcome change in the fortunes, for only six weeks earlier Pepys had noted that the Dutch had routed the English ships in a two day running fight between Dunkirk and Ostend. 'The Dutch do mightily insult of their victory, and they have great reason. Sir W. Berkeley was killed before his ship was taken, and there he lies dead in a sugar-chest, for everybody to see, with his flag standing up by him.'

In fact the Dutch were according a great honour to the body of Sir William, out of deference to his personal quality and courage.

They sent a 'trumpet' or herald over to England by the Calais packet, to tell the king that the States General had ordered the corpse to be preserved and to ask what wishes His Majesty might have for its disposal. Ruysch the anatomist had been ordered to preserve the body by injection, and he was to receive a good reward for his work.

At royal request the admiral's body was eventually brought to London for burial in Westminster Abbey, as well prepared as if it had been the corpse of a dead infant – though somewhat de-composed on account of the public exhibition in the sugar-chest before the work of embalming was begun.

Even if the people of Flushing once held de Ruyter in contempt, he is now remembered only as a hero worthy of his position on Walcheren's bastion against the sea. Nor have schoolchildren entirely forgotten his predecessor, the man with the broom on his mast. There is a round song, each line of which runs on the next higher note of the common chord, and which is really just one of those little housework ditties one might find in any land :–

> De bezem, de bezem,
> Wat doe je ermee, wat doe je ermee?
> Je veegt ermee, je veegt ermee,
> De vloer, de vloer!
>
> The besom, the besom,
> What do I therewith, what do I therewith?
> I sweep therewith, I sweep therewith,
> The floor, the floor!

But when I heard it sung by some small children marching away to school, the words as they passed our berth were not quite the same. *De vloer* had become *de Thems*. Perhaps the name painted on our bow had combined with a recent history lesson about one of the greatest of Dutch sea-commanders to turn the laughing children from mere mothers' helps into a crocodile of young van Tromps, off to sweep the Thames.

II

*The bells of Walcheren – Veere, port without sea – the
Elizabeth flood – the Delta Plan – creation of the Veersemeer
– avocets in the moat – the towers of Amsterdam – Elsje the
serving-maid – water-nymphs in the Amstel*

IF we had been doubtful about the mooring offered us when we
followed the sailing boat to the Flushing yacht harbour, our
fears were drastically confirmed at five o'clock on the following
morning. The previous day had faded calm but curiously still,
with an ominous sense of expectation. Perhaps the weather
deliberated with itself all night whether or not it was fair to catch
all the Easter holiday makers unawares. If so, it made up its mind
just before five o'clock and signalled the fact with a tremendous
crack of thunder rolling down from an apparently cloudless sky.
Within thirty seconds as strong a gale as I have encountered in the
wind-swept Netherlands was snatching up the tonnage of spent
shot blasting material and flinging it at us with all the violence it
could muster. I tumbled out of my bunk, and my wife out of hers.
I ran on deck through a blizzard of zinc and started the engines,
then we struggled on to the quay, more feeling than seeing our
way – for it was impossible to face into the storm of blasting
granules.

'Let go!' I called, with a hand in front of my mouth.

We jumped aboard as a rain of paper sacks fell on the deck, then
ran out past the end of the shipyard wharf into the water of the
main canal, where the wind was snatching the tops off the little
waves with such effect that I thought it was raining. Able to breathe
at last without taking in steel and manganese we looked back and
saw the dozens of little craft covered with drifts of brown deposit
and the water decked with shot-blast sacks and plastic sheeting.

As for the metallic dust, it filled my pyjama pockets and my
ears, it jammed the windows in their frames, it lay in little patches

in every cup and bowl in the china cupboards, it formed brownish beaches in the shower trays and lay in miniature mountain ranges wherever aboard the ship there was a wind eddy or some shelter. On our way down the canal I cleared it from the deck with the power hose, but three months later there were still patches to be found in undisturbed corners – behind the meat safe, under the gang-plank, inside the cowl of the galley stove. Yet by getting under way within twenty seconds we had at least saved our paint and our window glass from being dulled to a matt surface by the onslaught of the gale-driven shot-blast.

Straight and wide the Walcheren Canal runs across the width of the island, its long lines of bank faced with heavy hexagon crystals of Norwegian basalt, and every hundred yards or so there is a massive bollard formed from a cannon sunk muzzle downwards in the ground as though to show that the Netherlanders have finished for ever with fighting the Spaniards and sweeping the Thames or sending a broadside into the Duke of Albemarle's flagship. The canal runs past Middelburg, a very lovely place indeed, and if I felt guilty that we did not stop I still had at the back of my mind the northern countries nudging me to remember that if the *Thames Commodore* were to stop for every alluring Dutch city she would never reach the Øresund at all.

Every traveller has been charmed by Middelburg, and most have described it. The American Mary Waller sailed down the canal sixty years ahead of us and she insisted on staying there for two weeks so that she might hear 'those wonderful chimes that ring at all hours of the day and night, that talk to you at intervals of seven minutes throughout the twenty-four hours, that whisper to you in your sleep.' She arrived to the air of Mendelssohn's *Spring Song*, went to sleep with *I dreamt that I dwelt in Marble Halls* and awoke to *La fille de Madame Angot*. Her enthusiasm was not shared by the Englishman Frederick Spencer Bird, who stuffily wrote that 'to persons not particularly somnolent by nature, and who are, moreover, unaccustomed to being disturbed in the peaceful midnight hour, it is almost torture to pass a few nights in some of the small Dutch towns – such as Flushing, for instance – especially if lodged in the neighbourhood of the church.'

I sympathised with poor Mr Bird, but preferred Mrs Waller. There is a real charm about the carillons, and all along the Walcheren Canal we were just within sound of one or other as the bells of Flushing, Middelburg and Veere rang out in the clear air over a landscape bathed in the light of a Ruysdael sky. It is difficult to imagine the Netherlands without their belfries calling across the wide land spread at their feet, and always I have felt that they bring to that absolutely horizontal countryside some of its greatest beauty. Besides, the bells are in towers, and this provides the opportunity to climb panting to the roof of the church or town-hall belfry and see for as great a distance as the curvature of the earth will permit.

We had passed Middelburg once before, when fifteen years earlier the old *Commodore* had carried us along the canal from Veere. I remembered Veere as a very pretty little port with its fishing boats lying along the quay, their nets hoisted up the masts until the men should set out again to ride the sea outside and return with a catch of sole and plaice and cod. At the same time it was a quiet place, sad and faded, a mere shadow of what it must have been when fifteen thousand people lived there and the Scottish wool trade brought such wealth that the people could confidently start to build a church huge enough to serve a cathedral city.

It is partly the vast bulk of that church, almost but not quite derelict, which gives Veere its forlorn air. Within, the floor of the huge building is mere trampled earth, and the walls and windows have suffered at the hands of fire, English troops and French soldiery in turn. Slowly the place is now being metamorphosed into a museum, and on this Easter Sunday morning an old carriage and a broken-down fire-pump from ancient days held the floor near where the altar must once have been, while the modern congregation celebrated the greatest festival of the church in a small building which seemed to have grown on the outside of one of the buttresses like a barnacle.

If I recalled Veere as a run-down fishing port, that was a memory from days when it was still on the sea. But now the lock at the end of the canal knows no tide, and the water beyond it is that of the Veersemeer. The town has been so transformed as a result of Dutch engineering that not a fishing-boat is to be found in its pretty harbour, and the smoking and curing establishments have become antique shops. Yachts lie along the quay, and probably Veere is more prosperous than at any time since the Scots were there to trade in wool. And this alteration in the fortunes of Veere is merely a by-product of the vast enterprise of the Delta plan, by which the Dutch are transforming the whole area of Zeeland.

The villainous Duke of Alva once remarked of the Dutch that they were the nearest neighbours to Hell of any people on earth, because they lived lowest. No doubt this provided another excellent reason for saving them by roasting them in the fires of the Inquisition, but it is certainly true that the Dutch countryside is exceptionally low, and the fact that much of it lies below sea level makes the danger of flooding particularly serious.

Every year the River Rhine sweeping down from Switzerland through Germany carries in suspension half a million truck-loads of mud and one third as much of sand. If the Rhine could keep its pace, this material would be carried out to the oceans, but where it begins to collide with the salt water the opposing force of the tide makes the great stream falter and lose speed. The suspended solids drop to the bottom and the result is – Holland. Year by year across the ages river-borne silt has formed the fertile countryside through which the Rhine and Meuse have had to cut new outlets to the sea, forming a delta which once stretched from Flanders to Friesland but which in later centuries has been constricted by the labour of the Dutch themselves to the provinces of Zeeland and South Holland. Wind and tide and flood may have changed the channels, but on the low-lying patches of silty earth between them the people always lived as fishermen and farmers behind their dikes, menaced by the sea without.

'Diking against Neptune and his consorts is to wage a war, therefore we must be warlike.' So wrote a Dutch dike-master of the sixteenth century. Without dikes there could be no security, and far back in the history of the Low Countries it was the law that a state of 'Dike Peace' would be proclaimed when these ramparts were threatened. Then, if any man dared endanger the

public safety by indulging in a mere private quarrel he was
sentenced to death. The dikes were to be kept up and held at all
costs. The isles of Zeeland alone have consumed many times the
value of their land in effort and materials, but the Dutch cannot
afford to count the cost of dikage in florins and cents. If the sea
were allowed its own way the western half of the Netherlands
would vanish and Utrecht would be on the coast.

Although the Dutch have always diked and delved, exceptional
storms have sometimes breached the defences and inundated not
only the isles but considerable areas of the mainland. In the St
Elizabeth's Night disaster of 1421 seventy-two villages were
destroyed and the Biesbosch was formed – a swampy archipelago
which is now a favourite haunt of yachtsmen and anglers and bird-
lovers but which once was prosperous farmland. It is said that
nearly one hundred thousand people were drowned on that
occasion, and that the flooding was not caused by a storm breach
at all, but by the foolishness of a peasant who had a quarrel with
a neighbour and decided to pay him out by digging through the
dike in front of his house so that the sea would stream over the
property, as indeed it did. Unfortunately the wind went round to
the west, and the water poured through the gap so fiercely that all
efforts to stop it failed; and, as Samuel Ireland wrote, there was
'left to the humanity of those who bewailed a deluged province no
better consolation than that the author of this ruin was himself
swept away by the general wreck.'

Most inundations were the work not of aggrieved peasants and
farmers but of wind and wave and tide. It might be only once in
a century that these enemies combined for an attack, but sooner or
later the sea would return to its onslaught upon the land. Its most
recent successful sally was in 1953, when 300 miles of dikes were
broken or washed away and one tenth of the whole country was
put under water, with great loss of life, livestock, and property.
It was this disaster which made the Netherlands Goverment
finally decide to proceed with the Delta Plan. Not that the idea was
entirely new. Three centuries back, in 1667, a Dutch water
engineer had written that one day the people would be forced to
shut out the fury of the sea by making dams from island to island

along the Zeeland frontage. Now this formidable piece of work is well under way, and if it has at last been undertaken it is because three events gave the engineers the experience they needed.

The first was the successful blocking of the Zuyderzee, begun after a disastrous flood. Already in 1932 the 20-mile dike – which the *Thames Commodore* was soon to see – was completed, replacing 200 miles of sea-wall along the winding shoreline of the bay, adding new stretches of fertile farmland to the credit side of the ledger. The dike was laid in shallow waters with a small tidal range, but it provided useful lessons for the future.

The second experience was a result of war. In 1944 the Allies bombed the dikes of Walcheren to flood the island and dislodge the Germans. This was achieved, but Walcheren itself remained under water and more than a year passed before attempts to repair the damage could begin. Meanwhile the ebb and flood swept twice daily through the gaps until the breaches were so broad and deep that to close them seemed impossible. But it happened that Britain had some spare Mulberry pontoons, concrete tanks which could be towed into position and scuttled. They had shown their worth in building the invasion harbours on the coast of Normandy. Twenty-seven were brought to Walcheren, together with two giant Phoenix caissons, each weighing 3000 tons. They were sunk in the worst of the gaps, along with several old ships. The hole was blocked, and draglines quickly buried the scuttled obstructions beneath a wall of clay and sand, proving that in this way even the largest holes could be filled successfully.

The third piece of experience came from the 1953 flood. More than sixty gaps had to be closed, the largest of which was at Schelphoek on the island of Schouwen, where the tide quickly eroded an opening 120 feet in depth. This was comparable with the largest tidal gulleys which might be encountered in Zeeland, and to close it was the most formidable task the water engineers had yet faced. The largest repair fleet ever assembled converged upon Schelphoek, and within an arc of temporary dike the gap was gradually narrowed. At last two gigantic caissons of 7000 tons apiece were hauled into position at slack water, and their sea-cocks opened. They settled neatly, and the breach was closed. To connect the Isles of Zeeland no longer seemed impossible, and the Delta works were put in hand. The islands were to be linked near their outer ends by a series of stout sea-dikes, whilst various secondary dams would regulate the flow of water, prevent silting, and deal with the needs of shipping.

The first of these dams was built out from the two shores where the channel outside Veere opened to the sea. The limbs were extended until only one fifth of the original channel remained open, and then at slack water on four days the enormous floating concrete tanks were towed into position above a bottom which had already been flattened. The moment they were scuttled, suction dredgers began to pour sand into their cavities and against both sides until they were buried. When the last two units were eased into place the dam was complete. It was a fantastic achievement, but a photograph of the event in one of Veere's restaurants has the caption 'Veere's death-blow'. For this dam, like others of the Delta plan, closed off as a lake – the Veersemeer – an area of water where ships had plied for local transport and where for centuries the fishing-boats had returned home from the sea.

Some who know Zeeland as it used to be may shake their heads over the changes wrought by the Delta plan, yet in the long run action on the grand scale would have been unavoidable, for the simple fact is that the sea is actually rising. Measurements show that the continued melting of the polar ice-caps releases water enough to raise the mean sea-level by about one tenth of an inch in a year, and although this may not sound a very formidable shift of the highwater mark it has raised the water by more than fifty feet since 5,000 B.C. To the French and the British this has meant little, but for the Dutch the continuing rise would eventually demand that their low-lying land must be even more effectively walled in if it were not to be inundated and abandoned. Indeed, the relentless rising of the sea may one day force the Dutch to pump their country full of silt to a depth of thirty feet or more, but the engineers consider that this can be left to their descendants a thousand years hence. They have plenty to occupy them in completing the Delta works.

From the lock at the end of the Walcheren Canal we had merely to turn left round the edge of the town to run into the harbour. It was defended on the one side by the ancient Campveer tower – now an excellent restaurant – and on the other by a bastion. These fortifications are peaceful enough nowadays, and even the cannon on the bastion now has the pleasant use of serving as a riding-horse for children, but in the years when the Netherlands were striving to throw off the Spanish oppression Walcheren was the scene of terrible struggles, and even such a staunch protagonist of the Sea Beggars as the historian John Lothrop Motley was moved to say that the islanders found a fierce pleasure in acts of cruelty, tying the Spanish prisoners back to back, two and two, and hurling them into the sea. 'A Spaniard had ceased to be human in their eyes,' he commented. 'On one occasion a surgeon at Veere cut the heart from a Spanish prisoner, nailed it on a vessel's prow, and invited the townsmen to come and fasten their teeth in it, which many did with savage satisfaction.' This extraordinary scene was no doubt enacted at the very same quayside to which we now drew in, making fast below the trees and just across the cobbles from the two splendid fifteenth-century houses of Scottish merchants of the wool trade.

Veere has little to offer the landsman. All the while we were there the cars came across the new dyke and the families would park, wander over to the quay, stroll past the extraordinary town hall with its niches containing statues of local worthies of five centuries ago, and look up at the thin belfry tower which stands above the town like a minaret. It is very oddly proportioned, this building, and full of character; but when the visitors have seen it, and wandered into the depressing empty nave of the church, and had tea at the Campveer Tower, they climb back into their cars and drive on. They have done Veere. They have indeed, for there is nothing else there to detain them.

To the boatman Veere offers the same, adding only the harbour in which to lie for a while and do those hundred odd jobs which accumulate because they never need to be done just now. There is the deck to scrub, some lines to splice, the bell to polish and the windows to clean, fender tyres to be washed, a rail to be varnished, but none of these things are urgent. They can wait until one comes to a harbour with a particularly pleasant outlook where one is happy enough to occupy a few hours with such harmless jobs. Until one is in just such a place as Veere.

Where once the sea beggars sailed into the Veerse Gat to grapple with the Spaniards we found the North Sea now kept at bay by the huge rampart of the new dike, and it was only when I looked at that bank through the binoculars that I realised just how huge it must be, for what I took to be a little sheep track proved to be the main road and the objects creeping along it like little beetles were cars and lorries. The Veersemeer ran right to its foot, so I climbed a ladder down the ramparts by the harbour bastion and set off along the shore to see the bank from closer at hand. The edge of the Veersemeer reminded me of nothing so much as the Great Salt Lake in Utah, for the foreshore was as dead and barren as that desolate scene. In a way it was even more dismal, for in Utah the barrenness consisted in an utter absence of living things, whereas along the Veersemeer there was added the memory of countless millions that once were alive. With the change from sea to freshwater the seaweeds and the grasses of brackish environment had been unable to keep up the osmotic fight and had simply flopped dead where they stood. Down near the water there were drifts, sometimes almost knee-deep, of the shells of billions of little creatures slain by the decreasing salinity, shells pink and white and pale yellow. There must however have been something even now alive in the mud, for oyster-catchers were wheeling and calling, alighting to strut in their stilted fashion among the hummocks of the marshy edge and prodding the spongy ooze with their bright orange bills. A few gulls rode on the water, looking doubtfully at me as I walked past their private lake and crunched the dead shells underfoot, but they did not bother to visit such a poor beach when fresh sandflats were available beyond the dike itself.

It was not a very interesting walk, for the water's edge was even devoid of the debris washed up on any proper seashore, so on the way back I struck along the old supplanted dike of Walcheren towards the thin finger of Veere's carillon tower. Almost back at the harbour again I followed the rampart round to part of the

North Holland coast

moat which long ago had held invaders at bay, and there I was surprised to see some distance ahead a group of black and white birds sitting among the water lilies. They were larger than terns but smaller than gulls, and they were certainly not ducks. They were, I felt sure, some curious kind of wader.

'In exploring the tract which leads us, step by step, to an acquaintance with them (the *grallatores*, or wading birds), we must travel through reeds and rushes, with doubtful feet, over the moss-covered, faithless quagmire, amidst oozing rills and stagnant pools.' So wrote Thomas Bewick, and he was right. Pressing on with doubtful feet I skirted the boggy edge of the pool until I was close to the nearest pair. They saw me, discussed in glances whether or not I was a safe risk and decided to fly off. It was only when they rose and flew over me, trailing long black legs behind them and beating quickly with their thin and angular wings that I realised what these exquisitely graceful creatures must be.

I had not seen an avocet for forty years, and on that occasion it was only a fleeting glimpse of one among the reeds in the Blakeney marshes. But an avocet once seen is not easily forgotten, for it is not like any other bird. Thomas Bewick put it in a class by itself, the sole member of his 'Birds of the Avoset kind', and he also called it a Scooper, or Yelper. He described it as 'common in the winter about the lakes, mouths of rivers, and marshes, in the southern parts of England.' That was in 1804, and England is no longer a land where the avocet could be described as common, whereas at the beginning of the nineteenth century avocets were regularly offered for sale in Leadenhall market.

I suspect that the avocet is a creature with more to fear than to gain from the march of technology, but in the country between the Scheldt and the Elbe there should for many years to come be enough marshy flats to keep them happy. Yet a century from now much of Europe's wild life will only be known from specimens in preserves and zoos, and the notion that avocets once sat happily in the moat of Veere will seem almost as unlikely as the biological note recorded by Samuel Ireland, when he retailed the story that in 1276 a Dutch lady, the Countess of Hennesberg, gave birth at the age of forty-two to three hundred and sixty-five children at one time, this being the result of the imprecations of a beggar woman who, on being refused alms, cursed the noble lady with the wish that she should have as many children as there were days in the year. Not unnaturally, Ireland found the tale difficult to accept, although at the village church the bowl was still shown in which the Bishop of Utrecht baptised them, 'no bigger than shrimps'. Ireland thought the beggar woman's curse was more probably to the effect that the Countess should bear as many children as there had already been days in the year; and as the imprecation was made on January 3rd this reduced the number to twins.

From Veere we had merely to wind along the wilderness of the Veersemeer to where a new lock led us out into the familiar tidal channels between the isles of Zeeland. Some would find the voyage through Zeeland unbelievably dull, but I have always loved that particular run. It was now sixteen years since we had first made it aboard the *Commodore*, and how many times she must have passed through the Zijpe Strait I do not know. Already her successor had galloped three times past the same islands, and

B

though even now barely two years old she was once again bound through the Volkerak and Hollands Diep for Dordrecht and Gouda.

It was at a Zeeland port such as Hellevoetsluis or even Veere that the English traveller would often begin his grand tour, and there is a pleasant tale of how King George II was forced by bad weather to wait in Zeeland for a while when returning from one of his excursions to Hanover. When walking one morning in Hellevoetsluis he saw a pretty Dutch girl on the quayside and regally struck up a conversation with her.

'Good morrow!' he accosted her grandly. 'And what have you in your basket, my dear child?'

'*Eiren, Mijnheer,*' the girl replied.

'Eggs! And how much do they cost, my dear?'

'One ducat apiece,' said the girl.

'What, are eggs so scarce in Holland?'

'No, Sir,' the girl answered with a smile. 'But kings are.'

Twisting through Zeeland and up the familiar watercourses of the great rivers of the Delta the *Thames Commodore* sped on, only drawing breath when she had let the flow of tide carry her up the pretty River Ijssel to Gouda. The next evening she was turning into the inner harbour of Amsterdam, to spend the night in a favourite basin off the side of the Oude Schans, a waterway which is in constant use by motor lighters and refuse barges and is always the scene of busy comings and goings. The basin was well supplied with carillon music floating down over the gables of the warehouses ranged round the pool, and just across the water from our berth stood the tall form of a brick watch-tower, the Montalbaanstoren. This tower wore a Dutch hat in the form of a shapely rounded top that was not quite a spire, and early in the morning its neat coiffure would be lit by the rising sun and the gilt hands of its clock would glow to tell us it was time to be up and about our business, whether that were to take up the voyage or merely to walk out in the crisp coolness of the quiet streets to find milk and bread.

We had drawn in at the quay beside a forwarding warehouse, and as usual a number of people strolled over to talk with us and ask us whence and whither and how many horses in the engine. I also had a question, one that had worried me for years.

'Why is that tower called the Montalbaan Tower? Who, or what or where is Montalbaan? It doesn't sound Dutch at all.'

One of the shipping agents nodded. 'You are right. It is not really a Dutch name. It is said to be named after the castle of *de vier Heemskinderen*.'

I wondered who the four Heemskinderen might be, but his next words gave the clue. 'They built a castle at Montauban, in the south of France,' he added.

Montauban! So *de vier Heemskinderen* were the Four Sons of Aymon! Wherever she voyaged south of Scandinavia the *Thames Commodore* was for ever coming upon the trail of Bayard the magic horse, and the four brothers who rode him like the wind and outwitted poor old Charlemagne and all his men. Not that these heroes of legend had ever swept across the marshes of the Nether-lands, but what did that matter? There was a Bayard's Leap in Yorkshire, yet neither horse nor riders had ever crossed the Channel in the long course of their adventures.

Another tower, one by which we had passed whenever we took the more westerly entrance close beside the station, is still known as the Schreyerstoren or Crier's Tower. It is a massive bastion from the fifteenth century, and upon it a stone shows a wailing woman with ships in the background. Traditionally, this was the tower from which wives and sweethearts used to look out over the Y river and weep as the ship of their beloved faded slowly into the distance, to return months or years later after a voyage to the East Indies, or to Russia or America. Always there was the fear that the loved one would never come home but would meet his death from storm, ice, disease, American Indians, or the terrible English. The particular woman on the stone is said to be one who was no ordinary wailer, for it is told that long after the other women had retired and dried their eyes she stood weeping on the tower, wailing so inconsolably that all who passed near the place stopped and stared up at her. Only after nightfall did the sobbing cease as she betook herself home.

Next day she was there again, and the next also. Weeks went

by, and always the woman wept and wept. After months the news came that the ship of her loved one had been captured by pirates and all the crew murdered, but by this time the fate of her man meant nothing to her at all. She was a compulsive weeper, and as the years went by people ceased to be sorry for her, or even to find her sobbing a nuisance. She became part of the Amsterdam scenery, and when at the end of a long if not very productive life she died it was alleged that the upper storey of the harbour tower was filled waist deep with the product of her lachrymal glands. And as once again a curious quiet came over the port people began to miss the familiar sound of her weeping and to be sorry that she had gone.

Amsterdam is a city of towers and belfries, but even more it is one of canals. Indeed, without its hundreds of bridges the city would not be the same, for whether they are the yellow wooden bascule bridges that one associates at once with van Gogh, or the graceful stone structures with elegant curving rails, they complete the charm of almost every street in the older part of the city as nothing else could do. Often in the late evening we would see some young couple leaning over the parapet of any one of the bridges, an arm round each other's waist as they stood silent and happy, looking out along the leafy avenue of water with the gables mirrored in its black surface. There is nothing so pleasant as a bridge on which to pause in an evening stroll, and no doubt some of these young people would feel a little extra thrill when they stood together on one particular bridge, the Lovers' Bridge or Pont des Amoureux. Yet, if they knew it, the name has nothing to do with eternal devotion and plighted troths, but only with barges.

The ships plying from Amsterdam and Rotterdam to the towns of Belgium and northern France used to be of a particular type suitable for horse-hauling from the towpaths of the sometimes swiftly flowing Meuse and the Sambre. They were the 'Sambre and Meuse' barges, the *samoureuzen* of the Dutch and the *samoureux* of their French-speaking neighbours. Clusters of these craft would lie for loading by the bridge of the Hoogesluis, and so it was only natural that the crossing came to be known as the

Amsterdam

Samoureuzenbrug. It then required only the French occupation
in the days of Napoleon to convert the Pont des Samoureux into
the Pont des Amoureux.

Nowhere in the world can there be a more beautiful collection
of canals than those which form the fabric of Amsterdam, turning
little by little around the pivot of the palace like the strands of a
spider's web. The Heerengracht, Prinsengracht and Keizersgracht
are perhaps the most famous of them, and it is a delight to drop
the dinghy and row a leisurely course around their maze. Almost
every house along the quays is attractive and many are very fine
survivals from the days when wealthy merchants lived on their

own trading premises. Such a one is the de Geer house, the 'House with the Heads', its splendid classical gable decorated with the heads of the Greek deities of war and wisdom, harvest and hunt.

No doubt a rich merchant well versed in the classics could look up with pleasure at the range of Grecian heads which watched over the quay below, but the more ordinary citizens came to be so convinced that the heads were those of very different characters that eventually a story about them became strongly entrenched in the general store of knowledge which any burgher might possess, and everyone knew about Elsje the servant girl.

One evening that her master and mistress were out to dinner Elsje was sitting sewing when she distinctly heard a noise, like something scrabbling against the wall of the cellar. Not in the least frightened she tiptoed down the dark cellar steps and saw in the faint light which filtered through a small fanlight at the top of the wall that somebody was busy trying to break it open. Quietly picking up the heavy axe which was kept for splitting the logs of firewood she took up her position to one side of the opening.

At last the frame was pushed in, and the head of a man came slowly through the narrow opening. He had half wriggled into the cellar when he sensed that somebody was there.

'It's all right,' whispered the girl. 'I know where the keys are. Give me an equal share with the rest and I'll show you the way. There is plenty of silver and gold in the store.'

The thief whispered the good news back to his confederates, and told them to squeeze in after him. He had almost eased himself out of the window shaft when Elsje raised the heavy axe and took off his head with a neat blow. Then she hauled in the body.

Seeing the feet disappear, the second thief began to worm his way through the grating, and he too was neatly decapitated. So Elsje proceeded until she had six bodies on the floor. Then, having satisfied herself that the queue had come to an end, she replaced the axe, washed her hands and no doubt changed her shoes before going upstairs to continue her sewing.

When her master and mistress returned they asked her if all was in order, and she said it was. Only when they were about to retire for the night did Elsje remark that there was a certain amount of mess in the cellar and she thought that perhaps they should step in and see it. She lit a candle and took her employers down the steps, to where six bodies lay in one heap and six heads in another.

For her courage Elsje the maid was no doubt given a suitable reward, and according to the tale the heads of the six robbers – strangely classical in appearance, it must be admitted – were carved upon the gable to warn others that this was not a house to be burgled with safety.

The water of the Amsterdam canals is not of the cleanest. Though it does not actually seethe with corruption like the inky black fluid of Ghent, it has a particular tang of its own and if it were inhabited at all one would expect the only form of life to be eels, of which there are no doubt plenty. We were surprised to hear that the Amstel itself had once been the haunt of a very different kind of creature, the memory of which is preserved in a group of thirteen warehouses which extend along a quay in the old city, at the inner end of the Amstel.

There was once a barge contractor who had a flourishing trade both in lighterage and passenger carrying. His various craft were moored in the Amstel, and every night they would be checked over and ranged two or three abreast along the wall. One morning the barge-owner was astonished to find his ships all in disorder. The lines had been let go, the seats were wet, and instead of lying in neat rows the craft were now tangled together in a mass. Determined to teach a lesson to the hooligans responsible for such a mess the owner lay in wait for them the following night, armed with such a good stout stick as might bruise the bottom of any confounded juvenile delinquent who might dare to start fooling about among his boats.

Hours passed as he crouched behind a crate, and it was already after midnight when he suddenly became aware of movement in the water. Soon a host of graceful water nymphs had climbed over the gunwales. Darting quickly to bow and stern they began to cast the boats adrift.

'Get out of it,' roared the owner, leaping to his feet. 'Get away out of here and leave my boats alone.'

He leaped from the quay to the nearest craft and at once the figures dived over the side, but lunging forward he just managed to grab the hem of the diaphanous nightdress of the last of them. Tugging hard he hauled her inboard.

The nymph looked at him with tears in her soft and beautiful eyes.

'Please let me go,' she begged. 'We didn't mean any harm. We just like having fun in boats, that's all.'

Not even the roughest of men could have withstood the pleading of that beautiful voice, or the prayer in her troubled eyes. The contractor's heart melted, and more embarrassed than angry he let go his hold on the nymph's gossamer dress.

'Well, don't do it again,' he said, trying to sound stern.

She shook her head. 'Bless you,' she said. Then, with a quick smile that he never forgot as long as he lived she dropped over the gunwale with a plop, and the dark water of the Amstel rippled away in rings where she had vanished.

He watched the wavelets run outward, and it was several moments before he noticed the shine within the boat and realised that as a sign of her gratitude she had caused it to be filled with pieces of bright gold. With that same gold – for it was genuine enough – he soon afterwards paid the cost of building the row of warehouses, which still survives to this day.

I hoped that the same might happen to us, but I was disappointed. However intently I listened during the night I heard no other sound but that of the mellow bells calling across the silent city, and the voices of cats gossiping from their warehouse windowsills, or exchanging information on the progress of the night's ratting among the heaps of bales and barrels which lay along the wharf opposite the moonlit finger of the Tower of Montalbaan.

III

Before me lie dark waters,
In broad canals and deep,
Whereon the silver moonbeams
Dance restless in their sleep.
A sort of vulgar Venice
Reminds me where I am;
Yes, yes, you are in England,
And I'm in Rotterdam.

OR in Amsterdam, for Thomas Hood's lines could apply to any Dutch city with a tum-ti-tum name and a rhyme for ham. And if Amsterdam could never be thought vulgar, its canals are certainly broad and deep, their water dark. Beautiful they are, but practical also, and from the bustling harbour area near the station they carry the ships in almost every direction.

Some of the barges thread the town canals toward Schiphol and the south-west, others plug along the Amstel toward Gouda. The ocean-goers head westward down the ship canal to Ijmuiden and the big tanker barges and Rhine ships curve away south-eastward to the broad waterway which leads to the Rhine. Other trading ships leave by the Great North Holland Canal – no longer as great as once it was – or by the River Zaan which leads through Zaandam. Having some time in hand we let the *Thames Commodore* visit that town before taking up again her voyage to Scandinavia.

Zaandam is not a place of beauty, except that along its straggling waterfront some pleasant little houses survive, cramped between scrap-heaps or factory blocks. It is a place of tremendous industry with factories for everything from biscuits and chocolate to tractors and kitchen stoves, and it is famous for its shipyards. It has been so for centuries, since long before Pieter Zimmermann worked as an apprentice shipwright.

Pieter Zimmermann was none other than the young emperor, Peter the Great. This enterprising ruler had decided that the only way of raising his people from a half savage condition was by learning from the Western countries how to build ships and ports, so that the trade of the country could be carried on and its isolation broken down. He sent sixty bright young Russians to Italy to learn at Leghorn and Venice everything about shipbuilding and navigation, and forty more were sent to the Netherlands. At the age of twenty-five he appointed the first Russian embassy to the States General, and himself accompanied it as a mere attaché. However, the moment the party of two hundred officers, servants, secretaries and pages reached the Rhine he left it and sped down the river in a boat, dressed as a Dutch skipper. At Zaandam he visited the families of the Russian workmen he had sent in advance, and pretended to be a fellow-shipwright, but his incognito could not be kept up very long – if only because his diplomats in Amsterdam had a habit of calling on him in the yard and kneeling and bowing before him. Soon everyone knew that the fresh arrival who had taken a job in Calf's shipyard was the Tsar of all the Russias.

Pieter Zimmermann (as he called himself) was a man of tireless energy, and a Dutch writer of the time said that the people of Zaandam had never seen such a one for running, leaping, and clambering over the ships. Soon he had refitted a little yacht, and he delighted in sailing over the Zuyderzee, terrifying his companions and all the while gaining experience. An excellent carpenter, he also carried a case of surgical instruments and was always ready to draw a decayed tooth or tap a dropsy victim for fluid.

Peter eventually came to England to visit the dockyards, and he rented Evelyn's house, Sayes Court, at Deptford. He knocked a hole in the wall to give quicker access to the shipyard, and Evelyn's resident servant and caretaker disapproved of him as much as any good servant should. 'There is a house full of people, right nasty,' he wrote to his master. One of the Tsar's habits which he particularly resented was the way in which he would prove his strength and toughness by running full tilt at a favourite hedge with a loaded wheelbarrow, to burst through it. 'Which,' as the learned author of *Sylva Sylvarum* sadly wrote, 'I can still show in my ruined gardens at Sayes Court, thanks to the Tsar of Muscovy.'

In a tenuous way the *Thames Commodore* might have claimed a link with Peter the Great, for when the imperial workman needed to refresh himself at the end of a day's work in the shipyard he used to repair to the Tiger Tavern, close to the Tower of London. It was to the grandson of that Tiger (for the first inn was pulled down in 1893 and the second in the 1960s) that we would similarly repair for a meal after an evening of fitting out, either in the Regent's Dock or when lying at Tower Pier. The connection is not a very close one, considering that the site as well as the building has changed, but it is strengthened by the mummified cat and six rats inherited from Tudor times and now displayed in a floodlit cavity in the upstairs bar. They seem to be the only survivals from the original tavern, and if the master of the *Thames Commodore* were truly sentimental he would feel proud that the same little shrivelled curiosities had been gazed upon by the Tsar of all the Russias. But if the dead rats are the same I suspect that the food has greatly improved since Peter supped at the Tiger Tavern long ago.

When he had finished his studies in England he returned home, taking with him three naval captains, twenty-five merchant skippers, thirty Thames and coastal pilots, and a host of mechanics and smiths. Hundreds of Dutch joiners and masons were enrolled too, and enough Italian shipyard workers to construct a score of large vessels at once. With all these he quickly set about building St Petersburg on the model of Amsterdam – and even today Leningrad is the only city in the world which has more bridges than has Amsterdam.

However, the *Thames Commodore* could not forget that she was bound for Scandinavia, and soon she was forging up the harbour with yet another flock of shipping, making for the old Orange Locks which lead out into what is left of the Zuyderzee or Ijsselmeer, and sailing out by the channel that long ago was the seaport entrance to the city. The windlasses creaked, the gates wheezed open, and soon she was running down the broadening fairway to where the wide sheet of water lay faintly pink in the light of early evening.

There was little to be seen around the edges of this leaden expanse of former sea. The villages lay behind dikes no longer needed, and only their church spires peeped over the top. One of these was at Ransdorp, away to port as we slipped out past the lighthouse at the end of the long, curving mole, and it was not so much a spire as a rather dumpy tower.

If Ransdorp tower is squat, there is a good reason. Long, long ago it was the victim of a fight. The island of Urk, now rather sadly incorporated in one corner of the North-East Polder won by the engineers from the receding waters of the Ijsselmeer, was a stronghold of pirates and corsairs. One day there came sailing down the Zuyderzee a ship much larger than the caravels on which the Urkers were accustomed to prey, a craft so huge that although its name is not recorded I think it can only have been the good ship *Mannigfual* which will figure later in this voyage, when the *Thames Commodore* reaches Friesland. For the moment it is enough to say that the *Mannigfual* (or *Manifold*) was sufficiently broad in the beam to become jammed between Cap Gris Nez and the Dover cliffs on the one occasion when her skipper was rash enough to try to bring her through the Dover Strait. She was only extricated by clever seamanship, the captain ingeniously ordering the crew to spread her port flank with all the soft soap that could be found in the stores. He then hoisted full sail, and the boat slid through the gap.

If anyone should think this improbable the Frisians are ready to point out that sailing up the Channel one can actually see the yellow ship-soap still there on the Dover cliffs. I for one am quite ready to credit the tale, for two years after I first read about the *Mannigfual* we had the *Commodore* jammed half way out of a

German lock which was supposed to be nearly three inches broader than the ship. The lock was indeed large enough, but one of the gates would not open flush against the wall, and it was when we were tightly held in the gap that I remembered what the *Mannigfual*'s skipper had done. My wife and I liberally soaped the rubbing strakes on either side, and then I put the ship's engine at full speed ahead. She slid out very neatly, and I have no doubt that soap marks were for some time to be seen on the wall and gate of that particular lock.

When the great ship entered the Zuyderzee the Urkers set off in pursuit and soon the *Mannigfual* found herself chased by a host of busy little boats, all bent upon her destruction. But her captain was as resourceful as ever. Continually changing course he frustrated all attempts at boarding, yet all the while he was being driven further and further into the south-western corner of the Zuyderzee. Realising that the raiders were hoping to set his ship on the shoals he suddenly had the helm put over and came about. Swiftly the *Mannigfual* swung, and although she was so far inshore that her bowsprit struck the Ransdorp church spire as she turned, she was soon forging ahead to scatter the pirate vessels to either side and leave them far behind her as she swiftly made up for the open sea beyond Texel. And as Ransdorp lies just one mile behind the seadike, it is easy enough to calculate the minimum length of the giant bowsprit that felled its steeple.

I never tire of the Ijsselmeer. It is unpredictable. One day it will be smooth, and the next it can be stormy, its shallows making the waves sit up short and straight to slap a ship with surprising violence. Barges have been sunk by the waves of the Ijsselmeer, and altogether it is a water which demands respect. It also demands an up-to-date chart, for the Dutch engineers work so hard that what is broad and open water for ships to sail may only a month later be dry land. It was eleven years since I had last sailed up this shrinking sea and on that occasion the light buoys had been changed, and in the middle of the night we hit the island of Marken so hard that the old *Commodore*'s padded nose nearly knocked over a cow.

Out past Ransdorp the lighthouse of Marken soon appeared as

a tall finger rising from the horizon a mere hour's voyage to the north-east. That night when we ran down Marken it was still an island, so now as we rounded the cape and put in to its little harbour for the evening I was curious to see whether the change in its geography had much altered the nature of the place itself. For now Marken could be reached by car along a stretch of new dike, and this I thought was sad. There are few enough places still free from the noise and oil-drip of automobiles, and each time the motor-car vanquishes another outpost I find myself square enough to regret it.

It was still early April, a time when nobody in their senses undertakes an inland voyage, and when the travel agencies have barely begun to recruit their staff of maternal guides and helpful couriers who will see to it that no visitor to Amsterdam will leave Marken off his programme – and that he will have fifteen minutes dead to do the island. So, although the weather was fine and the sunset sky clear, we found the fishing-harbour exactly as I remembered it, quiet, and with only a miniature tanker and a German yacht berthed alongside the outer quay. The little wooden houses were shuttered, and light spilled through the hinges, but there was nobody about.

Yet in a curious way I was sorry for Marken. It was as though an efficient county council had cut a bypass through the parkland of some age-old manor, for in the old days people had at least to make the effort of a ferry journey if they were to see the place at all. Now they could drive in, peer out of the car windows, and drive out again without even stopping. It was only fortunate that a village originally built for fishermen about their daily business should have streets so narrow that visiting cars could not actually penetrate further than the enormous car park down at the new dike. But it may well be that a community which keeps itself as detached from life as Marken did is heading for extinction. The older people may like it that way, but I doubt if any young Markenaar has regretted the chance of taking his girl on the pillion, dressed not as an antique but in gay modern mode, whisking her off on his motor-cycle to the bright lights of a happy evening in Amsterdam. With the world a mere pop-bike ride away

I hope that the young of Marken may still want to live in their curious village homes, and that the coming of the dike-borne motor-road will have saved the community from a purely artificial existence, even if the dike itself has blocked the short water route from Amsterdam and so added a few miles to our own voyage.

Beatrix Jungman visited Marken at the turn of the century and wrote that 'every winter Marken is entirely submerged for a certain time. The islanders are accustomed to be awakened in the morning by a collision with some of the few pieces of movable furniture floating close under the ceiling of the room. A few years ago the indignation of the islanders was aroused by the high-handed action of an enterprising mayor, who insisted on the building of a dike round the cemetery, and the proper burial of the dead. Owing to the graves being shallow and the floods frequent and insinuating, coffins and their gruesome contents were left high and dry in the open on the waters subsiding. Frightful as this seems to our more civilized minds, the Markenites were accustomed to it, and considered it a desecrating innovation when the ridiculous fads of the mayor were translated into vigorous action.'

So in some ways Marken has certainly changed. The cemetery on its slight hill is peaceful and accepted, and since the conversion of Zuyderzee to Ijsselmeer people are no longer awakened by collisions with the furniture. Nor is one in mortal danger if taking a photograph. Nico Jungman made a sketch, but only amid loud murmurs of disapprobation from a sulky and angry crowd – for they had as great an aversion as have Arabs to making any kind of picture, believing it to be a flagrant transgression of the Second Commandment. A French artist was stoned and his canvases ruined by the shower of dirt thrown at them. Mrs Jungman recorded that before the people became used to the trip steamers from Amsterdam, photographers and artists went actually in danger of their lives, the infuriated Markenaars threatening to throw them and their apparatus into the sea.

The Markenaars did not even notice the arrival of the *Thames Commodore*, and when she slipped out of its pleasant harbour at dawn the village was still sleeping. By eight o'clock she was bearing down upon the most beautiful of all the harbour entrances of the

Enkhuizen

Ijsselmeer, at Enkhuizen. It was off this once prosperous port that
the Zuyderzee was at its narrowest, and if the raiders of Urk
commanded the whole expanse of water, so also the haven and
fortress tower of Enkhuizen held the key to the ten miles of sea
between North Holland and Friesland. For this reason the place
was often coveted by others, and particularly by the people of
Gelderland, who would resort to all possible ruses to take possession. It is said that early one morning an Enkhuizen man was walking along the quay when he noticed a number of ships lying
alongside, and very astutely suspecting that the craft came from

Gelderland he nodded to one of the captains and asked casually what cargo his ship was carrying.

'Malt,' said the skipper.

'A fine shipment,' said the Enkhuizener. 'And who is the consignee?'

But the Gelderland skippers had been well briefed, and the one who was asked promptly said the load was for the merchant Jan Groot Albert. However, this man happened to be the father-in-law of the questioner, who sauntered slowly away until out of sight, then ran to Albert's house and asked him if he were indeed expecting a shipment of malt. Albert confirmed that he had no such cargo coming, and with his son-in-law he set off to rouse the burghers. Soon a great crowd was racing to the quays, and the Gelderlanders very prudently wasted no time in removing their hawsers but cut them with axes. Poling out from the quayside, they hoisted sail and made straight out of the harbour, just in time.

Had it been on a weekday that we left Marken we would probably have run across the Ijsselmeer to Lemmer, but it happened to be a Sunday. Most Dutch locks and swing-bridges remain closed on Sundays, and so I had planned the route to avoid all closures. On the open water of the Ijsselmeer only winds and a bad sea might delay us, but on the farther shore the locks at every lake port were closed for the day and our only possible route lay through the huge enclosing dike which holds out the sea from any possible invasion of the Ijsselmeer. We knew that the locks near either end of the dike were manned day and night all round the year, for it would be impossible to keep a fishing boat or coaster hove to in the dangerous shallows north of the dike to wait for another day. We would go out into the salt water at Kornwerderzand Lock, I decided, and make round the coast to the seaport of Harlingen. And as I thought the wind would soon begin to shake off its sleep we took a quick breakfast in Enkhuizen harbour, then put out again to make Staveren for coffee.

Staveren is an exceedingly dull place. Once a great town and a member of the Hanseatic League, its modern glory consists in a wide harbour, a lighthouse, a lock and a handful of houses. As it was raining hard when we drew in to the jetty we did not feel very deprived if we stood warming ourselves at the galley stove and drinking hot rum-and-coffee instead of setting out to examine such a godforsaken place.

The term 'godforsaken' is of course an understatement, and as the damp steamed from my hair I remembered how an old sailorman in Enkhuizen fifteen years before had shaken his finger in the direction of Staveren, hidden across the water, and had roundly declared the place to be *onder Godes straf* – under the punishment of God. Its people, he said, had long ago become *godslasteraars* and *godloochenaars*, and all sorts of other nasty things. They had no respect for the Almighty, who in wrathful return had put the prosperous Staveren in its place. It was all due, he said, to one woman, the notorious female after whom the Vrouwenzand was named, a shallows which almost blocked the approaches and was capable of holding even the most powerful barge until the waves had pounded her to pieces. He had proceeded to tell us about the iniquities of this female of a bygone age, and since then I had heard the tale in much more detail, with the addition of the old man and his prophetic warning.

In the time of Staveren's prosperity its merchants were rich from their seaborne trade, and there developed between them a rivalry in houses, and finery, and ostentation. Richest and most splendid of them all was a certain widow of no great age, the proud and scornful Lady of Staveren – for it is a curious fact that riches and status-seeking seem always to have the effect of engendering pride, and scorn, and hardness of heart. If the northern coasts of Europe are well sown with legends on this theme, perhaps that is just because it is a true fact of experience.

When at last anyone who mattered in Staveren had gold on their doors, leather on their walls and priceless rugs of the Orient on their floors, it became more and more difficult to rise above the neighbours. Yet the Lady of Staveren was determined to keep her position, and so she entrusted one of her captains with a great sum in gold and ordered him to sail away to the farther end of the Baltic, calling at the ports as he went. His quest was to be the most expensive treasure in the world, and when he had found it he was to buy it and sail home to Staveren.

The good man set out, and around the shores of Scandinavia and what is now Poland and Russia he put in, inviting traders to bring their finest wares. Yet the ivory and amber, the rubies and gold and silks of Orient which were offered to him were already commonplace in Staveren, and after rejecting them he would sail on to another port and try again. After searching in every trading city along the coasts he had still found nothing, and it was probably a docker in one of the harbours who gave him an idea.

'The greatest treasure in the world, Captain? If you ask me, it's wheat. Plant a grain, and up it comes. God sends rain and God sends sunshine, and up comes the crop, ready for harvest. The staff of life, man. Bread! See what I mean? Without it we would all starve to death.'

Some such reasoning it must have been which made the skipper stop in his search and load his ship with wheat. Or perhaps he was tired of the fruitless hunt for fresh vanities and wanted to make his own protest. But however that may be, the tale says that he sailed triumphantly back to Staveren, and as the ship at last came into view, sailing down the deep water off Hindeloopen, the Lady of Staveren quickly put on her finest dress and had herself rowed out so that she might make a triumphal entry to the port, clasping a treasure which no other merchant could hope to possess.

When she discovered what her faithful and practical captain had done, her anger knew no bounds. The crowd was waiting on the quayside, and as she stepped ashore she ordered the vessel to be taken out of the harbour, and the wheat all to be poured overboard. In spite of the captain's remonstrance she pointed, icy and furious, to the sea outside. And the crowd watched, mocking.

It was at this moment that an old man pressed through to the front, an early forerunner of more modern prophets who have declaimed against crop destruction in rich countries whilst other lands are swept by famine. He begged her to give the wheat to the poor in the land, of which there were many. If she really wished to be more respected than the rest, she now had the chance.

The Lady of Staveren did not like to be instructed by the humble, or indeed by any. She thrust the man aside and ordered the crew to do as she said, and quickly. As the men cast off the hawsers the old man shook his finger at her, and at the crowd.

'Beware of pride,' he called. 'One day the proud will be made low, and you yourself, fine lady, will go as a beggar, asking for alms or a crust of bread. You, and all who think and live as you do.' His voice rose almost to a scream. 'This day will seal your fate.'

There was a hush. For a moment even the lady herself was silent. Then she took from her finger a priceless ring of eastern gems and hurled it far out into the water.

'Idiot! I declare that my ring will come back from the bottom of the sea before such nonsense will ever come to pass.'

Out went the ship, and overboard the wheat was duly poured. There must have been hundreds of tons of it, all told. The incident was closed, and Staveren settled down to normal. The honest captain was sacked, as perhaps the only revenge the woman could take for her own humiliation. It will not surprise the reader to know that within a year or two the ring should indeed return, either in the stomach of a fine fish served at the woman's aristocratic table or lifted up on a sprouting stalk of sea-wheat – for the story has many variants. That same day a freak storm overtook the whole of her fleet at sea and not a ship survived.

So much for the Lady of Staveren, who was reduced immediately to the beggary the prophet had foretold. But he had also castigated all those who thought as she did, and their fate was not far off. The bank of wheat caused sand to be deposited, and soon the harbour entrance was almost closed. For a while a channel was dug at low tide, but soon even this could not keep pace with the silting. Ships could no longer sail to Staveren and its prosperity collapsed. For centuries it lay decayed behind the barrier of the Vrouwenzand. And if now there is a dredged channel leading to the outer harbour and the lock, the memory of the Lady of Staveren and the pride which came before her fall is still there in the matter-of-fact words of the pilot book: – *A white occulting light (4 secs.) is exhibited from a mast to the north of the harbour. This light held in line with a fixed white light on the southern harbour dike, bearing 29°, leads clear of the western edge of the Vrouwenzand.* Besides, shortly after the *Thames Commodore*'s fleeting visit a new harbour entrance and lock was opened to deal with the ever greater quantity of yachts passing to and from the Frisian meres, and the roof of the keeper's smart control cabin was finished off with a strikingly handsome windvane in the form of a great bronze fish circled by a ring of gold, to recall the final incident in the strange series of events by which avarice is said to have brought about the fall of the wealthiest of women in what was once a vigorous and flourishing port with a trade which stretched across the known world.

We did not stop longer in Staveren than to decide that the place was certainly not worth the remainder of the Sunday, and in spite of the wind we would run out again and beat up through the drifting rain toward the enclosing dike. Half an hour up from the Vrouwenzand we could see the church tower of Hindeloopen standing dimly to starboard, almost hidden by the mist and cloud which drove across a cold and gloomy waterscape. This little town had also been overtaken by an awful fate, and like that of Staveren it was brought upon it by the acquisitiveness of its inhabitants, though at a very much later date. Indeed the beginning of the affair is fixed precisely to the year 1703, when Captain Auke Wijbes of Hindeloopen was at Amsterdam, his fleet ship *De Witte Windhond – the White Whippet* – lying at anchor in the roadsteads of the Y. This was long before the North Holland Canal was cut, at a time when ships bound for the city still sailed in past Texel or Vlieland and down the Zuyderzee, just as they had done in the days of the Lady of Staveren.

Captain Wijbes was about to sail on another lucrative voyage round the Skaw to the Baltic, when an alderman was rowed out to him with a letter which he was to carry to the port of St Petersburg and deliver to the Tsar of all the Russias. The skipper said he had never heard of the place, and the alderman replied that this did not surprise him. The harbour, he said, was only just being completed and no ship had yet berthed at its quays.

Wijbes took the packet and eventually set sail. The voyage was uneventful, and at last the ship hove to at some distance from the shore where the armies of imported workmen were still busy erecting the warehouses and dock installations. He surveyed the scene through his telescope, and no doubt somewhat mistrustful of the state of the unmarked channel he ran up what would nowadays be the flag G of the International Code.

Almost immediately a cutter put out from the harbour, and the sailors put over the ladder. The pilot climbed aboard, and they were surprised to see that he wore the clothes of a Dutch sailor. He nodded, stepped to the wheel, and issuing his orders in Dutch he took the ship up the winding channel and to the quayside. When the lines had been secured he turned to the skipper and asked his name, and where he came from. Wijbes told him.

'Then you are welcome,' the pilot said. 'And as your ship is the first to dock in our port I decree that she shall be re-named the *St Petersburg*, and that so long as her keel carries a ship she shall have freedom from all dues, and priority in the port. I decree this in the name of all the Russias.'

Captain Wijbes had often heard about the man who, dressed as an ordinary workman, had been apprenticed to a shipbuilder of Zaandam to learn the trade. This must surely be he.

'Your Imperial Majesty,' he said. 'I am your humble servant.' And he handed the dispatches to Tsar Peter.

Having filled his ship with treasures brought overland from India and the fabulous lands of the East, Wijbes was ready to depart, but before his ship sailed away the skipper received five hundred gold ducats as a present from the Tsar, and every member of the crew one hundred dollars.

The *St Petersburg* had a safe voyage home to Hindeloopen, and there Captain Auke Wijbes unloaded his riches and stored them in his house. This he also did on several later voyages, and as a result of his special privilege he soon amassed a fortune. At length the *St Petersburg* began to creak and groan with age, but remembering Tsar Peter's words the skipper took her to a shipyard and had her slipped. The ship was then stripped right down to the keel, upon which a new and even finer ship was built.

So the time passed, and when Captain Wijbes died he bequeathed the ship to his son. He in turn sailed on the Russian run, and after many years of trading had yet another hull built upon the same original keel. Then came the third generation, who did likewise, a swift and capacious cargo-carrier taking its place upon the keel which had first sailed into St Petersburg. But this was to be the last of the Wijbes line, for the young skipper's wife died when her baby was born, and the infant died also.

The people of Hindeloopen were not sorry. They had become envious of the great wealth the Wijbes family had built up in the Russian trade, and now they could see that there was none to inherit it. One day the last skipper of the *St Petersburg* would also die, they told themselves, and the vast riches stored in his heavily shuttered house would be there for them to raid. Soon Captain Wijbes came to realise what was in their minds, and that it was not mere idle curiosity which brought the Hindeloopers flocking to the quayside to greet him and see what new things he had brought home. And as he sat brooding and alone in his house he remembered how his father had told him that once in Russia a gypsy woman had gazed into the future and told him that Hindeloopen would fall asleep for ever in the selfsame night that St Petersburg should be engulfed by the waves of the sea.

The night that St Petersburg should be engulfed? St Petersburg, the prosperous city of Peter the Great? That was impossible. But *St Petersburg*, his own ship? Captain Wijbes sat morose and lost in his thoughts. Then on the following morning he had his men come to the house and carry down to his ship some sealed chests, which were placed in a compartment of the hold and cased in.

Every time the ship called at Hindeloopen more chests were carried aboard from the house with the heavy shutters. Then one day the skipper paid off his crew with double money and sent them down to Amsterdam to find other masters. When they had gone he betook himself on board the *St Petersburg*, carrying a bundle which contained the very last of the gold and jewels which he had stripped from his house. Flinging it down, he quickly hauled up some of the sails, flung a burning brand into the hold, cut the mooring lines, and at the last moment leapt back to the quayside. As the great ship swept out of the harbour before an easterly wind of winter he turned his back on her and hurried to his house.

Swiftly the flames spread through the vessel, and the citizens of Hindeloopen saw with horror how Captain Wijbes' famous ship drove burning over the water. The church bells rang the alarm and the men and women ran to the skipper's house to tell him the fearful news. But there was no answer, however much they called and banged on the door.

'Come out, Captain Wijbes,' they yelled. 'Hurry! Your ship is burning!'

Then as there was still no reply, they broke down the door. Skipper Wijbes was there right enough, stretched out dead upon the floor amid a sea of broken china. With the last of his strength he had staggered round the parlour, hurling to the floor the priceless porcelain he had brought back from Russia, all that remained of the great treasures of himself and his father and grandfather.

There was nothing left for the covetous Hindeloopers, nothing but a slumped body and a heap of smashed crockery, and the puff of fleeting steam out at sea as the fiercely burning vessel broke her back, her famous keel, and sank below the waves. And from that night forward the fortunes of Hindeloopen declined, just as the gypsy had foretold, and the little town sank into a perpetual, sleepy peace.

It would be difficult to find any place more desolate on an afternoon of downpour than the lock at Kornwerderzand, and I doubt if on a sunny day it would be very different. The immense barrier of the Afsluitdijk is broken only by a large lock chamber crossed by a road bridge, and on the 300-feet-thick dike itself stand the houses of the sluice-keepers. Otherwise there is nothing. The dike is a monument of engineering, and about as interesting as any other twenty-mile wall of concrete and rubble would be.

Arrived at the lock we showed our papers, the lock-keeper pressed the buttons to operate the sluices, and soon we were running out into the strange and rather eerie expanse of shallow salt water between the northern coast and the Frisian Islands. Away to starboard the marked channel known as the Boontjes twisted through the covered sandbanks towards Harlingen, only one hour distant, and hidden away in the drizzle on our port side were the long, low islands of Texel, Vlieland and Terschelling.

Among all the tales of avarice avenged and wickedness requited it is pleasant to come upon the story of what befell a certain ship as she was sailing through these same waters bound for England. Unlike ourselves her crew were basking in the pleasant sunshine and a gentle breeze filled the sails as the vessel forged through the channels inshore of the islands. Whether she was in the Boontjes or not I do not know, for the precise location is not given of the place where a sudden dark cloud appeared as if from nowhere and the crew barely had time to reef before the full violence of the storm was upon them.

The Waddenzee is no place to be caught in a storm, for its shallows will quickly set up a sharp and confused sea. Soon the vessel was rolling and pitching, and though all sail was struck and the skipper let the ship drive there came a fearful crack as the rudder was carried away by a wave. Out of control the proud ship was in danger of rolling on her beam ends or being flung on the banks, and the captain and his crew thought the last hour of their voyaging had surely come. So did the skipper's unhappy wife, as she clutched the rail of her bunk, feeling decidedly seasick.

Suddenly one of the sailors stared, pointing aft with a shaking finger. Over the transom there rose the dripping locks of a shaggy head. As an experienced seaman the captain at once recognized it as that of a merman, and making his way aft he addressed the apparition and asked it what it wanted.

The merman raised himself in the water, and replied in a deep subaqueous voice. It seems that like the merman who once cursed the island of Schouwen because the fishermen there had cruelly taken his wife on land, where she quickly died, he spoke in Dutch. The Waddenzee merman explained that he was the one who had made the storm, and to the astonishment of the sailors he went on to say that his wife was actually in process of labour. She urgently needed a midwife. The captain's wife must come to her aid immediately, he said.

The skipper pondered, then put his megaphone to his lips and called back. 'My wife is seasick,' he said. 'She is asleep. She cannot be roused from her bed.'

Perhaps he hoped in this way to satisfy the merman, but the fellow was far from mollified. With a flick or two of his tail he further stirred the water, to show that he would have no prevarication. Either the skipper's wife should come, or he would increase the gale to hurricane strength, he declared.

Far from being asleep the captain's wife had been listening. She was a courageous woman as well as a compassionate one, and bursting from the deckhouse she staggered aft. With a cry to the merman that she was coming she threw herself over the stern and disappeared beneath the waves. And as quickly as it had come, so now the storm was stilled.

On the strangely calm sea the ship drifted, none knowing what to do. No doubt the crew peered down into the silty water and perhaps the skipper muttered a prayer or a curse. Some of the men were probably for sailing on and leaving the woman to her fate, but without a rudder this would not have been easy. The skipper was a patient man and perhaps he also had a belief that the merman only wanted help and was not by nature wicked. He paced the deck in thought for a while, until suddenly one of the men called to him to come and listen. Making his way to the rail he leaned over it. Sure enough, a strange sound could be heard, a bubbly voice down in the depths singing what was unmistakably a cradle song. There could be no doubt about it now; a new merbaby had been born in the Waddenzee.

Suddenly there was a movement in the water, and the skipper's wife appeared beneath the counter. Quickly the pilot ladder was let go, and the sailors reached over to help her aboard. She needed help, too, for although her clothes were not even damp her hands were occupied in holding up the corners of her apron, which was loaded with gold and jewels. These she shared out among the crew, and while she was doing so the good merman recovered the rudder, repaired it, and set it on its pintles again. Then as he waved the ship a grateful farewell on its voyage to England, he called that never again should the vessel know anything but moderate and favourable winds as long as she sailed the seas.

I have never met a merman who did not tell the truth, and no doubt the ship which rendered such assistance to him was indeed vouchsafed many years of Force 3s and 4s, with a 5 when needed. As we sailed through the wind-driven rain along the Boontjes channel towards where Harlingen presumably lay hidden in the gathering gloom I wondered whether there was any chance of this incident repeating itself. We had on board for the run from Amsterdam to Kiel one of my doctor brothers-in-law and his wife. Douglas was said to be a good surgeon in cases of emergency, and his wife Prue had once been trained as a nurse. If I could buy a lifetime of calm voyaging for the *Thames Commodore* simply by persuading them to jump over the stern into the Waddenzee there was much to be said for it. But though I repeatedly scanned the water in our wake no merman had appeared when at last the cranes of Harlingen harbour pierced the mist only a short way ahead.

Of course the merman of the Waddenzee did not refrain from stirring up storms in general, and one of his most fearsome was raised on an October night in 1799. A certain French frigate which had been captured by the British had been refitted and put into commission by the navy, and she set out from Yarmouth to carry across the North Sea half a million pounds in gold which a London banker had advanced to pay the allied troops landed in North Holland as part of a plan to outflank the forces of Napoleon. Before dark the ship was off the Frisian Islands, bound for the channel which would lead her through to the Zuyderzee approaches. It was then that the merman set to work, and either because he did not like the merchant banking firm which had made the loan, or because he was on the side of Napoleon and his egalitarian imperialists, or perhaps just for sheer fun and to amuse his children, he stirred the sea most viciously. Between the isles of Terschelling and Vlieland the ship was driven off course, and in the darkness of the night when none could hope to thread a way in safety through the sandbanks she was cast on the shallows and smashed to pieces.

More than two hundred bodies were washed ashore on Terschelling, and others on Vlieland. The sole survivor was the ship's clerk, who confirmed the identity of the ship and then expired. And that was for some time the end of the matter, except that half a million pounds of gold cannot lie for long in shallow water without attracting the efforts of local fishermen and divers, and salvage men. Diving bells and dredgers and every conceivable device were brought to the area, but without result. Nearly sixty years passed before the first fifty thousand pounds was brought up, and just before the Second World War a gold bar with a stamped number came up in the haul of a Terschelling fisherman.

Late in the nineteenth century, however, two interesting items were salvaged. One was the ship's rudder, which was brought over to London and converted into a fine carved chair for the Chairman of Lloyd's and a table for the secretary. The bell was also brought to Lloyd's, and it stands there still under a canopy. It is still brought into service, and one ring on the bell of the ill-fated *Lutine* means that some ship has been reported a total loss. Two rings have a more cheerful meaning, and tell that an overdue ship has at last been reported.

Had the day not been one of rough wind and cold rain I had hoped to cut through the dike at Den Oever near its western end, and run over to the island of Texel to see the birds. Only four months later I was able to see that strange isle, not aboard the *Thames Commodore* but on the *Onrust*. Two years earlier we had taken Anne and Pete Carey from Farmington in Connecticut down the full length of the Moselle, and they had been so bitten with the idea of water voyaging that now they had themselves chartered a boat in Holland and had invited us to join them aboard for a week of voyage which was to cover some of the very few Dutch waterways my wife and I had never seen. So, one evening in August, we arrived at the cheese weigh-house in Alkmaar to see the *Onrust* lying waiting for us just where, fifteen years earlier, the *Commodore* had lain to await the dawn arrival of the barges and trucks loaded to capacity with ton upon ton of round and cartwheel Edam cheeses.

Alkmaar's Friday cheese market is one of the best known sights of Europe. In fact much of the dealing in the quarter million tons of cheese which Holland produces annually takes place over the telephone or in coffee houses, but enough of the North Holland product comes to Alkmaar's market place to bring several thousand visitors every week – all of whom may be counted upon to buy at least a baby Edam and some of whom will become lifelong eaters of Dutch cheese. Personally I find the Edam cheese rather insipid, and though the Gouda is stronger I would only select it if the sole alternative were the 'process cheese' invented in America. I have never been able actually to eat process cheese, though I have used it satisfactorily to grease a water-pump when my supply of more orthodox stuffing material had run out.

Alkmaar's guild of cheese-porters dates from 1604, and the dress of its members has not greatly changed over the intervening years. Their broad Italian straw hats, yellow, red, green or blue according to their section, flash bright in the summer sun, and their white overall suits give the members an air of being rather gaily dressed ambulance men. Nowadays the men are only porters on Friday mornings as a pleasant break from work in the insurance office, workshop, or coffin-builder's yard, and a porter may even decide not to report for duty if his own work is too urgent. Then his name is chalked upon the 'shame-board' in the guildroom behind the giant scales, and he has to pay a modest fine. But gone are the days when the porters gathered there for an evening of beer and song. The television has conquered that particular tradition, for ever.

Bargaining is done in public, but only in a whisper. Buyer and supplier stand facing each other, tapping each other's right hand as the matter proceeds. Maybe there is a hitch and one of them will turn away, but soon the negotiation is taken up again until in a crescendo of claps from palms hardened by years of practice the deal is concluded. Slap, slap, bang, and another ton or two is bought. The carriers hurry to load it on their sledge-shaped barrows and shuffle off to the scales. Weighed, the cheeses are tipped into handcarts and wheeled away to the warehouses, where some may sit for a year before they are properly come of age.

Cheese-selling is picturesque, but cheese-making is part of the great metabolic system of the Dutch nation. One of the largest factories is at Ursem, outside Alkmaar, and most of the cheeses on the market cobbles are in fact Ursem cheeses from the Prinses factory. Night and morning the patient Dutch cows are hitched to the pulsating suction pipes in meadows all across North Holland, and the farm lorries bump away to the factory to have the churns of warm and creamy milk loaded off to a roller belt. As each churn enters the factory it is set upon by the robot arms of one of two machines, which whisks it up, snatches off the lid, and turns the container upside down. Four hundred steel churns an hour each machine can tackle, and a river of milk flows through stainless steel ducts into the churns or into the storage tanks – for cows make milk seven days a week but men only cheese it on five days.

Further down the line the skimmed milk is run into such stainless swimming baths as would grace Florida mansions. Stirring arms swish it silently to and fro, and a man pours in a jug of rennet. Soon there is a basin of several tons of junket and the curds are dripping dry as they are extruded in an endlessly marching roadway of pale and flabby coagulate toward the guillotine. Flunk, and five more full-size cheeses are ready for the moulds. Flop, and another five jostle them from behind. Soon they are on their way round the long conveyor track to be squeezed a little more, then harder still, until they are ready to lie in the warehouse and be coated, slapped to see if they sound firm, and weeks or months later to be sent on their journey into the world outside.

Some of the cheeses are dipped in red wax. These are destined for export, and mainly to Britain. Long ago the idea took root in the mind of the English housewife that Edam cheeses were red, and no grocer could ever hope to convince her otherwise. Shown an ordinary Edam or North Holland cheese in its natural naked glory she will stoutly maintain that it cannot be genuine, just because it is not red, so the Dutch cheese-makers have to dip them, or in some cases merely wrap them in red plastic paper, to satisfy her.

Cheese-makers have their friends in the bacilli which are added to do the actual cheesing of the curds, and their enemies in farmers who are reticent about mastitis. When a cow is struck by this bovine malady the vet will often prescribe penicillin, and this excellent antibiotic has a tendency to pass through into the milk glands, unchanged. The cow then produces milk which not only will not cheese, but will destroy the busy hordes of cheese-making bacteria added to the batch at the factory. When this happens, the cheese-men may find themselves left with a few score tons of cheeses which obstinately refuse to do anything more than turn into richly mouldy junket. A farmer has only to state that he has a cow under treatment, and the factory will pay for his milk just the same and divert it to other uses.

But boers are often reticent by nature, and thinking it a reflection upon their animal husbanding to confess a sick cow they may keep quiet, and leave it to the batch-testers in the laboratory to find out in time, if they can.

IV

THE Great North Holland canal on which Alkmaar lies was cut early in the nineteenth century as a ship canal to save the port of Amsterdam from extinction when the southern part of the Zuyderzee began to silt and shoal. Once it was alive with shipping inward bound with strange exotic cargoes, but now its traffic is so slight that one may cruise for an hour without meeting another craft unless perhaps a dredger barge full laden with its giant pudding of grey and sandy mud. North of Alkmaar it is a rather plain waterway with only an occasional swing-bridge to break the long straight line of wind-swept surface before it runs to its end at Den Helder, where the Royal Netherlands Navy lies packed like a fleet of light grey sardines, each ship flaunting a mysterious black grid which no doubt has some ingenious electronic use but looks as though it were erected to prevent the gulls flying down the funnel into the machinery.

Den Helder is a naval base, its streets full of healthy young sailors, neat and tidy and very nautical and not quite sure that it is really Dutch and proper to whistle at their female counterparts housed in two ancient warships which have all the appearance of having been refitted by Noah himself. It is also a prosperous fishing port, and in the small hours the sturdy trawlers begin to crowd along the quay, bringing the catch of a week at sea. Their crews are young, very young, and there is still much to do before fifty ships have swung ashore the baskets filled in their holds and are ready for a wash down and a short rest for vessel and crew alike.

Endlessly the container trays are hauled into the auction hall, already sorted into sole and Dover sole, plaice, turbot, and odds and ends caught accidentally on the winding-in. The crews heave up their baskets and trays to overturn them on tables where four of their fellows stand, one at each corner, to snatch the fish in red rubber-gloved hands and swiftly place each flat-fish nose against a stop and note where the tail reaches on a grooved board which decides whether it is to be classified as small, small medium, large medium, or large. All down the hall the fish fly into their appropriate grade trays, which soon are filled and stacked down the centre of the building. There is not a moment to lose, for by seven-thirty the buyers are at their desks and the auctioneer at his microphone.

The lots stand piled in rows, each box with a label of the trawler's number slapped upon one of the fish. Above them is a great dial with a pointer, on which all eyes are fixed.

'Three guilders a kilo, gentlemen. Sole, first quality, large.'

The needle swings counter-clockwise, cent by cent, swiftly. Two seventy, two sixty, two fifty. At two forty-one it stops abruptly and below it a number in lights gives the identity of the buyer. He takes three hundred kilos, and a boy with a pole bearing pads of labels steps up and tears off a slip with the buyer's name and slaps it on a sole. The porters run to drag away the quarter ton of boxes, and already another lot is under the dial and the needle has come to rest. Within the hour it is all over, and a hundred thousand fish are on their way to the shops and stores across the country. The ships lie silent, or are chugging up the basin to fuel. Spare ice, stained and bloody, is shovelled into the harbour. The herring-gulls swoop upon the pickings of guts or crushed fish. The sweepers ply their hoses, and the Helder's fish-market is ready for another day's arrivals from the North Sea banks.

Den Helder lies behind its huge dike at the very tip of the Dutch mainland and so close to the nearest of the Frisian islands that the stout car-ferry can cover the distance in a bare fifteen minutes. We knew Texel to be the haunt of migrant birds, so we had arranged with the State Forestry Commission to be taken into their preserve at de Muy, two thirds of the way along the island. What we did not realise was that Texel is also a favourite camping

c

ground, particularly for the Germans – who find everything in the way of groceries and supplies very much cheaper than on their own Frisian islands.

Every half-hour the ferry-boat crossed the swift tidal current of the sound, and the moment it opened its lips the cars poured out in a double stream, seventy more families of campers to swell the holiday population. Nearly all were German, and they headed for the little towns lying at the back of the dunes, hurrying to acquire a licensed space in which to set up temporary home. The roads and lanes of the island were packed with cars, and just behind the outermost line of sandhills a great street of tents, bright orange and blue, stretched as far as one could see. Some of the visitors camped simply, but most had tables and chairs, and even bedsteads. A few had brought gas stove and refrigerator, and by the quantity of furniture we could only conclude that their homes back in the Ruhr had been stripped bare.

Texel is a broad, curving bar of dunes topped with Corsican pines and backed by a polder, its green fields spotted with sheep and its villages packed with sunburned parents hauling their children in hired wagons with soft rubber wheels. The chief articles of trade are ice-cream and beer, shrimping-nets and accommodation. One might wonder that so many people could be packed into the villages without the island sinking under the sheer weight of humanity, and yet the bustle of holiday-making leaves much of Texel untouched. Only a mile out of the crowded street of de Koog we found the isle silent except for the calls of oyster-catchers and curlews, gulls and redshank and sandpiper. A sandy track edged with willowherb and wild mint crossed the pastures to a copse of firs standing alone, the trees bent lopsided from the prevailing westerlies. This little wood had the curious name of Oorlogschip (or Warship) because from afar it seemed to have the shape of a ship of the line. Under the trees was a small green hut where the guide of the de Muy breeding sanctuary was awaiting us, dressed in dull green and almost invisible.

With a handful of others we set off, wondering that out of perhaps ten thousand holiday visitors not a dozen could be found who cared to see Texel's birds. He was a real naturalist, our cheerful companion, able to tell the name in Dutch or German, Latin or English, of any flower or bird we saw as we followed him into the marshes behind the dunes. Snipe, a nest of baby linnets, and then we came over a rise to just such a slack as one might see in the dunes between Liverpool and Southport. There were the same flowers too – ragwort, the open-eyed Grass of Parnassus, and the pyrola more delicate than lily of the valley. But the birds were Texel's own visitors, species which had used these breeding grounds for centuries.

'*Lepelaars!*' The guide pointed, and we stood stock still, staring at the curious and rather dodo-like creatures in the short scrub by the water. Yes, they were spoonbills right enough, and they stood languidly with bristling crests and their heads drooped as though tired of the sheer effort to support an oversized bill. We stared at them through our binoculars, but they did not appear to think the bipeds across the marsh worthy of attention. They knew that every day a small herd would come to gape, and that a wise State Forestry Commission saw to it that the curiously clothed anthropoids were harmless.

Though the Frisian Islands, both Dutch and German, are bright with the lights of holiday towns and camps, there is something strangely sinister about this wide area of sea in which the earth struggles to the surface only as a line of bleak sandy bars. Birds call weirdly across the emptiness when the visitors have gone to bed, and in the moonlight strange shadows flit across the shores laid bare by the falling tide. Somewhere out in the deep, Ekke Nekkepen, the merman king, may raise his head above the water and ponder whether or not to raise another storm to dash the frail ships of the seafaring nations to destruction on the banks, but nowadays his task is made more difficult by the efficiency of the lighthouses which flash, each in its own rhythm, to identify the beads in the bracelet of islands: Texel and Vlieland, Terschelling and Ameland, Schiermonnikoog, Simonszand, Rottumeroog, and Borkum lying off the mouth of the Ems; the line continues right up to the entrance of the Weser in the dangerous waters of the German Bight. These are the Electrides of the ancients, the Isles of Amber from which, in Nero's time, a Roman fleet collected five tons of the coveted substance in a single visit. Amber may not be so plentiful now, but at least one island (Ameland) has a name to remind us of the days long ago when amber was an important article of commerce. And besides their amber the isles must always have had something of an eerie character which makes it easy enough to imagine hauntings, and bewitchings, and horrors such as that of the beach where Ameland is relentlessly pounded by the sea.

It was long, long ago that a ship was sailing outside the isles when mutiny broke out on board. The crew rose against the captain and slew him, throwing his body to the waves. 'Good riddance,' they cheered as the corpse sank from view. 'And may the devil take any who fishes him out of the sea. Any man who finds him can keep him for ever!'

So the crew laughed and cheered in their success, and as soon as they had helped themselves to everything of value in the cargo set off upon a new course, steering northward into the falling darkness. Perhaps they had not reckoned with Ekke Nekkepen, for it must have been he who that same night raised such a gale as none of the men had ever known. They were able sailors, but not all their efforts could prevent the ship from broaching to the waves and being carried amid the foam to where the breakers pounded upon the banks. With a crack the ship was flung on the sands, which hereabouts are little softer than concrete. In a moment the vessel was nothing but a tangle of timber and rigging, and of her proud mutineers only two men survived. Clinging to planks they were washed ashore exhausted, on the long and beautiful white beach of Ameland.

In the eerie flicker of lightning from the departing storm they at last struggled to their feet and set off toward the village along the shore. Already the strand was strewn with wreckage driven ashore from their vessel, and perhaps from others sunk in the same storm. The two men looked among the debris in case there should be valuables, but the sea has a strange way of casting up odd bits of timber rather than coins and gold, and they found nothing. Nothing, that is, until they saw a bulky piece of wreckage bobbing in the edge of the surf, a shape which could only be the body of one of their fellows. They waded in and grabbed a hold, then dragged the body up to the sand to kneel beside it. Turning it over, they saw to their horror the face of their murdered captain.

If they had forgotten their light-hearted curse, it seems that the devil had not, for the arms of the dead man suddenly reached up and gripped them round their waists. Try as they would they could not tear them free. Struggling to stand up they were still held in the rigid grip, and in panic they set off, stumbling along the beach with the corpse dragging between them, its feet scoring a furrow in the sand.

Over the dunes and between the drifts of storm-blown sand they shambled onward, never able to stop. Always the captain held them tightly, his legs trailing behind them in rigor mortis. They have been roaming that deserted beach for centuries of night-times now, and whenever a storm dashes the waves against the banks any who may be unwise enough to brave the darkness of the gale-swept sands may suddenly see in the brief glare of a flash of lightning the two men struggling towards him, and the captain with his face turned up to the sky in a smile of age-long satisfaction as his murderers drag him this way and that in their efforts to rid themselves of a grip that will last to eternity.

Anyone looking at a map of northern Europe must wonder how these strange islands arose. Obviously they are the result of inundation, combined with the tendency of storm waves to build up banks, but it is only the Frisians who know just why the flooding took place. It was, they say, because a certain beautiful queen of England by the name of Garhoeven was engaged to be married to the king of Denmark, when he most treacherously went off and married another.

Garhoeven was not one to be so easily insulted. She schemed to ruin the land of her faithless betrothed, and set about the task with energy. At that time England was joined to France by a neck of land seven miles wide – a fact of prehistory which should place the events in this tale at a time not later than 6,000 B.C., for Britain was connected with the continental mainland until surprisingly recent times, and even the present ferry routes from Harwich to Esbjerg and Bremerhaven were dry land as late as 7,000 B.C., when the coast line ran roughly from the Humber to the Skaw. However, the Frisians assert that Garhoeven lived at the beginning of the seventh century A.D. The land bridge acted as a barrier to keep the Atlantic from inundating the lands of the North Sea shores, and Garhoeven put seven hundred navvies to work to cut through the isthmus. By working night shifts as well as by day they at last succeeded, and the king of Denmark had only been married seven years to Garhoeven's rival when the water poured through the gap and surged over Denmark to leave only those parts of it which are still above water today. The king, who lived in Jutland, escaped unharmed, but Garhoeven was herself drowned. Her natural curiosity to see the disaster had led her to install herself on a small island off the west coast of Jutland, and there she was overwhelmed.

If Denmark was largely inundated, the water also burst over the country of the innocent Frisians, whose coastal land lay even lower than Denmark. Many towns and villages were swept away, so that the Waddenzee came to lie where they had been. However, the Frisians were a fair-minded people, and realising that the ultimate fault was that of the untrustworthy Danish monarch they turned upon him and poisoned him. Then they set to work to build the dikes which would preserve the rest of their land from the fury of the sea the Queen of England had unleashed and which could never again be contained within its former bounds.

All the same, the islands seem already to have been there when the Frisians themselves arrived in strange fashion to inhabit them and settle the mainland behind them. Some of the legends see in the Frisians the vanquished Trojans, or the Assyrians, or even a crowd of refugees who left Jerusalem when it was besieged by the army of Sennacherib. But none are in any doubt that the Frisians arrived in that splendid vessel the *Mannigfual*, which we have already briefly met as a possible knocker-down of Ransdorp church spire.

The Frisians, the tale goes, were a seafaring people of the Levant, and when their land was threatened these independent folk decided to pack up and sail away to find their fortune elsewhere. The seas were uncharted, however, and there were no

Admiralty Pilot Books, and as the seamen were afraid of being scattered by fog or storm or darkness they decided to collect all their ships together, take them apart, and use the timbers to produce one giant ship which could carry the whole people over the seas. This ship was the *Mannigfual*.

I have already mentioned the incident in the Dover Strait, but a few more details will give a better picture of what the ship was like. It is known, for example, that to reach the stern from the fo'c'sl was a journey of several weeks and that young lads sent aloft to furl the sails at the yard-arms came back to the deck as grown men with beards. To sustain them on their long journeys among the rigging the sheave-blocks were hollowed out and contained hostelries, and in the crow's-nests herds of oxen were kept and fed until they were needed for food by the voyagers. One day there was a curious culinary incident, when one of the oxen broke out of its stall and fell headlong right through an open hatch into the soup. The cook had a boat at his disposal which could be swung out and launched in the soup-cauldron – which had necessarily to be of size enough to feed a whole nation – so that he could row about and skim off the scum with a shovel.

When the ox splashed in from a great height the boat was launched at once and the cook set out from the rim with a grapple to try to recover the body, but the skeleton of the beast only came to light at the bottom of the pot when the Frisians had drunk all the soup.

The captain of the *Mannigfual* was Frieso, and he rode from side to side on the bridge on horse-back. He had a raven on each shoulder, and these birds watched behind him and told him of anything he could not see for himself. They would soar when necessary and take a sight over the horizon. The skipper had two brothers, Saxo and Bruno. Saxo was the steersman throughout the voyage, but what special office Bruno may have had I do not know.

The Frisians set their course by some constellation in the west, and sailed right down the Mediterranean until they reached the Pillars of Hercules, where they had some difficulty in squeezing through the gap. Once out in the open ocean they were carried northward by the currents until they came into the area of fogs, which can of course only mean the coastal waters of Britain. After months or perhaps years they saw ahead of them a sailing-boat, which was probably a Viking ship returning home from a trading voyage or a raid. They followed it, and that was how the *Mannigfual* came to be stuck fast in the Dover Strait.

After soaping their way out, the Frisians rounded the Skaw and turned down the Kattegat and the Great Belt into the shallow waters of the Baltic. It was here that they suddenly ran aground – and I am not surprised that they did, for the *Thames Commodore* herself has cut across from one Danish island to another with the echo-sounder showing only four feet of water beneath her keel. But Frieso was a man of decision, and he rode his steed around the decks, giving his orders. The sails were run down, and all the ballast was hoisted and poured over the side to lighten the ship. This ballast was mostly composed of sizeable boulders, as anyone can see who visits the place where it was dumped and looks at the heap the Frisians left. The Danes own it nowadays, and call it Bornholm. Even then the ship did not come clear, and as a last resort the ash and clinker was scraped from the galley stove and thrown over to form the islands called Kristiansøn. Geologists have long known that these curious little isles are composed of ash, but like most scientists they have preferred to find a more improbable explanation and have always described them as being volcanic in origin.

Frieso could at last work the ship about, and he took her out of the Baltic as quickly as he could. He wanted deeper water close inshore, so having rounded the Skaw again he headed the ship due south until he came in sight of a low-lying coast. There the *Mannigfual* at last came to anchor, and the people were ferried ashore. Frieso and his own people, the Friesians, landed on one of the islands – probably Vlieland, off Harlingen. Saxo and the Saxons chose the flat marshy country between the mouths of the Weser and Elbe, the land which the *Thames Commodore* was to cross in the Hadelner canal. Bruno's people took their boats far up the Weser and into the Aller until there was not enough water to float them, and so they came to found Brunswick.

The Frisians, who had selected the land of islands and meres, were for centuries to be engaged in a war with the sea which the jilted Queen Garhoeven had unleashed. They built their dikes and raised refuge mounds to which they could flee when the waters broke into their land, and when next they appear it is as a pagan people led by the rough King Radbod. It was the English missionary Willibrod who first attempted to introduce them to Christianity, and he reached Radbod's camp at a time when the king and his people were gathered on the beach to watch the rising tide engulf two screaming boys who had been tied to stakes to propitiate the gods of the sea. Willibrod is said to have rescued them by praying the tide to keep within a lower range, but Radbod himself was not easily won over. Willibrod worked for long to bring him to the verge of baptism, and at last the king went so far as to place one foot in the water. But then he paused.

'Tell me,' he said. 'My Frisian ancestors, are they in heaven or in hell?'

Willibrod was perhaps not prepared for this question, or he would hardly have answered as he did.

'They are in hell,' he said. 'They were heathens, and so they cannot be in heaven.'

Radbod withdrew his foot. 'I wish to remain true to my fathers,' he declared. 'Where they have gone, there I wish to go also, that I may be with them.' And for the rest of his days he fought the Church with all his powerful vigour.

It was a Sunday evening, and the April rain was falling cold and steady as we turned the last buoys of the Boontjes channel and ran between the moles of the Frisian harbour of Harlingen. The chart showed the place to be a sizeable port with several basins, but I had not reckoned on the fact that the fishermen would all return to harbour for the week-end, and when we came round the corner to the long stretch of the Noorderhaven edged with its long row of beautiful gabled houses from the sixteenth and seventeenth centuries we found drifters lying two abreast along either side of it. The same was true of the Zuiderhaven, for more than one hundred fishing boats had come in from the North Sea to spend the week-end in their home port. The commercial harbour was well patronised by ships of the Scottish and English trade, for westward

of the Ems Harlingen alone is a port of any consequence within
the girdle of the Frisian Islands. No other can be reached by any
but the smallest ships, and Harlingen also had a stroke of luck
which made its fortunes very different from those of Staveren.
When the Dutch engineers finally closed the great dike which was
to shut off the Zuyderzee and convert it into the Ijsselmeer their
work spelled a lingering death to the little seaports of Hoorn and
Enkhuizen, and to the fisher fleets of Marken and Volendam. The
trade of these places declined, and was transferred to Harlingen,
and on the wall by one of the harbour basins a handsome bronze
plaque commemorates the closure which brought the town a new
prosperity and established its importance as a port. Men from the
other towns may view the plaque with mixed feelings, but the
Harlingers have no doubt about the blessing brought by the
elimination of their competitors, and they are not afraid to say so.

With the port so filled with shipping, the only place we could
find to berth the *Thames Commodore* was a patch of wall close
beneath the customs house, just outside the basins filled with
drifters. We could not have chosen a more attractive position, for
before first light on the Monday morning the fishing fleet was
getting under way. A heavy chugging, a ring of bells as the barriers
went down on the approaches to the lifting bridge by our bows,
and then the lights of the ships would glide past within a few feet
of the *Thames Commodore*'s flank. At each bridge-raising another
batch would emerge from one basin or the other, the crews waving
cheerfully to us as they sorted their gear for the first trawl of the
week. More than fifty ships had slid past us before I started the
engines to turn and head up for the Tjerk Hiddes lock which would
soon be opening at six o'clock to pass us through into the van
Harinxma canal towards Franeker and Leeuwarden.

The most romantic way to see Friesland must certainly be to
wait for a really hard frost, put on a pair of skates, and make the
120-mile tour of the eleven Frisian cities on the frozen canals
which link them. But the next best thing is to cross the wide green
country by boat, following in the wake of the big barges which
chug across the country from Lemmer or Staveren, or from
Harlingen itself. The rain had stopped and we were soon gliding

Harlingen, the Noorderhaven

across a green landscape with wide pastures grazed by the sleek Frisian cows which even now were in some cases still wearing overcoats of blanket-cloth. Across the meadows the peewits poked their skewer beaks into anything that appeared interesting.

Redshanks cried as they flew and bar-tailed godwits stalked over the wet grass, too intent on hunting to bother about a little ship like ours as it purred past them, whilst everywhere the oyster-catchers called with their strangely beautiful voices or strutted importantly away about the business of turning up worms and snails – for as Brehm once wrote, the one thing that is certain about the oyster-catcher is that it never catches oysters.

The canal passes through the old city of Franeker and round the edge of Leeuwarden before converging with the other main waterway from Staveren and the Frisian lakes. It was by this second route that we voyaged on the *Onrust* a few months later, and on the first evening we drew in to the edge of the little Frisian town of Sneek.

It happened to be Sneek Week, when even more than at other times Sneek is a sailor's paradise. There are said to be some five thousand sailing boats in and around the town and its neighbouring meres at normal times, but Sneek Week brings others from Germany and the southern provinces of the Netherlands. As we threaded our way through them aboard the *Onrust* I would not have found it hard to believe that there were ten times as many as five thousand. Happy and sun-bronzed their young crews tacked them to and fro across the waterways, confident in the belief that sail takes precedence over steam or internal combustion. And so it does in the International 'Rules for the Prevention of Collisions at Sea', but not every young dinghy sailor has tried to steer a 300-tonner. That was the modest size of a Groningen ship which happened to be coming down the narrow fairway when a handsome blue yacht began to cross the waterway only a few feet ahead of its bow. The light breeze faded, and even if the skipper of the motorship had put his engine astern he would have struck the boat just the same. However, he did not even slow his motor, thinking perhaps that a sound bumping would teach these mere amateurs a lesson. Probably it did, but the sound of the impact made me sorry for them none the less, and I was relieved to see that their craft was brushed aside and not actually overrun by the bigger ship's thrusting stem.

There is, I think, nothing so good as an eel, and the Londoner's way of jellying them has always seemed to me to be a ruination of a fish which is only perhaps surpassed by salmon. Cooked *au vert*, fried, stewed, coated in batter, or just plain smoked and eaten like a banana, an eel will attract the crew of the *Thames Commodore* as surely as the sound of a drawn cork will bring a customs officer to pay a casual courtesy visit – particularly in the wineless lands of Scandinavia. Until the Second World War the Dutch eel boats would stow their catch alive in a perforated hold and make for the Thames, and Sneek's attractive little museum of Frisian shipping has an oil painting in which a row of Friesland eelers lies off the quay of Billingsgate fish market, with London Bridge hazy in the background. They were among the most beautiful of all craft, these sturdy wooden boats with their leeboards and high rounded sterns, and London is the poorer now they have gone. Dutch eels may still be imported, but the deep-freezer has taken the trade from the *palingaken* which used to bring an air of romance and seamanship to the wharf above Tower Bridge.

The shipping routes from Harlingen and Staveren converge a little way west of the Bergumermeer, and from that point onward the waterway to Groningen resounds to the heavy throb of the motors of giant barges, Dutch and German. It is a pleasant but not spectacular voyage through farming country where herds of Frisians are held by their nipples to milking-machines and beyond them the white sails of yachts glide through the pastures, borne on invisible waterways. At Garkeuken there is a brief respite for a lock, and then the voyage continues into the city of Groningen, thirteen miles ahead.

I decided to take the *Thames Commodore* to the city by the orthodox route, pursuing the broad van Starkenborgh canal to its end in Groningen lock, then turning right at the next crossroads. But the lock was slow, and the only berth to which it led us was a small space between two laid-up and rusty barges. The reason for this vacant space was not long hidden. It covered a vigorous effluent which bubbled up from below and was probably the vent of the public lavatory system not far away.

With this experience behind me I asked the skipper of the *Onrust*, four months later, which way he intended to enter the

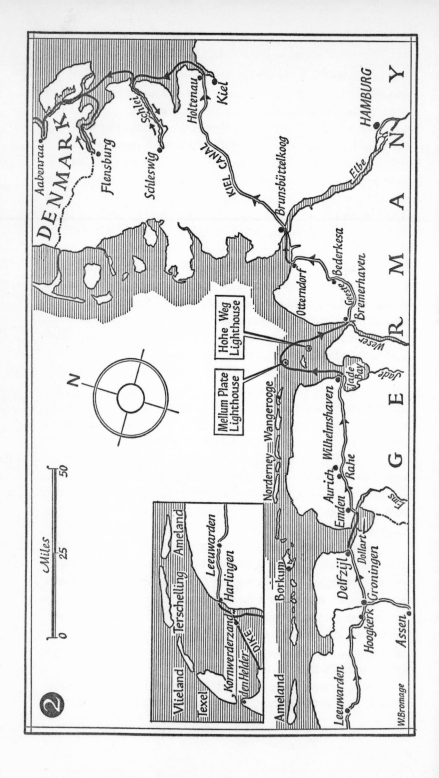

DENMARK

Aabenraa

Flensburg

Schleswig

Schlei

Holtenau

Kiel

KIEL CANAL

Brunsbüttelkoog

Elbe

HAMBURG

GERMANY

Otterndorf

Bederkesa

Geeste

Bremerhaven

Hohe Weg Lighthouse

Mellum Plate Lighthouse

Weser

Jade

Jade Bay

Wangerooge

Norderney

Wilhelmshaven

Rahe

Aurich

Emden

Ems

Delfzijl

Dollart

Groningen

Hoogkerk

Assen

Borkum

Ameland

Leeuwarden

N

Miles
0   25   50

Vlieland

Terschelling

Ameland

Texel

Leeuwarden

Kornwerderzand

Harlingen

Den Helder

DIKE

W.Bromage

city, and to our astonishment Captain van Amerongen said he had never been to Groningen by water. He had voyaged on the canals for more than fifteen years, but no charterer had ever wanted to go there, he said. Sneek was their usual limit, he explained, with just a hint of suggestion that nobody in their senses would want to go to Groningen anyway, and that the Careys and their friends Angus and Pat Gordon would never even have thought of doing so if I had not mulled over their plans with them and put such a silly idea into their heads.

'The Groningers are clods,' he said. 'Cow-peasants, clugs, thick as they're made.'

This, I thought, was a little hard on the Groningers, whose city sent coasters to ports in almost every country in the world, a thing few cow-peasants do. But the skipper was sure, and somehow he managed to make the whole idea of visiting Groningen appear like some ill-devised expedition into a land of cannibals.

We reverted to the problem of how to get to the place. The lock, I said, closed at eight. That meant we had to be there by seven to get through. It was now half past five and we could make it easily enough, but as all the town bridges would shut at seven we should merely end up by being stuck over the sewage again. Much better, I said, was to select one of the three turns to the right a few miles short of the city and take the place by stealth from the rear. I recommended the second of the three because it led through to a canal called the Hoendiep (or Hen Deep). The name appealed to me, and that was my only reason for suggesting the route at all, but I was careful not to tell the captain, who gave me the impression of a man moved by more nautical considerations. He was a great canal-runner and had done twenty-six locks at le Chesne in the Ardennes in five hours and twenty minutes, a very good speed for a barge; but he chose his routes according to depth and height, and whether the people along the shore were cow-peasantry.

My choice turned out to be a good one and we should have made Groningen that day if the very small scale three-colour map of the province had been better printed. Because the print did not register properly, the skipper thought we had to pass through a railway bridge and then turn into the Hoendiep, so the railway staff were roused to remove the bolts, jack the thing up, and swing it. In half an hour they had done so, and by the time we discovered that we should have turned before the bridge instead of after it they had put the works back again.

It says much for the railwaymen that after waiting for a train they set to work without complaint and opened the bridge again. But it was now nearly seven o'clock, and at the next roadbridge down the canal we were stopped for the night. Captain van Amerongen muttered something about Groningers, and drew in to the bank at a not very inspiring factory suburb which we found was named Hoogkerk.

The error about the railway bridge was our own fault for trusting a map too easily, and the captain made it good by setting off at six in the morning and reaching the city before breakfast. At eleven o'clock, he said, we were to proceed into the Noord Willems Canal. This choice of waterway was also ours and he seemed to doubt our wisdom. He had neither navigated the canal nor even heard of it, and when I told him that I had been through it as a boy nearly forty years earlier he merely smiled tolerantly, as though interested to know that my brain had already shown signs of derangement at such an early age.

Immediately round the corner from the junction of canals at the southern side of the city the Noord Willems Canal disappeared under a low railway bridge. The keeper came from his hut, smiled agreeably, and said we had missed the eleven o'clock opening time by six minutes. Trains were due, and the bridge could not be tackled again until twenty past twelve. The captain muttered something about Groningen bumpkins and curled up on his wheelhouse seat for a doze.

At midday I walked over to the bridge-house, for I have always believed in showing a certain restiveness when on the wrong side of a movable obstacle. The keeper was all smiles and said the bridge would after all not be opening at twenty past twelve. It would be a quarter to two, but only perhaps.

'Perhaps? And why not at the earlier time?' I asked.

The man managed to convey to me that there was a failure of power. The entire track was immobilised, and Groningen station was full of expresses which had been unable to leave. Looking down the track I could see them silently standing empty, a trifle sad. There were silver ones, and a green one, and at least two with blue international sleeping cars, and foreign rolling-stock. They cluttered the place like dead whales washed up by the tide. Their passengers had long since deserted them as though a prophet had declared that Groningen station were at any moment to have fire and brimstone rained upon it.

'All, all *kaput*,' said the bridgeman with a sweep of his arm worthy of the Duke of Wellington surveying the French forces at Waterloo. 'No current on all the railway.'

'Then you can open the bridge,' I said. 'If the trains are dead, why not open it now?'

The bridgeman then conducted a dumb pantomime with all the machinery to convince me that although the bridge was hand operated it was beset with a series of ingenious devices which prevented any possible error, but also made it impossible to open the span at that moment. When a blue disc was changed to a white one inside a little window about half an inch square, this freed a magnetic lock which enabled him to lift a lever. This bar turned a signal at the far side of the bridge, and when fully raised it also allowed a key to be withdrawn. With this key he could release the locks which held in place the bolts at either end of the bridge. This I could see was an excellent system from the point of view of the passengers in the trains, and I now began to understand why it was that Dutch expresses never took a dive into a canal. But he went on to explain that the simple matter of changing the little window-disc from white to blue was done electrically from the inner recesses of the station hierarchy, to whom he always telephoned whenever a ship arrived. He had indeed telephoned several times already but there was no electricity to move the blue disc and replace it by a white one. For the same reason all the station signals were set at STOP, even if there were no moving trains to be halted. The system was a 'fail-safe' one. It had failed, and everyone was safe, including ourselves.

There was no choice but to settle down to lunch. The bridgeman also departed, to help push up the barriers which had failed safe at a level crossing. After lunch I walked up to the station and asked to see the chief of Groningen's railways. Instead I was received by a polite official whom I addressed in English. I have always found this a sensible thing in Holland, for though the British are generally liked it is with that particular affection one reserves for dogs that are suspected of incipient rabies. People know they must play along with them, and not risk being bitten in the leg.

The station hierarchy said the bridge would be opened in forty minutes, current or no. I said ten minutes was my idea of the matter, and with an eye to hydrophobia they settled for fifteen. And sure enough, twelve minutes later there was a ring of the bridge telephone and the bridgeman came out to watch the disc suddenly metamorphose to blue. Four men in overalls leapt to work the bridge, and the *Onrust* was passed through.

Captain van Amerongen was pleased, but not for long. We soon came to a main road bridge, and he could see no trace of the keeper. I climbed up the buttress and over the boxes of petunias to ask in a greengrocer's and a barber's, a photoshop and a tobacconist's what had happened to the *brugwachter*. All agreed that the bridge-man should be there, and also that he lived the other side of the town, nobody knew where.

I hunted in vain for twenty minutes, but at last the man appeared. The opening times had, he said, been changed only that week. Anyway, from that point onward we would have no difficulty, he assured us. He dropped the barriers, raised the bascule, and passed us into the unknown.

We must have travelled a mile or two before we came to a place where another bridge was being taken away altogether. A grab was busily wrenching at the piles, drawing them like teeth, and a big muck-boat with no motive power was made fast in the gap to receive the debris. More than that, the canal was being widened by a suction dredger which carved up the land like cheese, sucked it in and pumped it through a long pipe to fill an unwanted marsh some distance away. It so happened that the machinery was on one side of the canal and the pipe outlet on the other, the two being connected by a long line of pipes straddling the water on a series of floats.

To let us approach the ruins of the bridge a navvy was sent down the canal with a small tug boat and a set of wrenches. He undid a joint in the silt pipe and towed one half of the line to the side of the canal. Then we had merely to hand the *Onrust* through the gap where the grab was drawing the teeth.

By now we had made at least three miles in five hours but I was glad to see that the skipper was entering into the spirit of canalling, and beginning to face each new difficulty with almost Nelsonian resolution. Indeed, as we squeezed through the debris of the bridge I thought there was a note of sadness in his voice when he remarked that we were now clear of all troubles. The bridges ahead had already been rebuilt, and the lock which soon came into view was so smart and new that a workman was still creosoting the piles at the entrance. We drew in, made fast, and the keeper pressed the button to shut the lower gates. Then he pushed the knob to open the upper paddles, and the motors whirred smoothly to turn the worm-gearing and lift the steel shutters. It was all very wonderful and modern.

The paddles had to be raised two or three feet, and they had covered perhaps half an inch of their journey when the whining suddenly ceased. The complex system of relays had somehow misbehaved itself, and all the machinery had become immobilised.

The keeper was a real countryman – a cow-peasant of Groningen province, no doubt. For all his life he had wound the windlasses of his lock-gates and cranked their creaking doors with large iron handles. Now, in his old age, the engineers had given him a new lock, and a new house, a set of pretty little indicator lamps in red and green, and rows of buttons. No more back-breaking work was to be his, for they had given him every electronic device that technology could provide. The only thing they had left undone was to provide an elementary course in electricity, about which he knew as much as Thurber's aunt. His first reaction to the failure was to stand on the gate looking extremely sad. Then, rather in the way that bystanders will kick the tyres of a motor-car which has passed out, he gently applied his foot to the smooth stainless steel plunger above one of the paddles, and kicked it.

The machinery heeded neither his sorrow, nor his boot, nor

even the expressions of anger in cow-peasant Dutch which followed. He lifted his cap, scratched his head, and explained that the nearest engineers were a day's journey away.

'Bring out the hand-cranks,' I suggested in charade. But he said no, the engineers had removed the hand spindles. One had first to dismount the motors, and that would take hours.

At either end of the lock stood a control house, and in its rear was a steel cupboard which covered one wall and reached to the ceiling. The keeper unlocked the door of the top-gate cabin to reveal a beautiful collection of little silvery mountings from which flowed bundles of wires, red and yellow, mauve, green, orange, black, white and blue. It was like a Wadsworth picture, and I thought the design would have made a wonderful wall-paper.

The keeper looked at the rows of relays and condensers, transformers and cut-outs, none of which were marked except with meaningless labels such as 'H23' and 'D12'. He then began at the top left and beat upon each of them in turn with his fists. From his decades of hand-cranking his hands were as hard as those of the blacksmith under the spreading chestnut tree, and it did not appear to hurt him. Nor did it make any impression upon the recalcitrant machinery.

Meanwhile the *Onrust* was definitely rising. The slight slit which the paddles had bared before they failed let in a small but definite amount of water, and in ten minutes the ship had edged up almost half a step on the ladder, and only had another ten feet to go. I thought that if the keeper left things alone there was a fair chance that during the night the lock would fill to the brim, and in the morning we could steam out into the head water. There was no question of turning round and going back, for the paddles were stuck open just far enough to cause a pressure which would make it impossible to open the bottom gates again – quite apart from any electrical interlocking designed to do the same. I began now to understand even better the meaning of the term 'fail-safe mechanism'. In this case it meant that when the works failed you were safe inside the lock until help arrived in the form of a man who understood electronics.

Having finished thumping the relays at the top end the keeper opened up the cupboard in the cabin by the tail gates and did the same. He then went into the cabin itself and pressed all the knobs in succession, but nothing happened. Each operation was relay-protected. The signal lights at the foot of the lock blinked twice, but that was all.

The honest keeper now began to explain to me in a mixture of dumb crambo and imprecations that they had never taught him what to do in case of failure, because to the engineers failure was unthinkable. At least, I believe that was what he was trying to convey, but he suddenly had another idea and broke off. In the top cabin there was a side cupboard with a vivid red flash of lightning painted on it, and having opened the double safety-lock he stood looking at the handsome copper conductors as though fascinated.

'*Hoe veel volt?*' I merely asked this because I saw he had his foot poised to kick a very powerful-looking transformer coupling.

He shrugged his shoulders. Six volts or two million, it was all the same to him, I could see. And in a way he was right, for a volt is to some extent only a conventional measure of illusion. The difficulty is merely that when crowded together the plusses and minusses of the make-believe have a way of rushing out of the copper conductors and biting anyone who kicks their home. I tried to explain this to him, and all the while there streamed across the blank screen at the back of my mind the pieces of sage advice in the nautical almanac. With dry hands a shock of 100 volts potential would contract the grip . . . unable to let go . . . leap high in the air and pull victim away, but only when you are off the ground . . . artificial respiration for ten hours – or was it twenty? I only knew that if I were to leap high in the air inside this cabin my head would go through the roof.

'*Mijnheer,*' I began, extending a warning hand. '*Mijnheer. . . .*'

The keeper shook his head, and suddenly began to pound with his fists every electrical gadget that was out of reach of his boot. There was a sort of hot fizz from behind one of the panels, and almost at the same moment a cry from aboard the *Onrust* in the pen. One of the six paddles had given up in its attempt to oppose the will of such a determined man. Smoothly, elegantly, it rose to

its full height, leaving its five disgruntled fellows where they were.
The water surged in, the level rose, and soon the keeper could press
a knob to open the gates for the *Onrust* to chug ahead towards
Assen, where early next morning my wife and I left her.

V

EASTWARD from Groningen the Ems canal cuts a straight line
across the swampy pastures to carry the coasters to the salt
water. It is a highly practical canal and not a picturesque one.
Running onward between its carefully graded banks it does not
hesitate for a moment, but aims directly for Delfzijl. One lock, a
smell of seaweed and fish, and the *Thames Commodore* was running
out between the long moles of basalt to let the tide put its shoulders
behind her stout rump and nudge her over to Emden.

It was a leaden afternoon, with shafts of sunlight spreadeagled
almost motionless in their angles through gaps in clouds which
seemed to be pondering whether to thunder or not. The light fell
here and there on a dredger or a muck-boat, for the approaches to
the Ems must continually be dredged to keep them clear for
shipping. Away to our left the horizon joined sky and water in a
line only made visible by the smoke of ships steaming out towards
Borkum and the open sea, their hulls receding into a wide blankness
which none would call beautiful – unless they were on a boat, for
there is something tremendously appealing about even the flattest
of estuaries, a romance bound up with the mere fact that here the
world of cities and farmers and nations slides slowly away into the
universal sea and sky. I think the more imaginative seagulls must
know this, for they congregate in estuaries more than over any
other waters.

We could not see Borkum, that weather-forecast name and the
island where at last the feared Black Rolf met his end. Black Rolf
was a raider. Though he was not in the same class as Störtebeker,

77

and so far as I know never left his name in any song sung by dutiful modern schoolchildren as that great pirate did, he roamed the waters of the Ems and terrorised the poor people of the Frisian islands at the river's mouth. He is said to have shared with Macduff the curious caesarian origin which rendered him invulnerable, and many a captain surrendered all that he had instead of risking a fight with one who must always win.

Black Rolf was not a man who restricted his attacks to wealthy merchant ships. He would land at villages and leave a trail of destruction behind him, and when he discovered that the men of Borkum had all gone on a whaling expedition to Greenland he considered it an excellent opportunity to attack the defenceless island and sack the village.

One of the women saw the ship approaching, and she quickly called the rest together. They do not seem to have been particularly impressed by the tales of Rolf's invincibility, for they quickly decided to teach him a lesson. Rather than let their homes be pillaged they swiftly changed into the land clothes of their sailor husbands and sons, and set to work to roll towards the shore an old cannon which had once belonged to a ship. Levelling the loaded piece at the raider, which was now close inshore, they lit the fuse and stood back. The ball flew out, and by an extremely lucky chance struck the mast of the pirate vessel and felled it.

They had few cannon balls left, but such as they had were fired straight into the side of the ship and caused such damage that Black Rolf himself decided that the choice lay between an armistice and sitting there immobilised until pounded to death or drowned. He chose to capitulate, and he called across to the defenders that they might take the whole ship and its booty if only they would let his crew land in safety.

The women were in a strong bargaining position, so they stipulated that all weapons should be left on board, and that the men were only to come ashore one at a time. Meanwhile they kept their gun trained upon the ship. Rolf agreed to the terms and his crew began to swim over, one by one. They were conducted away, and the moment they were out of sight of their fellows they were knocked down, bound hand and foot, and dragged off to be stored safely away in the tower.

It happened that there was one woman on board the pirate vessel, Black Rolf's own daughter. The Borkum defenders decided that they would allow her to go free, and as she promised to behave herself they did not tie her up along with her companions. All the same, to guard against accidents some of them rowed out to the ship and set it on fire, and before the evening was out it had burned to the water and sunk.

During the night Black Rolf's pirate daughter stole softly out of the house where she was lying. She succeeded in entering the tower, and set about releasing the whole pirate crew. The entire band of pirates then hurried stealthily to the beach and finding a small fishing-boat drawn up on the shore they pushed it down to the water, scrambled aboard, and rowed off. Unfortunately the craft was too small for so many and it wallowed heavily. When the men had rowed it clear of the shallows along Borkum and reached the deeper water, the dangerous sea of the German Bight decided to take another victim. The boat was overset. Black Rolf, his entire crew and his enterprising daughter were all drowned, and no doubt there were hilarious celebrations on Borkum when the men returned from their whale-hunt in the cold northern seas and heard what their womenfolk had done.

It was just after low water when we left Delfzijl, and close to us the Dutch shore of the Ems lay smooth and glistening like a walrus fresh from a swim. Across the flatness where the only wavelets were those left by a passing mud-barge the distant German shore lay as a thin wedge of darker grey, the lighthouse of Knock standing up stiffly like a sentry guarding the approaches. Further ahead and to starboard the coast above Delfzijl curved away to leave the rather sinister area of the Dollart half drying, a feeding-ground for sea-birds, and maybe for bad spirits of the waters too.

One has only to glance at a map to guess that this giant's bite chopped out of the Dutch coastline must once have been dry land, a part of the fertile Groningerland engulfed by the sea. In fact its flooding was not part of the general inundation wrought by the hotheaded and jilted English queen, for the Dollart was formed as the result of a complacent materialism which is historic enough to be associated with the name of one particular farmer, Tidde Winninga.

So rich was the country between Groningen and the Ems that the farmers became extremely prosperous, and somewhat like the traders of Staveren they began to rival each other in the gold and finery of their ladies, and the splendour of their homes. The granaries were filled, the grain sold at high prices to areas less well endowed by nature, and everything was in the favour of those who farmed the wide acres behind the dike. There were prosperous towns and villages, thirty-four in number, and two monasteries.

Along all the German and Dutch Frisian shores which faced the onslaught of the waves of the temperamental North Sea, each stretch of sea-wall had its *dijkgraaf* whose orders had to be obeyed. But it is a curious fact that material well-being always seems to decrease the respect for authority, and Tidde Winninga, richest of all the farmers, was not inclined to pay much attention to any mere local official who ordered him to work on the embanking. When one night the Winningas and their hinds were celebrating with a dance, the wind began to drive the storm waves against the coast, and the *dijkgraaf* called the council quickly to an emergency meeting. The church bells tolled the warning across the fens, and every able man should have taken up his spade and run to the dike. And so they did, except from the Winninga farm. The old boer ordered his people to carry on with their festivities, and when the *dijkgraaf*'s messengers came to his door to urge how serious the situation might be, he contemptuously offered money but refused even to send his paid hands. He would worry, he said, when he saw the water over his fields. Then he might think about helping. Meanwhile, the others could look after themselves. And with that he shut the door in their faces.

The other farmers and their hired men slaved to reinforce the weakest parts of the banks along the other stretches of dike, and everywhere they managed to hold the water at bay. It was about midnight when, at the height of the tide, part of the sea-wall fronting the Winninga acres slipped. The torrent quickly tore a wide breach, and burst in upon the revellers in the farm. How many of them were drowned is not recorded, but the farmer himself survived. In the morning he was the proud owner of hundreds of acres of shallow sea, on which floated a few pieces of driftwood and the corpses of his fatstock. Otherwise he had nothing to his name, and when some weeks later he furtively knocked as a beggar at the door of one of the monasteries, the monks generously took him in.

The rest of the land had in fact survived, but it did not remain safe for long. The other farmers mocked at the fate of Winninga and sat back in righteous self-approval because they at least had turned out, however unwillingly, to hold the dikes. They would have done better to consider how to protect themselves now that the sea had a salient in their territory, for only a little while passed before the storm waves rose again and came surging through the breach to spread out sideways and sweep away every house and farm, each church and monastery in all that part of the rich Groningerland.

Thus the Dollart was formed, and if for centuries it has been an area of shallow sea where the fishing-boats thread the gulleys to set their nets along the sandbanks, these fishermen have some- times been sure that when the light strikes obliquely through the water they have seen the outlines of streets, and churches, and farmsteads down below. But there, I think, they must have been mistaken, for on either occasion that I have voyaged along the edge of those same flat waters the sea itself has been so thick with the fine grey mud scoured by the tide from the bottom that I doubt if a swimmer could have seen his own finger-tips.

Others have heard in the stillness of the night the muffled ringing of church bells, down below the water. 'Hark,' they say. 'There are the bells of Torum.' The little town of Torum was one of the richest of all the communities which was swept away on that night long ago, and as the water burst into the houses the people who for long had cared little enough for the church ran in terror to fling themselves on their knees in prayer. And there they were drowned, for, contrary to their belief, the Almighty has never been one to repair miraculously the dikes which others have preferred to neglect.

Even if it may be difficult for sailors to distinguish between bell buoys and sunken steeples, there must indeed be bells lying buried in the Dollart mud. A certain peat barge once came down the river to Emden, and the skipper decided to drop anchor and wait for the start of the ebb. When the captain and his lad came to raise the hook again they could hardly turn the windlass. At last they managed to bring the anchor to the surface, and they found hanging from one of the flukes a heavy bell, on the skirt of which they could just make out the name Maria.

With great celebrations the bell was eventually landed at their home port of Rhauderfehn in the fens south of Leer, and soon it had been hung in the church tower to ring out as it had done centuries earlier. It is said to have had a wonderfully mellow tone when it was tolled, but its sound was not to ring out for long. Village youngsters were as energetic then as they are now, and one of the lads snatched the rope from the sexton's hand.

'Louder,' he cried. 'Louder, Maria!' And as he swung the bell ever more violently the girls cheered.

Suddenly with a terrible jar Maria split from top to bottom. After the hundreds of years in the murky bed of the Ems the exuberance of youth was too much for her tired old metal, and she fell in fragments to the floor of the tower.

The estuary of the Ems cuts clean through the lands of the Frisians, for the German province immediately opposite the Dutch shore is still known as Ostfriesland, or East Frisia. They were a rough and independent people, these folk of the *Mannigfual*, but soon they were to become a part of the Holy Roman Empire. Tradition says that they received their law at the hands of Charlemagne himself, who signed and sealed it at Aachen in the year 802. The great Emperor summoned the Frisian representatives to appear before him and propound a scheme of law for their people, which he would then discuss with them, but somewhat to his surprise they declared that they needed more time for drafting. On the following day they chose twelve select men to wait upon the Emperor for negotiations but when these had presented themselves at Aachen all they did was to insist upon a further adjournment. The law was an important matter, they said, and they were not inclined to be rushed.

Charlemagne agreed to let them deliberate further, but when after some days they had still no agreed proposals to put to him for his imperial approval he lost his temper.

'You can now have your choice,' he declared. 'You can either be put to death, or you may become bondmen, or you can be set adrift in your own tideway in a boat without oars or rudder or sail.'

The delegates chose the ship, and so they were duly set adrift. The tide carried them out of sight of the coast and it is hardly surprising if they began to be downcast. Then one of them suggested that they should ask their gods for a thirteenth committee member who would give them a true foundation for their law, and who would also steer their craft back to the land.

This they did, and when they looked up from their prayer a thirteenth was indeed present in their boat. He carried an axe, and with it he steered the ship to land against wind and tide alike. At the shore he flung down his axe, and proceeded to teach the other twelve what the framework of their law should be. The moment he had come to the end of his dissertation he simply vanished.

The twelve Frisians then betook themselves once more to Aachen. Charlemagne was surprised to see them, for he had thought — and probably hoped — that the committee must long since have been lost at sea. The men propounded to him the law which they had received, and the Emperor was pleased to approve it, promulgating it from his assembly as the *Lex Frisionum*.

This tale seems to contain elements of Christ, perhaps of Moses also, and certainly an admixture of nordic deities, including Thor. But there is no doubt about the law, the text of which has survived intact for more than eleven centuries. Some of its provisions are interesting, though they unfortunately do not apply within the realm of the Bundesrepublik today. For example, those who robbed holy places were to be dragged to the beach, where the malefactors' ears and genitalia were cut off before they were weighted and sunk in the sea as an offering to the offended deities. On the other hand the law was lenient on infanticide. A mother might immediately strangle or dash to death an unwanted child, without any punishment at all — a practice which was very naturally opposed by the worthy Ludger, who had just arrived from Monte Casino as apostle to the area.

In the days of Charlemagne the Frisians were still living in the low-lying land with no actual protection against the sea. All they had was their hundreds of large, flat-topped mounds, thrown up laboriously to provide refuges to which they could flee before the advancing water. Inevitably there came a time when this system was unable to meet the needs of an increasing population, and about the year 1000 the Frisians decided to start diking. At first they only built around their settlements low 'summer dikes', which kept the crops safe during the growing and harvesting season but were often submerged in winter storms – something which was an advantage, as each new flood brought a further layer of fertile silt to the fields. Then, as the sea level slowly rose, so eventually the people were forced to build up the entire coastline to resist the attack of wave and tide all along its length.

This process took centuries, for the work had to be done with spade and bucket or barrow, and the sea continually gnawed at the uncompleted work. But the Frisians persevered, and at last they could proudly proclaim *'Deus mare, Friso litora fecit'* – God created the sea but the Frisian the coast. Yet life behind the dikes depended upon hard work and a sense of community very different from the fatal complacency of Tidde Winninga and his fellow farmers of the Dollart.

De nich will dieken, mut wieken – he who cannot dike must yield. That was how the Frisian expressed it, and as soon as living behind the banks replaced the system of fleeing to the mole-hill there was added to the *Lex Frisionum* the very sensible and pragmatic code of the dike-laws, with its provision that any man whose dike was in such condition that he thought it beyond his means or strength to repair was to call the people together, stick a fork in the dike top, chop out three sods with a spade, and swear in public that he was through with it. His six nearest relatives could then take over the dike, and the farm and his possessions also. The famous German 'spade-law' went even further. Failure to repair the dikes was a capital offence, but a farmer who felt the upkeep of his section to be beyond his powers could drive his spade into the dike, for all to see. Any man who pulled it out and could make good the threatened dike might then take over the whole farm, stock, land, implements and all, without a penny payment.

We had never visited Emden before, but at least we had been past the entrance eleven years earlier, when heading northward aboard the *Commodore*. I remembered the glimpse up past the sea-ships toward the lock – a quick glance only, because the *Commodore* was sweeping past the moles at a higher speed than she was ever to attain again in her lifetime, even when descending the Rhône. She had sped past the measured mile just below the port at more than fifteen knots, half of them produced by her strangely reliable paraffin engine, another four by the tide, perhaps two by the lift and push of the strong waves behind her, and a final knot added by the lugsail of the dinghy lashed on her after-deck. It had seemed a pity to deprive her of the fun of such a gallop, so we had let her surge ahead up the Ems all the way to Leer. But this time I had decided to turn in at Emden and cross East Frisia to Wilhelmshaven through the Ems–Jade canal which I had seen on the map.

Being a German port, Emden was beset with regulations. I had looked up the directions in the pilot book and knew that we had to give 'timely indication of our intention by repeatedly sounding the appropriate signal by means of the steam whistle.' On approaching the pretty little red-framed lighthouse on the western mole the *Thames Commodore* dutifully uttered a clear — — · —, which meant that she was entering the Aussenhafen. She followed this with an imperious single toot to signify 'take that fishing-line out of the way or *Himmeldonnerwetternocheinmal* you'll get it run down.' Then she took a deep breath and bleated a — — · · · —, to signify that she did not want the lock-keeper to close the gate right in front of her nose. Had it been — — · · — it would have meant that she was aiming for the new lock on the starboard hand, but as the smaller lock was already open and contained a tug and two mud-hoppers, she added an extra pip in the middle to signify that she had the Nesserlanderschleuse in mind. She was anxious to do things properly, because she had heard of the awful fate that once befell a ship which acted outside the regulations.

In fact the seaman who may not know what he should blow on the steam whistle is nowadays likely to be received with tolerant good humour, even if the lock may not be opened until he has hit upon the right tooting rhythm. Long ago there was no outer harbour, and the Ems curved more closely against the walls of the town. The lock gates were then at the end of the Delft, the inner harbour which still leads up to the town hall, and it was the custom to open this lock only during certain hours and not after dusk.

It so happened that a considerable storm was blowing when a ship arrived home from a long voyage over the seas. She made the Emden approaches after the official closing time, but sailing up towards the Delft the captain managed to shout above the screaming of the wind in the rigging that he urgently wanted the lock opened so that he might berth in safety. All Emden was crowding the harbour walls to see the vessel arrive in port, but the lock-keeper refused to open up. The captain happened to be his particular enemy, so he merely retorted that the ship had arrived out of hours.

And so the vessel had to heave to, in a very dangerous position. At once the storm waves drove in, a squall caught her, and in a moment the ship was swept round and overset. The onlookers heard the cries for help and the screams of the passengers in the water, and they yelled to the lock-keeper to send out the watch-boat to pick up the drowning men.

But he was a regular union man, born before his time. 'It's after hours,' he said. 'Nobody's going to get me to send a boat out at this time of night.'

'Think of your son, man,' exclaimed an old sailor. For the lock-keeper's son was indeed one of the crew of the stricken vessel.

'It is their own fault for making port at this time of evening,' the man declared morosely. 'If you ask me, it serves 'em darned well right.'

There was not a single survivor from that wreck. And on nights when the storm wind from the north-west howls past Delfzijl and over the Dollart, then in the moments when the moon breaks through the gaps between the frightened clouds you may see a fine ship with reefed sails bearing down upon the Delft. Behind the moaning of the wind you may hear the megaphone of the captain, and beyond the scream of the herring-gulls the cries of the men and women as the vessel capsizes. The only thing you will not hear is a — — · · · —, for if that had been sounded in accordance with the regulations then I think the lock would have been opened, whatever the time or the weather.

A more pleasant event in Emden's history was the occasion when the Ems was frozen from shore to shore and the Dollart was one sheet of ice. As the frost continued, so skating gave way to dancing and revelry, just as in the Ice Fairs on London's Thames. Young and old were thoroughly enjoying themselves, and only a few of the most aged and rheumaticky had been forced to stay behind.

It so happened that one old man who was watching the scene from the shore was quite certain he saw the ice give a very slight but unmistakable heave. He hurried to tell the other gaffers, and they shared his fear that a ground swell from the north-west might be setting in, and that it would speedily increase in amplitude and smash the ice to pieces. Together they shouted and gesticulated, but in return they received only an occasional cheerful wave of the hand from children on a sleigh, or a salute from some boy on skates who sped by at a distance.

In desperation, one of the ancient mariners ran to the church and began to toll the bell. Then the one who had first detected the movement in the ice set on fire his own little thatched house which stood by the church. As the flames leaped upwards, the Emdeners out on the ice thought that the tolling was a summons to help fight the fire, and one and all they raced across the frozen river toward the shore.

They were not a moment too soon. Hardly had the last of them reached the river bank than the grinding and cracking began. Within minutes the long and powerful waves of the swell running ahead of the storm had heaved the wide expanse of ice into heaps of broken floes, which the tide swiftly swept far out to sea. History does not relate whether or not the Emdeners built the old man a new house; but as East Frisians are kindly people I am sure that they did.

The Nesserlanderschleuse obligingly waited for the *Thames*

D

Commodore to enter, and while the water level rose I went up to the customs post to explain where we were going, and why, and to ask where there might be a good berth. Nesserland itself is now a rather uninteresting outlying area of Emden and little more than a line of jetties overlooked by the big tanks of an oil storage depot, but the same place used to be an island in the Ems. That was before the engineers had confined the river with groynes and pushed it so far back from the city itself that Nesserland could be poldered off from the stream.

This island had a particular place in the life of the East Frisians, who used to go there to acquire a baby. Most people of Germanic race have children in a more familiar and biological way, by a process which takes the best part of a year. It seems, however, that on Nesserland there was a spring from which, as one might say, children sprang. A husband and wife would row out to the isle in a glass boat – though why it was of glass I do not know, unless that made it easier to see the shoals. Arrived at the eyot, the wife had to kneel and stare into the deep, dark water of the spring, which lay quite still. Her husband walked three times round the pool, and then the water would become troubled and suddenly rise as a fountain, so bright that one had to shut one's eyes. The splashing subsided, and when the couple opened their eyes again they would see a tiny ark or dinghy in the centre of the pool, radiant with light. Lying in the bottom of this little craft was a brand new baby.

When the baby drifted to the edge of the pool the man took it up and gently handed it to his wife to carry home. Full of joy she took the child down to the glass ship, but always she was so intent on the infant that on climbing aboard she slipped and broke her leg. That was why she had to have a few days in bed when the baby had arrived in its home.

If the Emdeners no longer increase their families in this original way, that may perhaps be because the island has gone and the spring has been filled up with rubbish. Or maybe an extra heavy mother fell like the rest, and broke not only her leg but the little glass ship which had served others so well for generations.

With customs formalities over, we were free to proceed down the long stretch of the inner harbour, past the side-arms where sea-ships lay along the quays and the herring-boats crowded up against the fish wharf. Soon we eased off to sound — — — —, which meant 'Please swing that wonderful iron-age railway bridge, if you will be so kind.' In fact the bridge only opened at certain specified hours, but the signalman cheerfully leaned out of his box to say that an express goods train was coming. Immediately it had gone by he would open up for us. Then we should be at the Rathaus quay in time for supper, he said. So, when the span was ready to swing, the signal arms flapped as though trying to keep warm on this crisp April evening and invited us to move ahead toward the most attractive berth we had found since Furnes in Belgium.

Emden must have been almost totally destroyed during the Second World War, for if there were still any buildings remaining from before the late 1940s we certainly did not find them. Most cities in such a situation would have been rebuilt in a way that made the most economical use of the space by filling in any pieces of harbour or canal which were no longer of commercial use, and the city fathers of Emden must have had a genius among them when they decided instead to deepen and widen the old Ratsdelft and build at its inner end a modern city hall but in the same traditional style as the old one. Instead of becoming derelict the Ratsdelft had been made into a feature right in the centre of the town, with promenade and seats for the locals to enjoy the reflections on the water upon a summer's evening. And just as though they knew that the *Thames Commodore* would one day push her nose into their city centre they had arranged a floral welcome by planting the banks behind the quay with tulips and wallflowers, pansies and daffodils and azaleas, just to delight her.

Nevertheless, the arrival of a Red Ensign in the Ratsdelft was enough to bring people scurrying over the square, and two young men in yachting caps drove up post haste from their club to bid us welcome to Emden. One of them gave us his motoring map of East Frisia, and with this we were able to have some idea of where we should be going when we set off next morning down the canal toward the Jadebusen, or Bosom of Jade.

I think these two kindly young men in their smart new-style caps were the only men we saw in Emden who were not apparently

Emden, the Ratsdelft

dressed as chauffeurs. Short and squat and usually rather fat, the
men of Emden would stand on the promenade or on the town
bridges to see this curious sight which had arrived in their town,
and each would have a brief-case or *Mappe* under his arm, and a
Mütze on his head. The Germans are a great nation of brief-casers,
and in Emden every man from the town councillor to the roadman
and the mere ancient mariner seemed to have one, either for his
papers, or his lunch or tools, or just to sit on if the seat were damp.
As for the *Mütze*, this is of course a particularly North German
type of headgear. It is like a discreet mayoral driver's cap, with
sometimes a piece of lacy garnishing on the front, but never a

badge. It seemed so universal in Emden that one of those with us asked if it were compulsory, but he was assured that the men wore this because they like it. What else could they wear on their heads? To judge by the window displays of the hat-shops, nothing.

If we only stayed one night among the flowers by Emden's city hall, that was because we were hastening to the Baltic. However, ships often used to winter in Emden, and on one occasion a skipper made a very strange discovery. He had brought his vessel into the port for the winter, and wishing to spend some time at home with his family he anchored her in the harbour and left the steersman living aboard as a watch. After some weeks ashore he returned on board to see that everything was in order, and he was surprised to see the ship lying in quite a different berth from where he had left her, so without rousing the steersman he climbed stealthily over the rail and hid behind one of the ship's boats.

Soon after dark the steersman came on deck and set to work to haul up the anchor. No sooner had he done so than the ship began to move, accelerating all the while until like a hydrofoil it rose to skim the surface. The captain clutched the davit as the vessel left the water and soared up into the sky, sweeping through the night air until at last it began to descend to land, the hull swishing upon the sea once more. The skipper saw that they were now close to the shore, and soon the steersman had berthed the ship alongside.

The steersman went ashore, but the captain stayed in hiding. He had no idea where he could be, but he saw a bush within his reach and he stretched over to pick a piece of it. He was surprised to find that it was Spanish bamboo. Eventually the steersman returned and the ship sped back to Emden just as she had come, except that shortly before landing there was such a bump as nearly knocked the captain overboard.

In the morning the captain challenged the steersman to explain how it was that he had been able to pick a piece of bamboo, and the man had to confess that he was not an ordinary seaman at all but a Waalrieder – a particular kind of spirit which haunts the northern lands of Germany. He liked travelling by night on the ship, he said, and he was sorry about the bump on the way back to Emden, but he had begun the descent too soon and had struck a

church steeple – probably, I think, at one of the villages behind the
Dollart, which are on the direct course for Spain. However, the
captain could satisfy himself that there was no damage to the hull,
he said. The skipper accepted the explanation because he saw it
must be true, but he thought it unwise to keep a Waalrieder at the
helm – for was there not always a chance that the creature might
interfere with the scheduled voyages and take the ship overnight
to the Canaries when she was carrying a cargo for Antwerp or
Hamburg? He gave the Waalrieder his papers and turned him off
the ship.

Emden was a modest port until the sixteenth century, when it
suddenly began to thrive upon the results of religious persecution
and economic depression elsewhere. When the Dutch patriot
rovers blockaded the ports of Holland to prevent their use by the
Spaniards during the revolt of the Netherlands, the trade which
once had been theirs tended to move to Emden. Soon more than
half the population was made up of Dutch refugees, to whom were
added others from Westphalia. With the return of more settled
times many of the Hollanders packed up and went home, but the
intolerance which later overtook their own protestantism sent a
new wave of refugees across the Ems estuary. Weavers, ship-
masters, craftsmen and merchants, throughout these periods of
unrest and uncertainty they flocked to nearby Emden, a port which
provided opportunity as well as safety.

With so much prosperity coming its way the city of Emden
dredged and buoyed its approaches as early as the 1530s, and a
lighthouse was soon added. The Amsterdam grain exchange then
moved over to Emden, and inland shipping upriver toward the
Rhineland was developed. Next to arrive was the continental base
of the English Merchant Adventurers Company, which had
previously been at Antwerp. Before the end of the sixteenth
century Emden had become – though only for a while – the port
which handled the greatest tonnage of all Europe.

Then came a steady decline, and only in the 1890s did the
fortunes of the city look up again with the opening of the
Dortmund–Ems canal, which enabled the heavy products of the
Rhur as well as the grain of Westphalia to flow down in large

consignments for shipping overseas. The large carrier companies became interested in the port, and soon it came to handle more ore and minerals than any other in Germany.

With its aqueducts and the famous boat-lift at Henrichenburg the Dortmund–Ems canal was a late-comer, but the traffic between Emden and the industrial basin of the Ruhr developed even more rapidly than the most optimistic canal engineers had expected, and within twenty years the waterway had to be widened and deepened. Yet Emden was already served by another route, the curious little Ems–Jade canal which cuts across East Frisia to link Emden with Wilhelmshaven. This was the route the *Thames Commodore* had selected for the next stage of her journey north, and she was surprised to meet several little barges chugging along its forty mile course. In fact the canal was still used to the extent of three or four thousand ships a year. This was of course only a handful each way every day, and if the shipping was a fraction of what it used to be, that was because the old smokers of the German navy had gone. They were scuttled in Scapa Flow.

Wilhelmshaven was built as a naval base pure and simple, and the canal to Emden was originally cut to take gun-boats from Wilhelmshaven to the Ems. Later it became a supply artery for the mighty Prussian iron ships which had their home in Wilhelmshaven, for these craft had to be supplied with coal, and even before the Dortmund–Ems canal was built to bring larger barges to Emden the smaller ships could descend the Ems itself and cut across country to the naval base. The fleet needed vast quantities of coal, and the Ems–Jade canal could carry it. But times are no longer what they were. The Bundesrepublik does not put its faith in sheer weight of iron-clads, and even if Wilhelmshaven is still a naval port the sleek grey ships now burn oil. However, there is enough internal traffic of peat and sand, stone and fertilisers, to keep the waterway going.

'No ways of pleasantness nor paths of peace are North German canals. The language of my diary is too highly flavoured for transcription.' So wrote H. M. Doughty in *Our Wherry in Wendish Lands*, an account of a voyage in 1890–91. He made the remark in the context of the Ems–Jade canal, which had only recently been opened, and what weighed so heavily upon him was the general moroseness of the people and the manners of the 'slugs and thickskins of bridgekeepers'.

I had read Doughty with interest, and everything he said about the waterway made me all the more determined to voyage through it, for the *Thames Commodore* was always one to accept a challenge and enjoy battling her way through difficulties and dereliction. Doughty concluded his brief account with a particularly vigorous outburst.

'The Ems–Jade canal done with at last! Blessed relief! Let no man of a full habit who cannot swear sail through it after us; at German bridge-keepers one must needs swear – or burst.'

These sentences happened to be my goodnight reading as I lay in my bunk in the Ratsdelft. Next morning I ran to the bakery for fresh rolls, then started up the engines and turned the ship round the corner into the Falderndelft, a broad canal which cut away behind the city hall. Only a hundred yards up it we came to the first of the road bridges, and I soon experienced something of Doughty's sentiments. We blew every combination of dots and dashes I could think of, and although a number of stout little men with brief-cases and blue caps stopped to look at our ship from the bridge or the bankside pathways there was no activity in the control box. At length I backed down to some piles, jumped ashore, and strode up to the bridge.

'Where is the bridge-keeper?' I asked one of the Emdeners.

'There.' He pointed to the control cabin.

Sure enough, the man was on duty, his feet on the table. The cabin was pleasantly warm from his electric stove, and he was reading a newspaper.

'Will you please open the bridge,' I said.

He looked at me as though I was a poor thing to be pitied.

'No,' he said. 'The bridge does not open till eight, because of the rush hour.'

'Then why are you on duty now, at half past seven?'

'My day has begun,' he said briefly. And he returned to his paper.

But sure enough, the moment the church bells chimed eight

o'clock he stood up. The barriers were dropped imperiously across the traffic and the bridge stood on end. Soon we were trailing through a narrow little waterway to pass a school.

Work for the day must have begun at eight o'clock, for as we drew up by the classroom to wait for the same keeper to arrive on his cycle to swing the next two bridges, the boys and girls rushed to the windows. I saw a teacher thump on her desk for discipline, but she then thought better of it and joined the spectators. It was a good start to the morning's classwork, and as a well-trained teacher she would know how to put it to good use.

'Write in your books:– Emden is on the Ems. London is on the Themse,' I could imagine her saying. 'Draw the flag, red, white and blue. Let us ask him. . . .'

The window went up. Which way had we come? How long had it taken us to reach Emden? Could one really cross the Channel in such a boat?

Only one of the children was upset by our arrival. In fact she was a mere four minutes late for school and with her satchel on her back she had just reached the bridge, almost breathless with running. Five seconds earlier and she would have been across in safety, but the man dropped the barrier in front of her.

'*Halt!*'

She was too young to swear but I thought she might burst, and into tears, too.

'Please, mister.' I could see her pleading and I knew how she must feel, marooned on the farther side of the water while the man got to work on the rusty bolts – for this access to the canal was rarely used and the barges usually came round from the docks by a branch a little further ahead. 'Please, mister. . . .'

He held up his hand. 'Back you go. It is dangerous to push through the barrier.'

And wait she must, until at last he had swung the creaking span and then put it back again.

'Thank you,' I said to her as we chugged slowly past. Her eyes were wide and troubled.

'We are going to Sweden,' I said. This would at least give her something to tell the others when she reached the classroom.

D2

She tried to smile, and the effort turned into a blush.

'Sorry we kept you waiting,' I added.

'Goodbye.' She waved her hand and we moved on one more bridge. Then we rounded the corner to the Kesselschleuse, the Boiler, Cauldron or Kettle lock – I am not sure which.

I had never before seen a lock with four exits. Three, yes, for at Bruges on the Canal de Gand and at Agde on the Canal du Midi I had been through round locks where a gate at right angles to the main direction of the canal gave access to another waterway on a different level. But the Kesselschleuse was a lock incorporating a water crossroads, for here the Ems–Jade canal crossed the town moat, which was also navigable. It was a week since any boat had been through, but there were three keepers on duty and they were delighted to see us.

'Are there any more swing-bridges?' I asked.

'Forty-three.'

Forty-three! I was not surprised that Doughty was blessedly relieved to reach the further end of the canal.

'Forty-three,' the head-keeper repeated. 'But they are all manned and will open immediately. You need not worry.'

We paid dues which amounted to a contribution of about twopence towards the salary of each of the bridgemen who would be ready and waiting for our approach. Then we set off down the canal towards the next lock at Rahe, twenty kilometres ahead.

VI

*The Ems–Jade canal – the bridal paths of Aurich –
Hilbertus and the hunting abbot – power from peat – the
plight of the Moorman – Wilhelmshaven – the Bosom of Jade
– down to the Mellum – Störtebeker's fate – the waves of
Mellum Plate*

THE *Thames Commodore* soon left Emden behind her and began
to wind her way along a canal which stood well above the level
of the land on either side and so gave an excellent view of this
curious part of East Frisia. A drearier, greyer landscape she had
never visited. Nor had I. The canal curved hither and thither as
though not quite certain that it really wanted to head for
Wilhelmshaven at all, and beyond its bank there extended on the
starboard side an immense sea of mud, which reached apparently
to the horizon. This vista of uniform grey was broken only by the
long lines of giant jointed snakes, as grey as the mud itself, which
were the pipes that brought the deposit and poured it out as a
continual dark and dismal flow at several points in the distance.
These pipe-lines led back to the harbour of Emden, where their
hungry mouths were continually fed by the dredgers and muck-
boats which had scooped the rich silt either from the harbour itself
or from the Ems outside. Until the 1950s this part of East Frisia
was a marshy morass, a haunt of ducks and duckshooters, of frogs
and insects and the birds that preyed on them. It was a waste land
without future until the harbour authority offered to provide free
of charge a continual flow of muck.

Year in and year out the mud was vomited out and allowed to
dry. Rainwater slowly leached out the salt, and pumps put the
brackish fluid over the bank into the Ems–Jade canal. Eventually
the ground would be covered with more than three feet of excellent
silt on which crops could flourish. The reclamation was a slow
process, but Emden's dredgermen could scrabble up enough wet

mud to make twenty or thirty acres of rich new farmland every
year – and there was still enough marshy desert south of the canal
to keep them busy for a century or two without the Harbour Board
having to bother its head about searching for a new disposal
site.

The mud dredged from the Ems is mainly silt, but it has an
admixture of other things – not merely the empty tins and beer
bottles thrown overboard from ships in the tideway, but small
fish not quick or strong enough to escape the suckers, and myriads
of soft-bodied little creatures which find their way through the
valves of the pumps and down the miles of trestled pipes to be
spilled out at last in the mudfield. And there they find waiting for
them oyster-catchers and gulls, but especially avocets. Avocets have
long stilts of their own and can strut gingerly on the soft surface
without sinking above their knees, and the spoil fields of the suction
line are a delight to them. They seem not often to see a Red Ensign,
however, for they would stalk over towards the canal bank as we
approached and stand there in groups of a dozen or more, their
heads slightly on one side as they looked at us over their aristocratic noses.

Beyond the pumping area and on the other side of the canal
some equally dismal-looking stretches of open water lay flat under
the heavy sky. One of them, the Grosses Meer, used to extend
right to the edge of four little villages, each of which had its church
set down at the water's edge. The lake and all the fenland ditches
and drains formed an inland waterway system on which the East
Frisians used to carry their farm produce in little punts, taking
butter and cheese, eggs and vegetables to market in Emden and
returning with the household shopping.

In such a flat and fenny area the fog would often drop down upon
the water, and as the Grosses Meer was two or three miles in
length the boatmen often lost their bearings.

'*Verdwolen*,' they would cry. '*Verdwolen!*'

It was the custom that any villager who heard a call from out
on the lake would run to the church and begin to toll the bell. As
its voice carried across the water it was joined by its fellows, and
soon the four churches were ringing their bells in different tones,

and the boatmen would pick up the oars again and row home on the correct course.

For nearly two hours the canal led us through mud and marsh, with only rarely a bridge on some insignificant roadway, but if when Doughty sailed the *Gypsy* along the waterway the bridgemen were asleep the *Thames Commodore*'s hooter carried far enough across the country for their more alert successors to emerge from their cottages, put on a uniform cap, and swing the spans before we arrived at the crossing. At last we came into a less waterlogged countryside and the canal led straight into Aurich, the capital of East Frisia. On the edge of the little town a pretty harbour awaited us, deserted except for a small gravel barge and a tiny cruiser.

Aurich has belonged to many different overlords, and most of them have left some impress of their character upon its appearance. Others stayed too short a time – as in the early nineteenth century, when the town was Prussian, Dutch, French, Prussian and Hanoverian, all within the space of ten years. From the point of view of organised tours of Europe it is one of those towns that nobody would ever visit, but it has a charm of its own just the same. It is in fact a busy little market town such as one might find in Britain, except that it has what was once the palace of the Cirkensa family, a nineteenth-century building which is now the seat of the regional government and which looks across to a baroque range of stables which must have made the Dukes wish that they were horses and not mere nobles. Once a year the East Frisians converge upon the town for a day of local nationalism, and then the place reverts again for another year of administrative efficiency, market days, and the chance for some stray and eccentric boatman from Britain to walk up from the quayside to buy milk, and bread, and pig-flesh.

There is a curious custom around Aurich, where on Ascension day the children lay out on the ground *Brautpfade* or Bridal Paths. A sandy area of a square yard or two is neatly edged round with moss, and then a design is laid in it, made entirely of flower-heads. Traditionally the children should only use buttercups and wild violets, and of course moss and leaves, but the designs vary. Some put hearts or crosses, others anchors and windmills, or sailing ships. In recent years teapots have been a favourite; and if it should come as a surprise that any German child should even know what a teapot might be, it is a fact that the East Frisians are such a nation of tea-drinkers that before the Second World War they accounted for something like ninety-five per cent of all the tea consumed in Germany. More than that, they made a proper brew instead of the insipid off-green fluid so familiar in German restaurants, and they probably picked up the habit from their trading contacts with the English and the Dutch, and their own voyages to the East Indies. 'East Frisian Blend' is the pride of old-established tea-importers, and its composition is kept a close secret. Indeed, the East Frisian is a three-cup man by habit, and if he likes to put whipped cream on his tea that is his own concern. He is as certain as any Englishman that tea-drinking is healthy, and if he has a pot always at hand he will live to a ripe old age.

The floral pictures of Ascensiontide are not there to advertise tea, nor are they specifically to do with Ascension itself. They commemorate an Ascensiontide long ago when the Cirkensas lived in their palace, and in one which preceded the building now to be seen. It was the wedding day of the beautiful daughter of this noble line, who was betrothed to a fair and noble young prince of some neighbouring land. She loved him as he loved her, and the people of Aurich shared the radiant happiness of the two young people. The children ran out into the woods and meadows to gather flowers and strew the pathway which the bride and bridegroom would take.

And so Aurich waited on that day of celebration, and the Cirkensa bride climbed up to the top of the tower so that she might be the first to see her young prince as he rode towards her home and his wedding. Sure enough, at last she could make him out, riding at the head of his retinue, and taking a red scarf she waved it in her excitement. The crowd cheered, and the bridegroom waved back to her. Then he spurred his horse that he might be beside her all the quicker.

There is to the east of Aurich a wood, just north of the canal. The bridegroom had only this short distance still to travel, and the bride saw him gallop into the wood. Excitement mounted as the news spread that the prince would soon be there. The crowd thronged the sides of the route and as the steed could be heard galloping out of the woodland ride there was a moment of wild cheering. Then a terrible hush fell over the people as the horse raced into the yard of the palace to which it had so often carried its master. Dragging from the stirrups was the bridegroom, who had been beaten to death. Neither the prince nor his bride had suspected that a certain young man who had been burning with envy because she had not chosen him for her husband had set an ambush of murderers in the wood of Egels.

With a cry the girl rushed forward and flung herself on her knees beside her lover. Then she collapsed, her gay young heart broken. Little by little the people of Aurich trudged sadly to their homes, and only the bridal path of flowers laid by the children remained. It was still there, faded and a little withered, when a day or two later the Cirkensas and all the people of the neighbourhood walked along it in the funeral procession of the two young lovers. And from that day to this the children have laid it every year when Ascension-tide comes round once more.

Near Aurich there once stood in the expanse of the Meerhusen moor a monastery which long since has vanished. It has, however, left one trace of its existence – or so the country people will tell. The story began with the passion of one of the abbots for hunting. Nothing would please him but to go coursing wildly over the countryside, hunting the deer or wild boar, the hares, or anything that moved. In this he was eventually joined by all the monks save one, and day after day the copses and moors resounded to the shouting and cursing of the hunters and the baying of their dogs. The more usual functions of the monastery were forgotten, except by the one anti-field-sports and devoted monk, Hilbertus.

Scandalised by what his fellows were doing to the reputation of the order and pained at their disregard for their vows, Hilbertus at last went to lay the matter before the bishop. This worthy man sent a severe reprimand to the abbot, who merely continued to take the monks hunting as before. He did not want any nosy prelate interfering with the sport; and as for Hilbertus, that peaching fellow was seized and imprisoned in the tower. If he wanted to spend his life in prayer – well, he could get on with it. Nobody would disturb his peace and quiet in that remote cell.

It happened that some weeks later the bishop decided to see for himself what was going on, and whether or not the sporting abbot had taken to heart his stern rebuke. He set out alone to ride to Meerhusen, and as he passed through a wood he heard a tumult of noise sweeping across the countryside. Soon the whole pack of monks and hounds came surging through the trees, the abbot at their head.

No doubt the good bishop raised his hand to call his subordinate to a halt, but what happened next was perhaps the fault of nothing more than equine instinct or animal mass psychology, for his own horse suddenly leaped forward and joined its fellows in the chase, racing through the trees with the unwilling bishop on its back.

Eventually the hunt came towards Meerhusen, and the din roused the humble Hilbertus to rise from his knees and peer through the bars of his cell. What should he see but the bishop himself, the man he had trusted, racing neck and neck with the abbot and leading the field. For a moment he stared in horror, then he raised his hands to heaven.

'Oh Lord,' he cried. 'Grant that these faithless men may hunt and hunt, ever onward until the day of judgment!'

And so it has been, for the abbot and his monks can still be heard wildly chasing through the woods and over the moors on stormy nights when the prevailing wind wails in the branches and the rain squalls flit over the marshy land. Surely that is fair enough, but it seems that the bishop is with them, too. This, I think, is unjust, and if there is a moral at all in this tale of the wild East Frisian land it can only be that a bishop should be careful and not go prying in his diocese. As for Brother Hilbertus, his fate is not recorded.

Within an hour of leaving Aurich harbour the *Thames Commodore* had left the fens far behind and was pursuing a long and straight course over the peat moors. Often she would be ploughing through a deep cutting between banks yellow with broom and flecked with heather, but on one of the rare occasions

when we could see for miles across the heathy landscape to starboard there appeared chimneys and cooling towers far away in the
middle of the moorland.

Like the marshes outside Emden, this vast tract of age-old peat-
moor once offered only the most meagre living to a scanty population. Then somebody had the ingenious idea that peat might well
heat something more than a poverty-stricken small-holding, and
sixty years ago Siemens decided that peat could indeed become
power. They built a generating station right in the middle of the
moors and ever since then some enormous machines like metal
dinosaurs have been roaming the moorland, patiently cutting the
sods and laying them out to dry, or picking them up for carriage to
the furnaces of the electricity works. About 100,000 tons of peat
are fed to the flames every year, and the land laid bare is then given
a coat of mixed peat and top-soil and turned over to cultivation.
So the Northwestern Electricity Authority produces not only kilo-
watt-hours but pasture for milk, crops of wheat, potatoes and
sugar-beet. Ever since the hot water from the cooling towers was
diverted to heat a huge area of greenhouses the range of products
has been swelled by a considerable amperage of cucumbers and
melons, mushrooms and kohlrabi, azaleas and begonias.

If the moorland has now a special economy of its own, to attempt
to cultivate the peaty wasteland was such a thankless task for the
individual farmer or crofter that the East Frisians had a saying
that the first generation won *Tod*, the second *Not*, and only the
third the *Brot*. Death, poverty, and only finally the bread – so ran
the fate of those who tried to work such intractable land, for the
ground had first to be cut away by hand as peat blocks, often to a
depth of many feet, before any soil was found. Not until the
seventeenth century was any serious attempt made to tackle the
area, when four merchants of Emden established the first fen
village at Grossefehn (or Great Fen) and cut a network of small
canals to drain off the water from the peaty mass. These waterways
also served for transport, and the peat cut away to lay bare the
land could be sent in barges to Emden, the boats returning either
with dredger-mud or with stable manure. In this way a richer
farmland was slowly established, and even today the same system

to some extent survives except that the motor-lorry has gradually been ousting the small barge.

This curious part of Germany is of course inhabited by its particular collection of strange spirits, and among them are the little Moormantjes, amiable little fellows who never harm those that leave them in peace and who perform all such friendly tasks as the more usual 'little people' do elsewhere – clearing up in the barn, helping overworked serving-girls to finish the washing, and no doubt cutting peat-blocks for poor widows. They have, however, one particular characteristic of their own, for they can only walk on the peat and not on ordinary ground.

Along this second half of the Ems–Jade canal we often came to areas where the peat had been dug away to a depth of twenty or thirty feet down to the silt beneath it, but here and there a farmer had left undisturbed a copse or a handful of trees to serve as a windbreak. These copses, together with the older farmhouses, stood on isolated islands, perched on their separate black cliffs of peat which rose above the surrounding land like the mesas of the Great Plains.

When the peat was first dug away the little Moormantjes retreated slowly across the country to find new homes. It sometimes happened, however, that one of them was taking a lengthy snooze in the heather and did not wake up in time to escape before he found himself isolated on one of these peaty islands. Unable to tread on the sand or shingle around him he could only pine away, separated from his friends.

The East Frisians were anxious to help, but they knew that the only way in which a moorman could be moved was if on Old Year's Night he were placed on a basket of peat turves and carried in complete silence to the adjoining expanse of moor. Once, a party of turf cutters had gone out on such a mission of rescue and they were well on their way to the moor when one of them fell over a root and let out a curse. He promptly fell in a ditch and was drowned, which seems a rather harsh fate for one who was only trying to be kind. As for the moorman, it seems that he managed to reach the safety of his island again, for he was later rescued by a smallholder who set out alone on New Year's Eve with a load of turves on his back. He called to the spirit to climb aboard, and strode off toward the moor. That he did the job thoroughly was at once proved by the success of everything he undertook from that day forward, for his stock would thrive when others were sick, his barge always found return freight after delivering loads of peat, and his crops were never beaten down by wind and rain nor ruined by pests. For the moormen were by nature grateful spirits, and they never forgot those who helped them.

Rahe and Wiesens up, Upschört and Wiesede down, the *Thames Commodore* had only four little hand-worked locks to pass on all her forty miles of journey between the Emden Kesselschleuse and the beginnings of Wilhelmshaven at Mariensiel lock. Had she not stopped at Aurich she would have achieved the whole stretch in one day, but evening and closing-time overtook her just beyond the last of the forty-three bridges had been opened for her by their attentive keepers. She had to contemplate Wilhelmshaven only as a glow in the sky and wait until the lock-keeper came on duty early in the morning. Yet she missed nothing by being barred from the port itself, for even the most patriotic East Frisian would find it difficult to praise Wilhelmshaven, a town that is a mixture of naval dockyards, surplus bombed quaysides, and all the architectural taste which one would expect of the Wilhelm Kaisers. Wilhelmshaven is in fact best left unseen, or quickly forgotten. If we waited there for six hours it was to allow the tide to stream out for an hour or two, emptying the vast bay to the south of the town before we set out to catch the tail of the ebb out to sea.

The huge expanse of sands and watts at the mouth of the insignificant River Jade is in every way so very similar to the Dollart that one would naturally expect it to have had its own Tidde Winninga whose careless confidence in his own riches brought disaster and flooding to the area. And so it had, only with the difference that there was no lack of warning of the danger which threatened.

Like the Groningerland, the country now buried under the sands and channels of the Jade Bosom was one of rich harvests and self-satisfied farmers. One day there had been a baking at one of the farmhouses, when a beggarman came to the door, lured perhaps

East Frisia

by that same irresistible aroma of fresh bread which has often made the captain of the *Thames Commodore* set out at six in the morning into some canalside village. He asked for some food, and the servant girl who was drawing out the loaves was just about to give him the little loaf made of the odds and ends when her mistress turned upon her and snatched it away.

'I would rather my spare bread became stone than that it should be given away to the first sot who comes to the door,' she shouted. This was a foolish thing to say, and she might have known what would happen. The whole batch of loaves from the oven was found to have become petrified.

This portent would have alarmed many people, but it apparently left the local farmers unperturbed. So did a similar event when the beggar called at another farm and the beer all turned to blood. The farmers went their accustomed way, and are said even to have shod their carriage wheels with gold because a surfeit of the metal was becoming quite an embarrassment. The *dijkgraaf* himself became careless of his duties, and when at last the inevitable northerly gale drove the sea up past the Mellum Plate he was as sound asleep as the rest.

And that was when, in a single night, the Jadebusen was formed. How many were drowned when their villages were swept away is not known. Some say it was twenty thousand, others one hundred thousand.

There was one disadvantage of taking the Ems–Jade route, and I was aware of it before I made the decision. The neck of land separating the Jade and Weser estuaries is only seven miles broad, but it has no canal cut from one side to the other. Looking at the map one might think it only necessary to chug quickly round the tip from Wilhelmshaven to Bremerhaven, a journey which might easily be accomplished in an hour and a half; but a sea chart gives a very different picture. The German shore is beset with great areas of dangerous sands, and to reach the Weser from Wilhelmshaven even a small boat has to run at least twenty miles out to sea to pass round Alte Mellum, a wild area of desolate sands and marram grass which is declared to be a bird sanctuary. None but a seabird would wish to haunt such a dismal area, except perhaps the nature warden who lives a life of ornithological loneliness in the only small building upon the island – though it seems that he may occasionally have unexpected visitors, for at the inner end of Alte Mellum there is a pyramid pierced by a seventy-foot pole, and as the North Sea Pilot so pleasantly puts it *'the upper part of the pyramid is boarded in to form a shelter for shipwrecked people.'*

The wide nick in the German coastline which contains both the Weser and the Jade mouths is of course open to the north. Nobody in their senses would attempt the trip from one river to the other in windy and northerly weather, but we were so berthed in Wilhelmshaven that it seemed to me that the wind, if any, was very light. And so I believe it was, but the wind has a curious habit of holding its breath until the *Thames Commodore* is under way, and then getting to work in earnest. When the huge gate of the new sea-lock moved back to allow her to run out into the estuary I could see from the smoke of a cargo vessel at anchor that the wind was blowing it away sharply. The breeze was also whipping the wavelets so violently that it blew their tops right off. The scene reminded me of the last time I had entered the Weser. That was nine years earlier, aboard the *Commodore*, and we had an unexpected meeting with a waterspout. I remembered it very clearly, for a waterspout is almost as rare in European coastal waters as is a merman.

On that occasion we were running round the corner from Cuxhaven toward the Weser. As usual, the German Bight wind hid itself until we were well out from the coast and then suddenly let go its lungs and drove up some clouds of a beautiful deep violet blue, crossed with weaving lines of lightning. The old *Commodore* rolled so that she rang her own bell without any assistance, and after tolling her way round the Knechtsand and its pattern of wrecks she was able to turn down for Bremerhaven with the wind and waves at last on her flat rump and the storm filling the sail of her dinghy. It was just then that there appeared a little to one side of our course a curious conical projection which hung quivering from the bottom of a strangely angular and menacing cloud. Suddenly this finger groped down to the sea and plucked at it, so that at once the water began to stream up until it formed a solid pillar twenty yards or more across and several hundred feet high. The salt sea surged upward with a roar, the cloud swelled, the surface beneath it appeared to boil, and then the thousands of tons of water fell as a salt downpour of great violence. Some of it fell on our deck, bringing with it the curious gift of seaweed from the heavens.

Now, as we steamed out of Wilhelmshaven and past the tanker jetties I wondered whether the little squall playing on the water heralded another freak performance. It did not. It was merely the lead-in to a storm.

The third small wave beyond the harbour entrance was so mentally unstable that when the *Thames Commodore*'s stem pushed into it the water lost its temper, leaped straight over the bow, cleared the foredeck and windshield in a single bound, and poured down my neck by the front, back, and side entries. As I happened not to be wearing anything more waterproof than a pullover and shorts I was decidedly wetted. Never mind, I thought, we can take a joke and there won't be any more waves. It was but the slop in the harbour entrance, I told our ship's company.

As soon as I had turned the mole I began to have doubts, and

sure enough within a minute I was as wet as if I had fallen overboard. I decided to close the sandbanks on the farther side of the
channel, which here is no more than a mile wide, as I thought this
would make things more comfortable for the visitors. As for the
water landing on the deck, it at least would serve to wash off the
dirt which had rained upon the ship from the dusty dereliction of
Wilhelmshaven.

We had taken the tide just right, and the Bosom of Jade was
milking at a fine pace through the strait. The tide was of course
running strongly in exactly the opposite direction to the wind and
this made the water a little more humpy, yet the boat soon settled
down to a not unpleasant motion and if I was continually soaked at
least I did not have time to become chilled in the strong and almost
freezing wind before another wave would jump over the windshield to cheer me up with its slightly warmer water. Half an hour,
and the promontory of Butjadingerland was fading round to the
right, leaving an open view of Bremerhaven tantalisingly close to
starboard. Another forty minutes, and East Frisia had run to its
end a mile or two away on the port beam. Over the starboard bow
I could see between the flashes of spray the low flat of Alte Mellum,
with its pyramid beacon and the low, storm-swept dunes with the
square house of the bird-watcher. Over the sandhills the sea-birds
rose to roller-coaster on the wind for sheer enjoyment, and above
the sounds of the storm I could occasionally hear them screaming
in their delight. Northward the island faded off gradually into the
great and notorious area of the Mellum Plate, still lying under
water.

The wind was increasing now, and the thought crossed my mind
that we were not in any urgent hurry to reach the Baltic and it
might have been wiser not to come out on that particular afternoon,
but to suffer for one more day the dismal Hohenzollernery of
Wilhelmshaven. I knew that the *Thames Commodore* shared my
liking for an occasional frolic with the waves and that her Perkinses
were always anxious to show what they could do, but it seemed to
me that the water was becoming continually rougher and the
waves rather more insolent. However, another hour should bring
us clear of the banks and then we could turn the corner to head up

the Weser. If now we were to turn back for the Kaiser's haven we should have to fight a strong ebb for most of the way. No, we would go on.

Had I at that time made the acquaintance of the *Hai* (or *Shark*) I would perhaps have decided differently, but it was five months later that the *Thames Commodore* came to lie for a while in the peaceful little inland harbour of Verden on the Aller, made fast alongside the powerful ice-breaker of the Water Authority of the Middle Weser. The *Hai* was a fine craft, black and grey and weighty, and she must have been twice as long as the *Thames Commodore* and six times as heavy. She had once been sent down the river and out beyond the Mellum Plate to take provisions to the light vessel '*Bremen*', and round the Mellum the waves had smacked away the whole of her superstructure. Probably it was good that I did not know this, or I might have become anxious.

My wife had given me for Christmas a 'Seafarer' echo-sounder which registered with a soft little pinkish glow the depth of water below the point under the galley floor where its business end was mounted. Such a device may make a steersman on the Rhine nervous when he shoots between a rock on one side and a two-thousand ton load of coal on the other and discovers that there is no more than two feet of water below the keel, but for sea areas such as the western Baltic and the German Bight it is invaluable. One can cut certain corners in safety, knowing exactly how deep the sea is at any moment. Studying the chart I noticed that there must be at least one fathom of water over the whole of the Plate northward of the light tower which rose from its wide surface, and I was sure that with the clever little electronic gadget I could clip the corner as soon as we had passed the lighthouse itself, and so save a long and increasingly uncomfortable run all the way out to the light vessel '*Bremen*' a few miles ahead.

The great square tower of the Mellum Plate was already in sight, looking like an office block that some careless developer had dropped down in the middle of the German Bight. I cut it as close as I dared without risk of being driven into its base, and I was surprised to see that here we were already as far out to sea as the Frisian Islands. The low shape of Wangerooge was now not far away to port, and I could make out a lighthouse and a church projecting from the bar of sand where, no doubt, a few early holiday-makers would be finding the sea breeze a bracing tonic after a winter in the office. Somewhere on the further end of that desolate strip of land must be the remains of the tower where Störtebeker was said to have stored much of the booty he had seized from ships in the Bight – Störtebeker, the pirate with eyes so sharp that from the tower on Wangerooge he was reputed to be able to scan the English and Danish coasts, miraculously bending his vision to follow the curvature of the earth.

The famous pirate was one of the results of the endeavours of Queen Margaret (later of the 'Three Realms') to add to her provinces of Denmark and Norway the crown of Sweden. The Swedes declined the honour, and Stockholm was besieged. To help the city, Rostock and Wismar undertook to supply it by sea, and a league of blockade-runners was formed which later had its headquarters in Visby.

The Hanseatic League eventually helped Queen Margaret to take over Sweden, because the blockade-runners were a danger to their shipping and trade. So, with the coming of peace, a fleet of gallant ships manned by aristocratic toughs and swelled by German mercenaries no longer needed in Sweden was left with nothing to occupy it – except piracy. These Vitalienbrüder (Brother Victuallers) now made the life of the sailor and trader a dangerous one. Only Stralsund had the courage to mount an expedition against them, and this enterprise was so successful that with the destruction of Visby in 1398 almost all the Victuallers were captured. Only a few escaped – notably Klaus Störtebeker and Godeke Michels, who betook themselves to the German Bight, and with Heligoland as a base in the fairway played havoc with the trade of Hamburg.

Skilled these two leaders were, and they were served by many faithful lieutenants. One, Master Wikbold of Rostock, was an Oxford graduate. The might of Denmark, of England, of the Hansa itself failed to capture the roving ships of the gentlemen turned pirate. The corsairs sailed down as far as Compostella, where they stole along with other treasures the bones and dried tongue of St Vincent, which Gödeke Michels used as an oracle. It remained for some of the individual traders and clients of the Hansa to urge effective action, and it was a cheese-wholesaler of Utrecht who eventually provided his own new-built ship for the task. And so it came about that *De Bonte Koh* (*The Spotted Cow*) was held ready in Hamburg against the moment when an opportunity should arise.

The *Spotted Cow* had not long to wait. Störtebeker was at last brought to book when a fisherman sailed up under the stern of his *Roter Teufel* (or *Red Devil*) and lay there for shelter. Waiting until the pirates were no longer suspicious, he quickly poured over the rudder pins a cauldron of molten lead which he had been boiling up, pretending it to be his supper. When the raider found himself encircled by his enemies he also discovered that his ship could not be steered, and his effort to free the rudder with boiling oil was too late. Along with his eighty-three ruffians he was taken in victory for public execution in Hamburg.

The authorities rejected all his attempts to buy his freedom, but at least they agreed to what seemed a foolish last wish. They would grant him the lives of all his companions past whom he could run after his own head had been struck off. He stood ready to sprint, like an athlete waiting for the starter's pistol, and as the swordsman struck off his head with a single blow he was already moving. He had passed eleven of his comrades before his body fell to the ground, and those eleven were spared. The remaining seventy-two were quickly beheaded. And Hamburg's women cried and cried in their sorrow for such unprincipled rascals – as women always will. That was the end of Störtebeker, except that in 1851 an opera appeared in France under the title *Claus Störtebeker, Lord of the Seas*.

It was of course a great day for the executioner, who had never before had so many heads to top on a single morning. But it was hard work, too, and after he had come to the end of the row he appeared before the city council for his wages and overtime payment. One of the councillors asked him how he felt after so much labour.

'Fine, worthy Sirs,' he exclaimed. 'I enjoyed it so much that I could have gone on and topped the whole of the council and aldermen too.'

Sad to relate, the councillors of Hamburg were a humourless lot of men and they had the fellow condemned for insulting them. His own head was the next to fall – to the less practised hand of his successor in the interesting if not very exalted position of Hamburg's municipal swordsman.

Klaus Störtebeker was a mighty pirate indeed, even if he only roved the German Bight for three years. From prints and medals one can see that he was a powerful, bearded figure, every inch an aristocrat. In fact Störtebeker (or Empty-the-Beaker) was only a nickname to cover an identity too refined for a rough pirate, and he had it from his capacity to empty at one draught a gallon jug of wine. He nobly gave all those he captured the alternative of paying a huge ransom, or – if they could not do so – of drinking the measure in one, or being thrown overboard. Only one man ever escaped by the drink, and Störtebeker had his name engraved on the goblet:

Ik, Jonker Sissinga van Groninga, dronk dees Heusa in een Fleusa door myn Kraga in myn Maga.

I was glad Störtebeker had gone, because I doubt if at this moment I could have emulated the worthy Mijnheer Sissinga of Groningen and emptied the draught 'in one flush through my neck into my stomach'. Not that pirates were the only menace to shipping in this area, for even closer than Wangerooge I could make out the diminutive and uninhabited islet of Minsener Oog, with another beacon partly boarded in 'as a shelter for shipwrecked people'. Close to this was another and larger refuge, a hut on piles which the Pilot Book reassuringly told me to be 'furnished with necessaries' for the survival of shipwrecked mariners.

Despite all this harping by the authorities on possible catastrophe I never for a moment doubted the *Thames Commodore*'s ability to climb any waves she might meet, or the determination of the Perkinses under the saloon floor to keep going without a hiccough. Choosing a bearing on which, by the chart, there should be never less than two fathoms of water, I slanted her across the outlying sands of the Mellum. Dead ahead and about one mile away I could see a very odd distortion in the surface of the sea, quite unlike anything I had experienced in nearly twenty years of small boating. Taking up the binoculars I took a quick look at it between successive blasts of spray, and then considered what it could possibly be.

The sea over an area of a few acres was transformed into a series of jagged peaks, from the top of which something looking like whipped cream was continually being flung into the air. The wind, I told myself, could never do that. Either Ekke Nekkepen himself had lost his temper with somebody, or else he had got wind of the fact that we had a surgeon on board and was once more going to ask for help. Or maybe the sea-witches were at it again. However, there was no need to speculate, for in another few minutes we should be there and could see for ourselves.

Although I had never seen such an extraordinarily confused patch of water I did not wish to turn away from it. The good ship was plunging and rearing nobly, and once or twice already I had been thrown up from the bar stool which I sat on to steer, but it was the choice between perhaps one mile of very mixed-up and nasty-looking waves or an extra hour and a half down to the light vessel and back. The ship was not downhearted and nor was I, and of those down below two were prostrate and no doubt wondering in a dazed sort of way whether boating was really such fun as people insisted, whilst my wife and brother-in-law were busily chasing tins from the store lockers, grabbing the table and chairs as they galloped past them, and trying to pile in relative safety on the floor such pots and pans and dishes as had not already leaped down from their shelves and cupboards unaided. I do not like the sound of everything breaking loose down below, but chasing tins and bottles gives people something to do and diverts their attention from what can be seen out of the window, which at this moment was rather menacing.

When we ran into the sharply bounded patch of watery peaks I was surprised at their steepness. So were the coils of lines, the boat-hook, and the Cambridge punting pole I had marked off as a measure for sounding. In their astonishment they leaped cleanly into the air, and before they could regain their seats a great mass of water caught them and whisked them away like straws. The only thing left on the foredeck was a fine fat motor-tyre on a rope. It jumped up, somersaulted, and landed flat on its back just ahead of the saloon windows. I would have been sorry to see it a victim of the Mellum Plate, for it had a particular sentimental value. Before the *Thames Commodore* sailed on her maiden voyage to the Moselle she had lain near the zoo monkeys on the Regent's Canal. Fred Doerflinger, who had shared most of our voyages for twelve years had rowed us along that peaceful cutting below the roar of the rush-hour traffic and he had salvaged the tyre from beneath the Avenue Road bridge, to serve the ship as a good soft fender at low quaysides. It had accompanied us in six countries already, and had become quite a favourite.

I eased off enough to reduce the bucketing motion to manageable proportions, and all the time I kept an eye on the cheerful little pink line of the echo-sounder. Whenever a particularly nasty wave lay across our course I tried to sidle it, and soon I noticed that most of the waves were not moving at all. They were just going up and down, but otherwise standing almost still.

The soft pink glow on the dial moved up, then down, and over one wave it announced eighteen feet at the crest but only four feet in the trough. These were the depths below the transducer head, which was mounted under the lettuces beneath the galley floor, and I knew that the bottom of the belly was about eighteen inches lower. At the trough of this wave we had only just over two feet of water between ourselves and the Mellum Plate, a discovery which I found not very reassuring.

'One foot less, and I'll turn, whether the next wave is on the beam or no,' I said to myself. The idea of twenty tons of ship being dropped from a height of ten or fifteen feet upon a notoriously hard sand did not appeal to me.

The next wave was smaller, and so was the next. We only leaped eight or ten feet instead of fourteen. Then we had another larger visitor, quite as high and steep as the first, but in the trough we now had five feet of water. Soon after that it rose to six at the bottom of the hills and I was decidedly relieved. Continually the measure rose until there was never less than two fathoms on the dial, and I knew the worst was over. Another few minutes of violence and the ship passed over the foaming frontier into deep water where regular wave trains were chasing each other out of the murk beneath the northern sky. We were now in the edge of the Fedderwarder Channel, and as soon as there was a chance of turning her to get the waves astern I did so. Then I pulled back the throttle and let the good ship roar ahead, the waves hardly overtaking her.

I could now see a large ship well to our right, but I was not tempted to follow her, for she seemed to be in a position where the chart showed no water at all. She was an old-fashioned vessel with a high smoke-stack out of which, I noted, no smoke was coming. Later I discovered that she was the Liberian-registered *Balmoral*, and she had gone aground only two weeks earlier. She had run straight on the Mellum Plate 'as a result of faulty navigation', as the report said. When some months later we passed within a mile of her aboard the ferry *Prins Hamlet* bound for Harwich, she was still there. Every attempt to move her had failed, and she had been knocked down to a Dutch firm of breakers, who would dismantle her where she lay.

It was almost dark by the time we overtook our first tramp. I passed within yards of her, and the old skipper at the wheel smiled cheerfully and made deprecating signs at the sky. Ahead and to starboard the Hohe Weg lighthouse bore down quickly, standing where once yet another wealthy community was overwhelmed by the storm waves. Not on account of negligence in diking, the story goes, but for their blasphemous behaviour in making a pig drunk with corn spirit, dressing it in a nightshirt and tucking it up in bed before summoning the priest – who must have been rather short-sighted, I think – to administer the last sacrament to a dying woman. Now in the gathering gloom beneath the storm clouds the lighthouse stood friendly and reassuring, waving to us like a giant doll, its collection of masts and arms and dials telling the direction of the tide, the depth, and the strength of the wind in the Heligoland and Borkum sea areas. Both pointers were set to north, and I could just count the grade-bars sticking out from the side. It was force 6 at Borkum, force 8 at Heligoland, these fingers said, and I was glad we were inward bound.

We overhauled another coaster, a barge which had hoisted a reefed sail to steady her. Then the *Prins Hamlet* came surging out, the rows of lights burning brightly along her saloon decks. Her wash made enough commotion to show that we were already in much calmer waters, sheltered by the long line of the submerged Robben Plate (or Seal Bank) to port. Ahead, a row of cheerfully winking lights made a pleasant avenue down which to steer. One hour more, and we should be in. Meanwhile, I tried to warm myself with thinking about the standing waves over the Mellum Plate.

It seemed impossible that waves fourteen feet high could run over water so shallow as to leave us only about two feet under the ship, and yet it had happened. Or very nearly, for the secret lay in the fact that the waves had not actually run at all, but had stood. They were 'standing waves'.

The dial had shown eighteen feet at the top of the wave and four at the bottom. Add two for the depth of the transducer below water level, and that made a depth of twenty at the crest and six in the trough. This meant that there was a mean depth of thirteen feet – or just over two fathoms, as the chart suggested – and the wave was oscillating to give a peak seven feet above and a valley seven feet below that level. The fact that the waves over the Plate had been more or less stationary heavings showed what was happening, and how these steep hills and valleys of water were made.

With the storm bearing down from the north, a ground swell of quite modest waves bore down upon the Mellum, splitting at the tip of the nose of the Plate to run past it on either side. But Newton's Laws and a few other physical phenomena of a perfectly regular and predictable kind had slowed the edge of each wave which was running in the shallower water over the sand, and so had swung the waves inward. The same regulations had also made the waves bunch up higher – for all waves have to remember that kinetic energy is something real, and is made up of mass and velocity multiplied together. In this quite simple way the Mellum Plate brought it about that two halves of a swell which had perhaps been no more than three or four feet high had split, turned, steepened, and run straight at each other as two seven-footers. And twice seven is fourteen feet – a fact of arithmetic which can be rediscovered by any who may care to leave the Bosom of Jade on a day of northerly wind and cut round the sands of Mellum.

I was still pondering this arithmetic when I realised that we were surging past the Columbus quay and the bright lights so close beside us were on some great liner lying alongside. Soon the *Thames Commodore* was bearing down upon the red light tower at the entrance of the River Geeste, and after executing a pirouette to avoid colliding with the dark shape of the ferry-boat as it came gliding out between the piers she slid inside and made for the open door of the lock into the Fischereihaven.

Soon afterwards I was able to wring out my clothes and take a hot shower before settling down to supper and a sound sleep, lulled by the delight of being in port and the satisfaction of a resolve that wherever our Baltic voyage might take us the return trip would be by the inside route. We had seen the Mellum once. And once was enough.

In Holstein

VII

The Baltic blue – the Klabautermann aboard – Thames Commodore *reaches Denmark – flag of the Danes – the executioner of Sønderborg – Broager's spires – the Flensburg fjord – Black Margaret and the Swedish king – the case of the brook rescue – Glücksburg – the giants of the Als Sund*

THREE days later the *Thames Commodore* was nearing the end of the Kiel Canal, along which she had been running all day, dipping on the wash of the little timber ships, Polish ocean-goers and Russian giants which surged past her, westward bound. Already the high bridge just short of the locks at Holtenau was in sight, and as soon as we had locked out with the shipping which shared the giant pen with us I looked up the log of our earlier voyage to the Baltic and found that Holtenau had been the twenty-fifth lock the old *Commodore* had passed after leaving the Thames. This time it was our thirty-first, for we had swelled the number by our wanderings across East Frisia and over the Hadelner land between Weser and Elbe.

There was another difference, too. All those years ago I had thought of the Baltic as a remote sea overhung by dismal cloud, a greyish sheet of water bounded by shores as bleak as those of Norfolk, its gloomy waves driven by a chill northern wind to heave and threaten, and at last to break upon the shallow coastline. And yet when the little ship had chugged out of Holtenau to run down the Kiel fjord into the open sea we had found ourselves in water as brilliant and azure as the allure of Bahama holiday posters, its surface perfectly smooth, as seemingly painted as the ocean of the *Ancient Mariner*, its skin of surface tension broken only by a rare float above a net, or by our own wake. It seemed almost improper to cut the mirror of this perfect sea, its water so clear that one could stand on the bow and look right down to see the little fish floodlit by the sunshine and watch them suddenly dart to escape the intrusion of the fat-bellied anti-fouled monster forging by overhead.

I recalled the jellyfish, too. Like eels in the Sargasso depths, it seemed as though all the scyphozoans of the seven seas must have been born and bred in the Baltic, to return there in old age to die. Large and small, pink and purple, violet and translucent blue, the water was filled with these delicate and slowly pulsating bells, some just idling, others trailing behind them a yard or more of filaments, private minefields with their myriad microscopic and trigger-happy stinging cells ready to send out poisoned harpoons to secure any little fish who might be day-dreaming. Beautiful beyond belief these creatures were, dressed with a loveliness to which I must have been blind when, a quarter of a century earlier, I had had to study their nerve-net and reproductive system in the zoological laboratory to satisfy some all-important syllabus. We even had to weigh a jellyfish, I remember, and a piece of blotting-paper, then leave the one on the other until the poor creature had simply soaked its soul away and evaporated to leave only a slight residue. Two per cent, I think it was, that the balance revealed at the end of the experiment. Two per cent of salts and proteins with a good seasoning of inaccurate weighing. This showed us something very important, but even then the lesson somehow escaped me. I was no lover of jellyfish, but I could not help wondering what figure the professor would turn up if we were to bake him slowly on a fat pancake of blotting-paper.

The Baltic had been breathtakingly beautiful on that June morning long ago. But now it was April, and the sea into which the *Thames Commodore* made her exit from the Kiel Canal was different indeed. Gone were the blue, the sunshine, the clearness of the water. Instead there was a sheet of slowly heaving grey, bounded by shores which looked as bleak as those of Norfolk, its wind-tossed surface over-shadowed by dismal clouds driven by a chill northern wind. It was precisely the Baltic I had imagined when first I ever heard the name of this Eastern Sea, and it certainly did not look inviting. The jellyfish were there as I had remembered them, but they too had lost their glamour. Cold, ugly and glutinous they crowded the water, bobbing in the effluent of Kiel. The scene was altogether so uninviting that instead of running ahead to the Danish isles we turned down to the harbour of Kiel itself.

Next morning the wind had lessened but a cold fog lay over the Kiel fjord, and as the harbour bulletin said the fog would continue for some days we took out the *Thames Commodore*'s green dressing-gown of tarpaulin and laid her up while we went home by the Esbjerg ferry to Harwich.

Six weeks later I was back in Kiel. My wife had a round of meetings which could not be broken into, and as we had promised to remove the *Thames Commodore* from the harbour before the beginning of Kiel Week, when every square inch of the port and fjord would be needed for other craft, I returned aboard to set off again in a way I had never attempted before. I would be alone. A few days later I was to be joined by Bill Gardam, the chairman of the River Thames Society, and I had arranged to call in one day at Flensburg to meet his train, but until then I would have to run the ship single-handed.

There is nothing heroic about taking a twenty-nine-ton motor-ship alone on the sea. It is not a Chichester or Slocum undertaking, but it has certain difficulties of its own. A sailing ship can be made to run on a reasonably straight course, and with the sails set and the helm positioned she should need little attention. This is even true of the better-built model craft which I have often seen from my study window as they run the length of the sailing lake at the Highgate side of Hampstead Heath and make a reasonably correct landfall at the further shore. But a motor-boat will not steer herself. She has no such equilibrium between sail and helm, and will not run straight for a hundred yards without a hand on the wheel. With no keel, the least wave will deflect the bow slightly, and if the sea is perfectly smooth the craft still has a mysterious tendency to turn circles, even if the radius is a large one. Such calm meander-ings do not matter (except in busy shipping lanes, where they may be inconvenient) but in rougher water the ship has to be steered over every wave and cannot be allowed to broach and roll on her beam ends. This makes it difficult to undertake much cooking when under way – particularly when the galley is down two sets of steps from the wheel.

I realised that this would be so, but I thought I could prepare a good meal and eat it without throwing the anchor or waiting for a port. I also decided that it might be imprudent to walk round the outside of the vessel for any reason at all when she was under way, for if I were to trip over something and fall overboard I should merely surface to have a fine view of the transom as the ship disappeared toward the horizon while I floundered among the myriad jellyfish of Kiel Bay. The ship would normally describe a circle and pass within hailing distance again, but what use would that be if there were none aboard to answer? The *Thames Commodore* would become a second *Marie Céleste*.

For these various reasons I tried to see that every little job both inside and out was done before leaving the harbour. On deck I

secured the lines, put a safety hitch on the anchor chain, and checked that the dinghy could not start swinging. Below decks I carefully put the lamps on the floor, laid anything breakable on the
bunks, and packed down the china and glass in the saloon by
stuffing the settee cushions on top of the piles of plates. At the same
time I wondered at my own caution, for it was a fine summer's
afternoon of sun and light breeze, and when at last I set out from
the Olympiahafen with the sealed blessings of the customs officers
I thought the sea would be almost as smooth as it had been eleven
years before. There was a curious little heaving swell in the harbour,
but I took it to be some sort of meteorological hangover.

Out we sailed, the *Thames Commodore* and I, happily running
past the roads where the ships were drifting to await the signals on
the Holtenau locks. Abreast of Laboe the water was still calm and
everywhere the anglers were in their little rowboats, sitting peace-
fully on the surface of the bay, half asleep in the sun. Jellyfish,
mauve and azure, flowed past in their thousands just as I remembered them. I set the nose for the open sea and darted below
to put on a kettle, then ran back to the wheel. The slight undulations I had noticed at the inner end of the fjord were still present,
giving a dreamy lolloping motion to our progress.

The moment we were clear of the shelter of the eastern shore
beyond Laboe I realised that the swell was no hangover at all,
but nature's own warning to mariners that out in the open water
the Baltic was throwing one of its characteristic epilepsies. Ahead
a smart German sailing yacht was bucketing in a surprising fashion,
her nose throwing sheets of spray over her oilskinned crew. I
slowly overhauled her, and as I did so I heard a clatter and hiss
as the kettle fell off the stove. Then the pans went down, and began
to fight each other. Next, the saloon chairs rolled on their backs.
I heard a crash which I knew could only be the dining-table
turning over in sympathy.

Soon a sound began which reminded me of the ingenious
thunder machine in the Drottingholm theatre, where cobbles and
stone cannon balls are rolled down a wooden trough with most
realistic effect. I realised the store lockers had come open and a
month's supply of marmalade and peas, canned potatoes and

coffee, tinned fruit and soups and sausages were rolling down to
the galley and plunging from side to side, yet I dared not leave the
wheel for a moment to try to secure anything.

There is nothing worse than the noise made by pans and brushes,
cans and bottles, dishes and furniture when they work themselves
up into a frenzy in their cumbrous efforts to dance the hornpipe.
Each crash and thud sounds like a fearful blow of destruction, and
the only sensible course is to take the ship as swiftly as possible into
still water. Choosing a suitable gap between two of the combers
blowing down from Estonia I spun the wheel, put on full power,
and swung the ship to take the waves on her stern and ride them
home into the inlet.

The German sailing yacht had already done the same, and
together we cantered happily on the lifting of the crests until the
waves fell away and we could turn the corner of the shallow spit
of sand to aim for the pretty harbour of Laboe in the shelter of the
beautiful fjord of Kiel.

Next morning I decided to be up and away before the wind was
stirring, and with this resolve I awoke at three o'clock, and started
the engines. It seemed almost indecent to set the sleeping harbour
throbbing with diesel at such an hour, but I tried to assure myself
that fishermen were used to it, tramp skippers slept soundly, and
yachtsmen would be either too lazy or too good-mannered to
object.

And now the Baltic was at its loveliest. Somewhere towards
Siberia the sky was aglow with almost electronic colours as the sun
climbed the far side of the hill of the earth to peep over the top
and see what sort of a day the winds were going to make. The sea
lay perfectly still, deep purple and jewelled with the ruby and
diamond flashes of the buoys winking to each other across the
stillness. The stars even now shone brilliant in the twilight sky of
the Nordic deities, and their reflections stared back at them from
the water until they faded in the growing light of the coming dawn
and the sea itself became mauve, then greenish yellow, and at last
the most intense and delicate blue.

By this time I was off Bülk Point. The lighthouse on the cliff
closed its eyes and went to sleep, leaving me to head up the coast

alone, without so much as a fishing vessel on all the sea as far as the horizon. I had a curious, elated sense of owning the whole world, unseen by anyone. Earlier in history I should have been watched, for at Bülk the sea-brigand Störtebeker had one of his hide-outs, a castle from which his sharp eyes roved over the water in search of booty, but now I was alone unseen except perhaps by the Klabautermann who was my constant companion.

I must explain about the Klabautermann, for such little fellows are not usually found aboard British-registered ships. They are much more Germanic. A Klabautermann usually makes himself known by the strange noise he makes, and that was precisely how I slowly became aware of his presence aboard the ship.

Sometimes when steeering the *Thames Commodore* at night I could hear a curious knocking sound. During the first season I took this very seriously and at the end of a run I would examine the propeller-shaft for looseness and creep down between the engines and twist my torso into contortions to inspect the solid rubber cores which formed part of the mountings by which the tons of machinery was held to the bearers on either side of the keel. I even went so far as to tell Tough Brothers of Teddington and Perkins Engines of Peterborough that I thought there was too much move-ment and that at certain speeds the engines had a tendency to rock and shake and clatter. They took the matter as seriously and studiously as I had done, for like myself they had either forgotten about the Klabautermann or had not even heard of him.

The Klabautermann is a knocker, and he just clabouts about, particularly at night. He is about eighteen inches high and he always carries a hammer, and this he uses when he emerges after dark to do all the jobs that the crew have not finished during the day. In fact he is the good spirit of the ship and only the most boorish seaman would be so stupid as to throw a block of wood at him, or try to hit him with a rope's end, for then he might be angry and leave the ship. Without its Klabautermann a ship is as good as done for, and the East Frisians know of a case where a member of the crew has overheard two Klabautermänner on adjacent ships whispering to each other at the moorings. One was heard to say that he was packing and looking for another vessel, as his present ship would sink in the English Channel. The crew member reported this to the captain, then he signed off and took his papers, but the officers and crew merely laughed at him – which was foolish, for the ship within a week became part of the ground obstructions embracingly shown on the chart of the Dover Strait as *numerous wrks*.

Our own private Klabautermann has never been seen – at least not by myself. If I have given his size and can also mention that he has large eyes and a grey cloak and a hat pulled over his ears that is only because these characteristics are regular to the breed. Not everybody can hope to see a Klabautermann – in fact very few can do so, for one must be born at midnight on the 22nd day of February. As for the ship, it is important that she should not be launched on a Monday or Friday, as the little men do not like those days. The *Thames Commodore* was actually launched on a Tuesday.

Even if he is unseen, one can easily realise that the Klabautermann is there right enough, for apart from tidying up unfinished jobs he also acts as a warner when danger threatens. On such occasions he bangs or rattles with his hammer on the hull itself, and every time we have run aground in a river I have heard this curious noise just in time to put the engines astern and take some of the way off the ship before she has struck and slid smoothly to a halt. In the Thames tideway, too, the little fellow has sometimes thumped loudly to tell me that some massive piece of driftwood is just about to run through the propeller blades.

All the same, it was surprising to have a ship's spirit of this kind aboard the *Thames Commodore*. With her predecessor it was a different matter, for the *Commodore* had a wooden hull and was built (for the Royal Navy, her first owners) in Wales.

It seems that Frisian mothers used sometimes to murder their unwanted children – and if the Frisians did it I expect the Welsh did too. The guilty mother would often bury the body under the roots of an oak or some other tree, and as the tree grew so it took up into its body the essence or spirit of the child. Later the lumbermen would come, then the sawyers and the shipwrights, and the infant spirited into the tree would be distributed among the planks of a ship. When the vessel was fitted out the spirit would become reconstituted down in the bilge, and that is how a Klabautermann was born. This was all explained to me in detail by one of the men aboard the German sailing yacht which had turned back and made for Laboe. As the *Thames Commodore* had a smooth and straight flank I signed to the crew to come alongside, and it was while he was waiting for the coffee to be brewed that the skipper stepped over and told me about the origin of the Klabautermann in infanticide. He was a pleasant, donnish man, and I think he was an anthropologist or something of the kind. Certainly he spoke about *Schiffsgeister* with authority.

Now, the *Thames Commodore* was not built of any sinister wood, but of steel plates – eleven tons of them. I pointed this out, and the German nodded thoughtfully.

'He must have joined the ship later,' he said sagely. 'Maybe he was aboard a wooden ship and it became old and leaky.'

'A Thames barge,' I suggested.

He nodded. 'Could be. Yes, he might have come from such a ship.'

'Except that I've never heard of any English coasting barge having a Klabautermann,' I said. 'I don't believe they live in our part of the world.'

I saw that he took the point. 'That's true,' he said. He thought for a while, staring out across the fishing-boats clustered in the corner of the harbour. 'Didn't you say that your ship was fairly new, and made her first voyage early in '65?'

'Yes,' I said. 'But what has that to do with it?'

He chuckled. 'And you sailed down the Thames below London? Well now, did you happen to notice a wreck of any kind? A big ship, laden with buses for Cuba, wasn't she?'

'The *Magdeburg*! Yes, she was lying on her side in the fairway.' I remembered her very well.

'Well, suppose you were a ship's spirit, and they messed things up by sinking the ship. You would have to find a new home, wouldn't you? My guess is he hopped aboard your craft as she went down the river.'

'Except that the *Magdeburg* was a steel ship, too,' I pointed out.

'Of course. But the Klabautermann wouldn't belong to her in

E2

the first place, because she was from the Zone. Can you imagine any decent spirit wanting to live in the Zone, or on a ship with the D.D.R. flag? He had just stowed away to escape, and when the *Magdeburg* went down he jumped ship.'

'Hm,' I pondered. 'Are you sure about that?'

He grinned. 'Are you sure you have a Klabautermann?'

On this early morning I was steering across the mouth of the Eckernförde bay when the Klabautermann began to give a few little taps with his hammer. I looked astern, and sure enough a severe blow was coming from the south-east. In the distance I could see the surface of the sea thrown into serrations like a badly made saw-blade, though ahead the water still had only small wavelets. Dark and menacing clouds appeared as if by magic, and soon we were rollicking and rolling, pitching and heaving almost as much as on the day before.

The Baltic is curiously capricious. When E. F. Knight wrote *The 'Falcon' on the Baltic* and described his journey from Hammer-smith to Copenhagen in 1897 he had very much the same experience of the weather as we were to have aboard the *Thames Commodore*. 'The Baltic is a treacherous sea,' he wrote. 'Settled weather can never be depended on, gales spring up very unexpectedly. We soon discovered that whenever the wind means mischief in these seas it shifts to the north-west. We never encountered bad weather from any other quarter. Another discovery we soon made was that a dangerous sea can get up in the Baltic with extraordinary rapidity. This is without doubt not only due to the shallowness of the water but also to the small proportion of salt contained in it. A well-pickled ocean is always more sluggish than a fresh-water lake.'

With the wind rising, the ship beginning to lunge and the saucepans and crockery capering through the saloon I had no choice but to forge ahead to the shelter of the inlet of the Schlei. This wonderful fjord is thirty miles long and no more than eighty yards broad at its entrance, and if I do not describe it here in any detail that is only because if I were to do so this particular volume would run no further than to Schleswig, at the inner end of what must be one of the most romantic stretches of water in the world, rich in the memories of the Viking trading ships which made it their base. The Schlei must wait, and we shall merely put in there to shelter and to sweep up a little broken china and glass before returning to a sea once more as calm as a mirror and running an hour further up the coast to cross the invisible frontier line in the mouth of the splendid Flensburg fjord and introduce the ship to her first port in her eighth country, Denmark.

There is a magic about Sønderborg which comes entirely from its position, for in fact the main street is that of a busy county town with stationers, ironmongers, builders and plumbers, paper and paint and gift shops, and no particular charm. It is the water-front which makes Sønderborg what it is, and this lies tucked away round a kink in the entrance to the Sound of Als and remains hidden until the very last moment. When steering towards the port from Kiel Bay one can make out a factory chimney, a wind-mill, then some rather dull commercial buildings, and a few grass-grown emplacements on a hillside which rises steeply from the water, yet all are on the Dybbøl side of the sound, which is the mainland. Sønderborg itself is on the island of Als at the other end of the swing-bridge which spans the narrow channel. A turn round a black buoy, a doubling back to pass behind a red one, and quite unexpectedly the view opens out to a scene which has no equal in any other Danish port. To starboard there stands right beside the quay the great mellow brick castle where long ago King Christian II was imprisoned to ponder through many years his treachery in inviting the Swedish nobility to a party in Stockholm and then having them murdered almost to a man, beginning with the bishops as protocol demanded. Even in those distant times it was a fearful deed of ruthless deception, and it cost him his kingdom and paved the way for the secession of the Swedish provinces.

Immediately beyond the castle stands the rather elegant pink-washed building of the customs house, and then in the elbow of the harbour the stages where the steamers come and go all through the day – for this is a part of the world where ships still provide the easiest and in many cases the only means of communication between one town and another. Danish and German, the white vessels swing round in the current that always flows through the Sound of Als and head away for Glücksburg and Flensburg, or for Langballigau across the widening fjord. Behind these busy ships the quay curves round to a very matter-of-fact but beautiful row of buildings standing across the street from the jumble of yachts and fishing-boats. There is a sailmaker, and Siddy's laundry, and the two ship-chandlers, Hansen's and Tingleff's, with their array of ropes and anchors, charts, oilskins and sweaters, fishing-gear, and everything from potatoes and eggs to caviare. Sønderborg is a place where one can pull in right beside the shops, and on her several visits to the town the *Thames Commodore* would acknowledge with a toot the wave of Mrs Tingleff's hand from the upstairs balcony where, like a Störtebeker of more generous purpose, she could look out across the approaches or up the sound to see whatever boat might soon be bearing down upon the quays. Nothing was too difficult or too much trouble for her. She could whistle up a tanker of diesel oil at nine o'clock on a Sunday morning, or conjure up a baker's boy with hot rolls fresh from the oven. She knew the yachts and their owners, and at once she made them feel that this was a port where they were ever welcome.

Although so close to Germany there is something quite distinctive about the appearance of this harbour frontage of Sønderborg, and it does not take very long to realise that the difference lies partly in the colours. Pale ochre, buff, brown and black and copper-red, the houses could be nowhere but in Scandinavia, for their tints are those of Danish handicrafts. The half-timbered cottages of the fishermen are bright in their hues of blue and green; and over the whole scene, on ships and houses, across the bridge and up by the church, on the castle turret and high over the sad monuments of the Danish-Prussian war on the Dybbøl hillside there floats the splendid red flag with a white cross, the famous 'Dannebrog' of the Danes, an ensign brilliantly offset by the quieter colours of the Danish land and the gentle blue of its cloud-flecked sky. If ever a flag had a right to fall as a gift from heaven, surely it was this.

> *Vift stolt på Codans bølge. . . .*
>
> *Wave proud o'er Baltic's billows*
> *Thou Dannebrog blood-red!*

Every Danish child can tell how King Valdemar II (Valdemar the Victorious) set out to chastise the heathens of Estonia, and how he landed upon their shores and told them what was in store for them if they should resist. Very wisely the pagans appeared to be enthusiastic toward the new religion he brought to them, and they queued up for the baptism which would ensure their safety. At the same time their friends began to assemble secretly in the woods nearby, and after three days a formidable army was ready to rush out upon the Danish camp from all sides, swinging their deadly clubs and slashing furiously with their hefty swords. Many a Dane fell before any defence could be mustered, and the fate of Valdemar and all his army was hanging in the balance when like some latter-day Moses the aged Bishop Anders Sunesøn climbed up to the hilltop with his fellow priests and their clerks. Raising his hands to heaven he implored deliverance, and all his companions fell to their knees so that they might lay the weight of their prayers in the scales to tip the balance of the fighting. That at least is how the ballad tells the tale, and it goes on to relate how the Danes still held out until, as old Anders tired, he could no longer hold up his arms in supplication. As he dropped them, so also the fortune of the Danes began to fail, but the clergy quickly saw the cause of the reverse and they crowded round the old man to hold up his arms when his own strength failed. And as long as they did so the Danes again prevailed.

In the confusion of battle the Danish ensign had been lost, but now the famous miracle happened. A scarlet banner with a cross in white came dropping gently down through the cloud base and a voice proclaimed that under that sign they should conquer. *In hoc signo vinces* – so ran the celestial reassurance of which Constantine had long before dreamed when threatened by his rivals, and no doubt there must have been echoes of that Roman emperor in the tale of the Dannebrog as it came to be handed down.

As for the Estonians, they were very rightly amazed. They were also frightened, and as panic spread among them they fled. The Danes pursued them and cut them down, baptised or not, until the field was deep in their bodies; then the weary soldiers of Valdemar knelt around the miraculous banner and the king there and then instituted the famous Order of the Dannebrog, dubbing thirty-five knights upon the battlefield. That was seven and a half centuries ago, and the order is still one of the highest in the land.

Beneath the glinting red of its Dannebrogs Sønderborg is a bustling place, with a smell of fish and diesel oil down by the harbour. Nowadays it is peaceful enough, and nobody is imprisoned in the mournful cell of its castle. Beheading is a thing of the past also, but there was a time when Sønderborg was renowned for the brilliance and skill of its executioner, who was such a mild and kindly fellow that he liked to meet his ordained victim, chat to him, and suddenly slice off his head with a single deft swish of his sword before the condemned man had even realised what was about to happen. So skilled was he that stories accrued about him, and one of them relates how he happened to chop off the head of a victim upon a very cold winter's day when even the swift water of the Sound of Als came near to freezing. The cut was so clean and neat that the head did not even fall from the torso, and as the air was extremely chilly it froze on again. Naturally the offender was very relieved to find his head still attached to his shoulders, and he at once went into the nearest inn to celebrate with his friends over a hearty glass of beer.

The inn was warm, and after a while the man became conscious of a trickling down the back of his neck and his throat, a sensation which unfortunately made him sneeze. Like all polite individuals he sneezed into his hands – and so for a moment he held his detached head in his own palms before he fell dead on the floor. His companions had to pay the round.

Then there was the occasion when the victim happened to be a fanatic for skittles and chose as a last favour before his execution the chance to challenge the swordsman of Sønderborg on the bowling alley. The game began happily – or as merrily as was possible under the circumstances – and yet the executioner had so stiffened himself up with liquor before performing a job he found distasteful, that when his opponent bent down to pick up the large wooden ball the temptation was too much for him. With a lightning blow of his sword he chopped off the head, just in time for the victim's hand to catch it and bowl it along the alley.

It was a masterly shot, too, and as the pins fell in all directions the detached head shouted excitedly 'All nine!' One must presume that the torso was considered to have won the game if nothing else.

I had arranged to pick up Bill Gardam in Flensburg late that afternoon. It was a day of bright Scandinavian sunshine and the *Thames Commodore* galloped over sparkling water flecked by just a pleasant touch of stiff breeze which came first one way and then the other as she turned the promontories of Danish Broager to starboard and German Hölnis to port. The shores were splendidly decked in beechwood, or sloped back to wide expanses of pasture with fields of mustard traversed by trains of golden waves running before the wind. The low cliffs of boulder clay were topped with rich farmland, and here and there on the Danish shore a white-washed church stood out against the backcloth of woods and meadows, its step-gabled tower wearing a gay hat of bright pinkish tiles. Right in the centre of the high land of the Broager peninsula stood the church I remembered as such an excellent landmark, and this had no stepped tower but two steeples huddled close against each other.

This church is said to have been the work of two sisters, and probably it was. A more popular and picturesque story associates it with a noble and godfearing knight who had put the work in hand before he left on a pilgrimage to the Holy Land. As a pleasant touch he asked his wife, who was having a baby, to arrange for a tower if it should be a daughter and a spire if a son, so that when homeward bound he might know and rejoice while still far out at sea. The event, as all can see to this day, was twin boys; and the fact that the spires are not alike in every respect is, I think, an indication that the twins cannot have been identical but were fraternal.

The building operations were watched from afar by a *Jaette-kvinde* or giantess, and the expression 'from afar' means in this particular case from at least twenty miles away, for that is the distance to the promontory of Horneland, the nearest point on the island of Fyn on which this oversized individual happened to live. Often she would look out in anger over the approaches to the Little Belt and work herself up into a rage at the churches which

were being built all over the Sundeved, the area beyond Sønderborg. Just why she should have been so infuriated I do not know,
for female giants were usually rather good-natured. Perhaps she
was an ardent admirer of Freyr, or just extremely conservative and
opposed to anything new.

One day this giantess noticed a building being put up on the
Broager headland and she was mightily relieved to see that it
was not to be just another Danish church, because it had two
towers. She assumed – for she was a simple soul – that it must be
a castle, and not until she heard the bells ring for the consecration
did she realise her mistake. In her anger she picked up a great
stone, but she soon realised that even she could not throw it so far.
Then she thought of a catapult, and taking off her suspenders
(for Danish giantesses were curiously avant-garde in wearing
suspender-belts) she put the rock in it and let fly. But just as she
did so the elastic broke and the stone fortunately fell short. It can
still be seen where it landed, on the hill of Dybbøl at the very
edge of the Sundeved.

The Flensburg fjord is one of those rare stretches of water which
becomes continually more enchanting whichever direction it is
navigated. Outward bound there is the ever wider vista of the shores
opening out toward Als and the sea, and on the inward run the
banks become higher and more wooded all the way beyond the
Hölnis narrows to the final reach which leads up to the port. Here
at last the beautifully moulded line of the beechwoods begins to
give way to radio masts and barracks on the German side, but on
the Danish shore the enchantment remains right up to the edge
of the German city.

Now in Denmark, now in German waters, the *Thames Commodore*
ran cheerfully up the inlet on water stable enough for me to cook
the lunch as we went – dashing below to fill a pan, then again to
light a burner, and yet again to stir. I tried to set her on a straight
course each time I did so, because here we were not alone. We met
several cargo vessels, and a small tanker, and several of the once
sailing-ships, the barques and schooners by which so much of the
trade of the Baltic is carried on. Passenger steamers came and went
continually from the little beach resort of Glücksburg or the

Flensburg

woodlands of Krusaa, from Sønderborg and the little village of Graasten with the summer residence of the Danish royal family. There were white sails, too, for the fjord is a wonderful water for sailing, and twice I had to ease off so that the wash would not disturb eights. In Danish waters one may often meet eights and coxed fours on the sea, and this suggests that the water must always be smooth; but of course these row-boats with only a few inches of freeboard rarely venture far out in the open waters and they can turn and run for shelter very quickly if they need to.

Flensburg makes up for its relative dullness by the beauty of its position at the very head of the fjord. Besides, any port is attractive to a boatman, and the Flensburg fairway has plenty of life as the ships come and go along the quays right up against the town. It was at Flensburg that I first realised the full wonder of a tideless sea, with buildings running right down to the water's edge like the boathouses of the Cam, and no muddy foreshore or line of tide-dumped refuse. I like the unexpected about a tidal harbour, with the ebb slowly exposing the sewers to delight the gulls, but for a quiet night and the chance to leave a boat without fear of her being dumped on the bottom or trussed in her own mooring-lines there is no sea better than the Baltic.

Flensburg is a city of some size which seems not to be quite sure why it is there at all. Once it was a famous northern port and hundreds of ships were based there, but nowadays the shipbuilding programme is not very large and without the navy the yards would have an even thinner time. This is partly because in 1920 the Flensburgers voted to be German and all their hinterland elected to be Danish – an awkward situation for any place which tries to maintain itself as a trading centre. National rivalries in Europe are not what they used to be, but the fact remains that the frontier at the edge of the town is not just between Germany and Denmark but between the Common Market and the EFTA communities. So to some extent Flensburg is backward-looking, stuck up the creek of its own fjord.

The city was once dominated by the Duborg, the castle built by Queen Margaret in 1411 and named after one of its first wardens, Jens Due. If all trace of this fortress has gone, that is perhaps not very surprising, for long after the days of Due himself it was the abode of an ungodly knight who committed the un-forgivable sin – the precise nature of which has very much varied as theology has evolved, so one cannot be quite sure what he did.

As a result, the entire castle sank into the ground and was covered by a bottomless lake. Yet every Old Year's Night it is raised again on the stroke of midnight and it has no doubt been seen by many Flensburgers as it stands there for the first whole hour of the new year, the lights burning in its windows and the lords and ladies riding round the dark blue lake in procession before returning through the main portal. The cavalcade is well timed, for the last rider has just passed the portcullis when down it comes, the bells of St Mary's chime one o'clock, and there is nothing there but the lake. Plenty of Flensburgers have seen this midnight show, but I am not certain that the apparition is unconnected with the fact that Flensburg has more than thirty rum distilleries, and that the favourite local drink is not wine but grog.

If Flensburg is associated with any one character of history or legend, that individual is *Schwarze Gret*, or Black Margaret, a particularly unscrupulous lady who was once the Queen of the peoples of Southern Jutland. One of her favourite occupations was to close harbours by putting chains or stakes across the approaches, and she is said not only to have put Flensburg and the Schlei inlet out of commission, but also Kiel itself and even the mighty estuary of the Elbe. Yet she seems to have been something of a heroine too, for to her is sometimes attributed the building of the Dannevirke, the massive rampart which bridged the distance between the Schlei inlet and the River Treene, and so protected the Danes from the attacks of the Holsteiners.

She had not completed this undertaking when the Germans attacked. The resourceful Gret promptly had a row of cows placed in the outer ditch, and when the stupid Germans saw the horned heads peering over the rampart they very naturally took them for helmeted northerners and used up all their ammunition in firing at them. Meanwhile her army hurried on with the work, scooping up earth in their helmets and carrying it up to the embankment until in a matter of hours the whole huge fortification was completed.

Gret had a son – though who his father was I do not know – and this son she sent to Sweden so that the Swedish king would teach him to hold the reins of government. However, the Swede thought

differently, and having promptly had the boy murdered he also
had him salted down and returned to Jutland with a brief message
that the lad was being sent home as full of learning as he ever would
be.

The furious Queen threatened to attack the Swedes, and the
self-confident King thereupon sent her a measure of salt, adding
that he had as many soldiers as there were salt grains. The next
diplomatic note was in the form of a measure of pepper from
Black Gret, who said she had as many men as there were pepper
grains, and all just as fiery too. They would soon make the King
of Sweden sneeze on the other side of his face, she hinted. After
these pleasant discourtesies the armies eventually took the field,
and Black Margaret's forces were successful. The insolent
Swedish King was taken prisoner, but instead of confining him
in a prison the Queen humiliated him by using him as a footstool.
Each time she went out riding or drove in her carriage he had to
crouch on the ground while she used his neck as a step. There
must have been a great temptation to bite her in the leg, but
prudently the King restrained himself. He probably knew about
the fate that had overtaken a Duke of Holstein who had unwisely
set himself in opposition to the fiery queen.

The tale of Gret's victory over the Duke of Holstein is one
which does not show her in the best of lights. Presumably the
incident occurred before the building of the Dannevirke rampart,
as otherwise she could hardly have found herself threatened with
invasion. The story tells that Queen Gret was confronted by forces
much greater than her own, so she ingeniously sent a messenger
to tell her opponent that it seemed a pity that so many good and
worthy men should fall in battle on either side, and she would
much prefer that he should chivalrously give her the opportunity
of meeting her in single combat. The Duke could hardly refuse
this request. Besides, he probably thought the victory would be
easy. So the armies watched as the duel began.

After only a few blows the queen said she needed a moment
to adjust the fit of her helmet. This, too, was granted; but Gret
said she did not trust the Duke to refrain from attacking her while
she was unprotected, and to show his honesty he was to thrust his

sword up to the hilt in the ground and leave it there until she was ready again. Even this the Duke foolishly agreed to do. It was his last act, for the moment he had disarmed himself in such trusting fashion the queen abandoned all pretence of arranging her helmet. Rushing at the poor gullible man she decapitated him with one hearty blow and thus became the heroine of her own soldiery. To commemorate the victory they scooped up earth with their bronze helmets and built a mighty mound in her honour. As for the Holsteiners, they presumably melted away in defeat to pay their homage to a new and more prudent Duke.

Black Margaret is often so confused in tradition with Queen Margaret of the Three Kingdoms – under whom Scandinavia was briefly if not very effectively united – that one cannot always be sure which is which. It seems, however, to have been Margaret of the Three Realms, the same Margaret who built the Duborg, who had a councillor of Flensburg broken on the wheel after accusing him unjustly in order to rid herself of a man who was not afraid of opposing her. Just before he was beaten to death, the story goes, he pointed at Queen Margaret and declared that within three days she would have to account for her misdeeds before the judgment seat of the Almighty. Queen Margaret wisely decided to cut herself off from contact with any who might fulfil this prophecy by poisoning her, and she retired quite alone to a ship at anchor in Flensburg harbour. And there, at the end of the three days, her servants found her – dead. Presumably this event occurred somewhere near the rather effluent-laden corner of the fjord in which the *Thames Commodore* had ranged herself against the quay to await the arrival of Bill.

If most of the tales of Flensburg are connnected with violence and murder and deception, there is at least one more pleasant story concerning a difficult legal problem. Behind the city the wooded hills tail away into the wolds which gradually slope down toward the North Sea, which is not thirty miles distant. Clear streams wind their way down gentle valleys, and one of these brooks – probably the Risaa, but nobody seems to be very sure – was once the scene of a curious incident. The stream had cut a gulley in the soft land through which it flowed, and one day a man who was walking along the path on the bank slipped, or tripped, and fell headlong into the water. He found himself in a position where he could not climb out, and all he could do was to shout for help.

By good fortune another traveller was within earshot, and this man hurried to the spot. Seeing the fellow struggling in the water he quickly found a long stick, and leaning over the edge of the little ravine he pushed it down so that the man could grab hold and pull himself out. The rescue succeeded, with only this one little blemish, that the man who had fallen into the brook had one of his eyes poked out with the stick.

He lost no time in arraigning his rescuer before the local *thing* or council, demanding satisfaction for the loss of his eye. But the elders were not ready to find on his behalf against a man to whom he certainly owed his life; nor on the other hand could they merely dismiss the matter, because there was no doubt that the fellow had lost his eye. They debated the matter without coming to any conclusion, and in the end they decided that the case was beyond their own competence to judge. They referred the matter to the prefect or bailiff of the district, who was to decide it in public at the next assembly.

This good man turned the matter over and over in his mind, yet could not decide what verdict to give. The rescuer might perhaps have been careless, but had he not succeeded, at danger to his own life, in extricating the plaintiff from a dangerous situation? When the day of the next *thing* came round, at which he was to deliver his judgment, he was still undecided. With sorely troubled mind he mounted his horse and rode slowly across country to where the people would be gathered to hear his decision.

On the way he happened to come upon three boys sitting on a heap of stones beside the path. He drew rein and watched them as they put their three heads together and whispered and nodded.

'What are you doing, my lads?' He brought his horse close to where they were seated.

'Playing a game, Sir,' one of them answered him.

'Hm. And what game are you playing?'

'We're playing judges,' said the boys.

'It seems a serious case,' said the bailiff pleasantly.

'It is,' answered one of the boys. 'We are trying the case of the man who lost his eye in the brook.'

The bailiff had been about to ride on his way, but at this he seemed for a moment to be lost in thought.

'I see,' he said. 'Yes, a very difficult case, I suppose. And have you reached a decision?'

'Yes. We think the man should be taken back and thrown in the water again at the same place. If he can climb out unaided, then he should have satisfaction from the man who poked out his eye by a mistake. If he cannot, then he loses his case.'

The bailiff tossed the boys some coins and rode off, pondering this piece of juvenile common sense. When the council and litigants and all the people had been called together he pronounced exactly the judgment the boys had provided. The plaintiff was to be thrown into the stream, and everyone would see whether or not he could extricate himself.

So the man was taken off and dropped into the pool in the ravine. He struggled to climb out, but he could not. He drowned – and that decided the matter once and for all, to the satisfaction at least of the onlookers and the bailiff.

The *Thames Commodore* had arrived at the Flensburg quay in good time, and from then onward she and I were no longer to voyage alone. With Bill Gardam aboard and her crew doubled in size she was panting to get under way, if only because she did not like to lie in quite such a soup of drainage as seemed to seep into the harbour from well concealed pipes. However, the myriad jellyfish made such short work of the consommé that only a few hundred yards down from the quays we were surging through the familiar clear water of the Eastern Sea and peering down to the very bottom. This clarity of the water is a wonderful help to the yachtsman, for when he enters a small harbour he can see the bottom very clearly, and even without an echo-sounder we would have had no trouble in finding our way into the yacht harbour of Glücksburg, a short way down the fjord.

It was early evening, and on the crescent of sandy shore the couples were sitting half asleep in the two-seater wicker chairs,

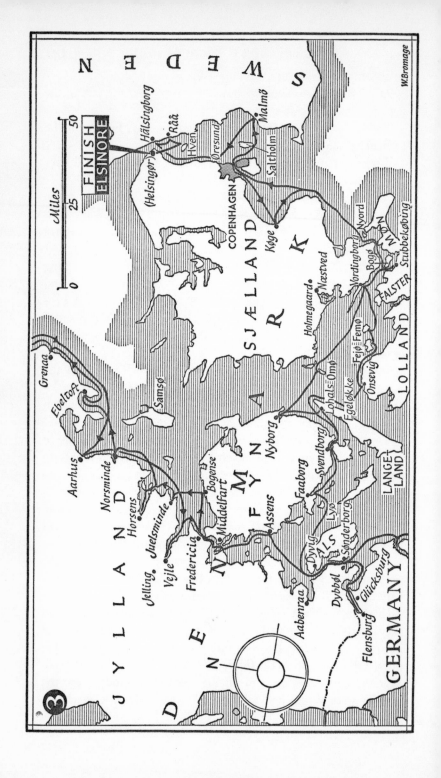

FINISH
ELSINORE

Miles

50

25

0

W.Bromage

SWEDEN

Hälsingborg
Råå
Hven
Øresund
Malmö
Saltholm

(Helsingør)

COPENHAGEN

Køge

SJÆLLAND

MØN

Nyord
Vordingborg
Bogø

FALSTER

Stubbekøbing

Næstved

Holmegaard

Feji
Femø
Onsevig

LOLLAND

Ω

Grenaa

Ebeltoft

Samsø

FYN

Lohals
Omø
Egelokke

Aarhus

Norsminde

Horsens

Bogense
Middelfart

Nyborg

Svendborg

LANGE
LAND

Jelling
Vejle
Juelsminde
Fredericia

Assens
Faaborg

Lyø
Dyvig
ALS
Sønderborg

JYLLAND

N

DE

Aabenraa

Dybbøl
Glücksburg

Flensburg

GERMANY

their faces turned to the glow of the sun as it fell towards the line of the Danish woods across the water. Children were busily repairing the ramparts of their castles for the following day – and not only the children, for castle-building is a great activity of the German seasider. Camp is pitched, and soon the family is as active as Gret's soldiery, shovelling up the ground to make a rampart two or three feet high which will exclude all comers for the duration of the holidays.

I am sure that several doctorate theses must already have been written about the subconscious territorial urges or the sheer possessiveness which this habit demonstrates, but I think it is perhaps a much less Freudian activity than people may suppose. There is often a cool breeze in the Baltic lands, and to shut it out by a windbreak seems reasonable; but more than that, the absence of tide makes castle building really worth while, and if the day's work is not recurrently wiped out once every twelve hours and twenty minutes, as it would be on our own beaches, there is really no excuse for building a castle of any lesser size. But to a stranger the effect is very curious, and I still cannot explain why the Germans throw up these huge earthworks and the Danes and Swedes do not.

Ten years earlier I had written of Glücksburg that if ever I should want to convalesce I would go there to lie beneath the pines on the warm sand shining pink in the evening sun. I had never needed such rest therapy, but once again the sheltered bay with its wooded headland had the same gentle allure. Just after darkness had fallen as far as it could on such a Scandinavian night in June we strolled along the foot of the cliff and climbed a path between hedges of roses to a small café among the pines. The scene was quite Mediterranean, yet without the creeping, relaxing amnesia of the southern lands. The stars were brilliant, far more intense than ever they could shine when they tried to pierce the haze and dust of the atmosphere over Britain, and the scent of resin drifted down the slope and out across the harbour where the jellyfish still flumped in the darkness along the sides of the scores of idle yachts, scouring the water to keep it Baltic and blue. In the woods behind us the nightingales – at the northern limit of their summer territory – sang tirelessly, as though determined to tell us that the northern lands were as warm as the south, and between ourselves and the Oxen Islands off the Danish shore a motor ship cut the smooth water into furrows and sent the serpents of its starboard green and mast-head white to wriggle over the surface and expire on the deserted beach below us. It was so peaceful and still that it came as a surprise to discover on the following morning that in that same strait the wind was setting up such a slop that the *Thames Commodore* washed herself down in the shower bath of the waves and another smaller cruiser sailing out in our company had to turn back for fear of being sunk.

We did not stay long in Sønderborg, for I was determined to spend the night instead at Dyvig, a voyage of two hours and a half through the Sound of Als. Except for the fact that some large tankers and other craft were laid up in its deep water this Sound of Als might have been the Upper Thames somewhere above Pangbourne, so little did it resemble the sea, and when some months later we again passed through it the similarity was even greater because except for one ancient Liberian so rusty that I wondered if they had been unable to get her going, all the ships had gone. The Arabs had ganged up against Israel, the Israelis had trounced them all in a five days' *blitzkrieg*, and the result for the maritime world was that the Suez canal was once more out of commission and the spread of shipping over the much longer course round Africa meant that many more vessels were needed. The ships idle in the Sound of Als, like those in the Blackwater estuary in Essex, could blow three hearty cheers on their hooters and begin to earn their keep once more.

Nydam, where the famous Viking ship was dug out of the bog, lay just behind the trees on the port hand where the Sound of Als began slowly to open out into the broader Als fjord. Still further back stood the steeple of Sottrup, another spired church but with a peculiarity different from that of Broager. Long before the Christian X lift-bridge was installed at Sønderborg the passage of the narrows was watched over by a giant on the Dybbøl side who would issue from his cave to hurl stones at the farmers on the ferry and the sailors who tried to force the passage of the channel in their boats. This boorish behaviour naturally incensed the good men of Als, and they prevailed upon another and more public-spirited giant on their own side of the water to challenge their tormentor to a duel. The Dybbøl giant accepted the challenge, and the fight was arranged to take place on the Dybbøl hill.

However, the two giants both insisted that before they actually fought they should be allowed to have an eating contest. The farmers could only agree, and from both Als and the Sundeved the men brought up cartloads of beef and bread, beer and porridge, and as fast as it arrived the giants ate it. Only when the land was almost destitute of victuals did they reach satiety – and both at the very same moment, so that the result was a draw. All the same, the two overfed and bulky champions were now ready to set about each other in earnest and the fight began, but after their eating match they were so fat and weighty that the earth trembled under the violence of their wrestling. The Isle of Als itself shook, and across the water in the Sundeved where the struggle was being fought the countryside trembled so that the spire of Sottrup's church nearly collapsed. At last the giant of Als gave a final and mortal blow to his opponent, who fell to the ground with such a thump that the Sottrup steeple was tilted by the impact and never recovered its former poise.

Still, it was in a good cause, for the crossing of the sound was safe at last, and ships could safely pass through it – just as they can today if they remember to sound one long and one short blast on the hooter to warn the keeper of the Christian X bridge that they are approaching.

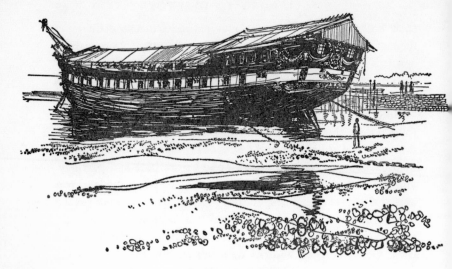

Ebeltoft, the frigate

VIII

*Dyvig bay – the night wedding – Peter Willemoes of
Assens – Christian III and fashion reform – Middelfart's
levy – Bogense and Vejle – the stones of Jelling – from
Horsens to Norsminde – Ebeltoft harbour*

WE would never have discovered Dyvig if the German
yachtsman sheltering alongside in Laboe had not told me
of it, the same man who told me the origin of the Klabautermann.

'You must go to Dyvig,' he said. 'I will show it you on the map.'
He searched the chart in the area behind Als and pointed to a small
inlet which led through a very narrow pass with only just one
fathom of water. 'There is an inn there, nothing else,' he said. 'And
you can find there the best food you have had in your life.'

Boatmen have often recommended me to places, and I have
sometimes done what they suggested but more often not. It all
depends on the informant. Some yachtsmen are great bar-proppers
and their interests turn no further. Others are happiest when
hanging head-downward in the sump of an ancient engine. A few –

particularly in the smarter yachting waters of Kiel and Cowes – think it beneath them to do any actual work and like to leave the running of the ship to a professional and often scallywag crew. Still others are unsophisticated cruising men whose advice will correspond very much with their own tastes, and among these are many who somehow manage to convince me before they have even spoken that they are sure to have sensible likes and dislikes. (By 'sensible' I mean, of course, tastes similar to my own.) The German sailing man I met at Kiel was such a man. He had an academic politeness, too, and instinctively I trusted his taste. That was how the *Thames Commodore* came to sail into Dyvig one summer evening.

Dyvig is mentioned in the Baltic Pilot as a locality where 'water and small quantities of provisions may be obtained' – a description applied to almost every village or jetty in the Danish dominions. And there is nothing else that such a book could say, for Dyvig is hardly a place at all. A few tiny boats lie at anchor, a score of gulls float half asleep on the water, the warblers sing in the copse at the side of the almost landlocked bay, and bugloss and cornflower sparkle richly blue in the waving fields of grain. There is a *kro* or inn with an excellent deep-water jetty of its own – for eight feet of water is a good depth in Denmark – and apart from a cottage or two away to one side that is the total extent of Dyvig. It did not take us long to discover that the German's forecast was correct, and on later occasions when we passed within reasonable diesel-distance of Dyvig we would always put in to this curious creek, thread the narrows by the fishermen's cottages, swing the *Thames Commodore* alongside and order as good a meal as I have ever met with in Scandinavia. A few local people from the nearby electronics town of Nordborg might manage to find their way by road to Dyvig, but otherwise it remained the discovery of such boatmen as had learned from others that there was something to be found up that unlikely passage between the cows and the stake-nets.

The first time we sailed out of Dyvig it was on one of those rare mornings when the Baltic was determined to show us its dreamlike features at their very best. At six o'clock the sun was beating so steadily on the deck that it had long since whisked away every trace of the heavy dew of the clear, genesis-firmament night which had passed so quickly between a June twilight and the dawn. In the meadows at the end of the Dyvig bay the cows were about their rhythmic grazing, and in the shallows along the beach the small fish were frisking into the air to look at the world around them. The inn was still asleep as we took in the lines, and to the sound of the larks high over the wheatfield behind the trees we moved down the enchanting inlet, through the strait by the fishermen's cottages, and out between the widening shores to the utterly still water of the Als fjord in which the stakes of the nets were so perfectly mirrored that we seemed to be in a strange world of perfect symmetry as well as of no motion.

Over the side of the ship one could see the mauve jellyfish floating past, and now and then a fish would jump as though forgetting that this was the sea and it should behave in a proper marine fashion. Out from the Alsen shore a fisherman was tending his nets, his little white row-boat doubled in the water like an empty mussel shell. A flight of ducks came over from the Jutland side to land with a splash on the water and look at us more closely. They had heavy triangular heads, the national ensign of the Eider duck. Ahead a pair of Black-throated divers watched us out of the sides of their heads, then decided they would be safer to go for a long underwater swim.

As the mouth of the fjord widened towards the Little Belt a tramp came gliding out of the haze to port, an old ship laden with pigs and heading for a bacon factory in Germany. At least, I presumed that would be her cargo and destination for she was coming down the Aabenraa fjord, and when we had lain in Aabenraa eleven years earlier our sleep was broken by the squeals of the reluctant passengers being driven aboard their ships for a voyage to the slaughterhouses and curing factories of Holstein.

Each of the Jutland fjords is beautiful, with its cliffs and woods and the soft curve of the low hills behind. There is an almost incredible peace about these inlets – and perhaps that is well, for most of them have a history of dark deeds of violence and treachery in the early centuries of Danish history. But the Aabenraa fjord has an even stranger story of how the pastor of a village church by the shore was one night woken by two sailor-men who spoke in some foreign tongue but who made their meaning clear enough by dangling before the preacher a bag of gold and at the same time brandishing a hefty sword. Prudently the minister chose the gold, and quickly dressing and putting on his robes he accompanied the men to his church. Already the candles were lit and the nave was filled with foreign seamen, all of them armed. Everything was ready for a service, and the pastor soon discovered that he was to conduct it. In fact it was made clear to him that he was to perform two ceremonies, one after the other. The first was a wedding, and there now appeared at the chancel steps an officer in full uniform, tall and powerful. By his side stood a girl, pale and trembling. The pastor was used to wedding nerves and no doubt he did what he could to smooth the path of love.

The moment he had married the couple he was ordered to conduct a committal for the dead. This also the good man did, then he hurried home as fast as he could. There had been no corpse at the burial service, he had observed, but he had not long left the portal of the church before he heard behind him a shot. He did not turn round, but ran and locked himself in his house, and it was not until the morning that he summoned two trusty neighbours to go with him to the church. There they found an open grave, new dug, and in it the body of the girl whose wedding the minister had conducted. Far out at sea a ship with three tall masts was sailing before the wind toward the open sea beyond Kiel Bay.

From where we joined it, the Aabenraa fjord held out its arms to a wide sea without haze or ripple, and so blue against a sky of the same colour that there seemed to be no horizon except where the lump of Barsø broke it on the port bow. We set course to strike twenty-five miles across the hazy water of the Little Belt to Assens. After one hour of a painted sea cut only by our ripples we began to overhaul a trading schooner, and by breakfast time we could see our destination in the distance, just where the compass thought it should be – a fact which never fails to surprise me each time it happens.

Assens is a pretty little market town and port on the large island of Fyn, very similar to all the other pretty little market towns and ports which are scattered in such numbers around the Danish shores. It is a place of ferries and tall grey grain silos, of fishing-boats and half-timbered houses in dark red or ivy green, but it also has two particular possessions of its own. One is the curious little cooking-house on the quay. Such was the danger of fire in Danish harbours that an accident in the galley could sometimes cause a conflagration which would burn down a whole town, and Assens was one of those which used to forbid any fires to be kept burning aboard ships in the harbour. A little brick cookhouse with an open chimney was provided, and there the ship's cook might roast and boil and stew as many dishes as he wished, but otherwise a cold menu was the order of the day for every ship in port.

The other pride of Assens is reflected in the statue of the gallant and very young naval officer whose family house still exists as the most attractive of all the buildings in the town. His name was Peter Willemoes, and when I asked the grocer who the young man might be he seemed surprised that I did not know Willemoes to have held up the bombardment of Copenhagen so effectively that the great Lord Nelson himself had asked to be introduced to him.

The attack on the Danish fleet is one of the less creditable episodes in British naval history, but without it Willemoes might never have become a hero. It was a fierce battle that raged before Copenhagen. 'Thank God I still have whole limbs, which I never expected to have; for I had round my little battery Admiral Nelson and two English ships-of-the-line, which both kept up a steady fire with grape-shot, round-shot and bar-shot.' So wrote Sub-Lieutenant Peter Willemoes to his mother and father at their home in Assens on that April day in 1801. At the age of only seventeen this boy with the turned-up nose and auburn hair had commanded 'Floating Battery No. 2', a vessel carrying 120 men and 24 guns, and he had directed all the fire and force of his curious vessel against the flagship of the victor of the Nile. How he came to be in command at all is not known, for the Danes did not usually appoint youngsters. Like most nations they relied more upon old sea-dogs.

The ship Willemoes commanded was unique, a sort of raft 140 feet long and 40 feet wide, with a make-shift breastwork instead of bulwarks, pierced for the muzzles of a dozen 24-pounders on either side. There was no rudder, no rigging, and the floating fort could only be moved by a sweep, like that of a Thames lighter. It lay so low in the water that many shots from the English ships passed right over it without striking it.

Willemoes manœuvred this cumbrous contraption near enough to the English flagship to score a number of direct hits between wind and water. Nelson, looking through his telescope, was amazed to see such a youngster inflicting so much damage upon his proud vessel, and to prevent the English flagship being sunk he ordered two of his captains to bring their ships to his aid and close in upon the young Dane to attack him. At the first broadsides many of the crew of the float were killed, but the Danes fought on until more than a third of them were killed or wounded.

Nelson had used six flags in succession at the Battle of the Nile, having a new one hoisted as each in turn was shot away, lest any should think the ensign had been struck for surrender. At Copenhagen Willemoes had only one spare, and after that had been shot to pieces he ran up the scarlet tunic of a dead marine. This rallied the crew, who fired their guns with even more determination until the Danish flagship broke loose, ablaze from stem to stern, and Willemoes had to cut his own cables and let his frail battery drift right down the English line under heavy fire until he could bring her safely into harbour.

A few days after the battle Nelson requested that the lad who had commanded the battery should be presented to him in the Crown Prince's palace, remarking to the Regent that the young man should be made an admiral for his bravery.

'If I were to make all my brave officers admirals, I should have no captains or lieutenants in the service,' the Prince answered. To which even Nelson could think of no reply.

And indeed, Willemoes was not singled out for eulogy by the Danish command. He was merely promoted from sub-lieutenant to a full lieutenant – and that only after six years. Yet he was so popular a hero that the ladies of Kiel (then in Denmark)

F

subscribed to give him a sword of honour. The Willemoes curl down the side of the cheek became a fashionable coiffure, and children were christened Petrea and Willemoesina in his honour.

He was not yet twenty-five years of age when he served on the last of the Danish ships-of-the-line, the *Prins Christian Frederik*. Three British ships attacked her off Sjaellands Odde, and in that epic little action Peter Willemoes was killed.

Assens was – and still is – a ferry terminal for traffic across the southern end of the Little Belt, and it was there that the extra-ordinary meeting took place between the Danish King Christian III and the deposed Christian II, the monarch who had been im-prisoned in Sønderborg after his treacherous onslaught upon the Swedish nobility, to spend the next seventeen years in a confine-ment relieved at first by a dwarf and then by a kindly old trooper, but finally with no other company than the miniature portrait of his dead mistress Dyveke (or 'Little Dove'). Seventeen dismal years, and then at last King Frederik I died and Christian III came to the throne, a man of a fine and generous character who at once arranged for the captive to be moved to less harsh quarters at Kalundborg, and travelled to Assens to meet him and assure him that anything which could make amends for those years of cruel and solitary confinement would be done. Indeed, he treated the former king with such genuine kindness that when some years later Christian II heard of the death of his successor and rival he burst into tears and prayed Heaven that his own time might be short. His wish was fulfilled, for he died the same month, the chronicler Hvitfeld recorded.

The same recorder noted that Christian III was not only generous but austere. The king strongly disapproved of extrava-gance of dress, and at first he hoped to sway his courtiers and the nobility by his own example of sober clothing. Yet it was an age of splendour, and people of quality preferred to wear finery, with rich cloaks of silk and satin. As the fashions became con-tinually more outrageous the king tried to put them down by ridicule, but again he failed. He then issued an edict forbidding them, yet still the nobility paid no attention to his attempts to impose his taste, even when backed by the law. The king then had scissor-men appointed who were to roam the streets and cut away all unnecessary pieces of garments on those who appeared over-dressed. The edict was then obeyed, but the king can hardly have been popular in fashionable circles.

From Assens northward the Little Belt is less wide, and it tapers away toward the twisting narrows where the road and railway leap across it on the famous Little Belt Bridge. It is incredibly beautiful, this sound through which the current sweeps out towards the Kattegat, and the fine beechwoods start right at the water's edge where the channel splits around the isle of Faenø at the foot of the dark green slopes by the chateau of Hindsgaul. The water runs deep – twenty fathoms and more, which is rare indeed around the Danish isles – but the reverse flow of heavy salt water along the bottom strikes against reefs and shoals on the deep eroded floor and prevents it being as still as such deep water proverbially should be. On the contrary, this hidden undercurrent heading inwards comes boiling to the surface to cause eddies and swirls, so that even on a windless day the water of the Little Belt narrows appears to twist and writhe and seethe, as though anxious to escape from the confinement of the Baltic and reach the freedom of the Kattegat which lies some way ahead.

So tight is the curl of the channel that within a few minutes of bearing up north westward the *Thames Commodore* was running southeastward to pass under the span of the bridge and aim for Middelfart, with its harbour set at the foot of a slope where bright-coloured fishermen's cottages have their little gardens of holly-hocks and petunias propped up terrace-fashion with walls of brick and stone, just as though they were in Cornwall. Middelfart has a somewhat German-sounding name, and perhaps that is because across the ages the old Danish ferry terminal of Melfar handled so much German traffic that the name became meta-morphosed to a German edition of the same meaning – Middle Crossing. Middle, because there were other crossings at the narrows of Strib to the north, and at Føns to the south.

This little town must always have been a busy place of ferrying between Jutland and the second largest of the Danish isles. It is said that Christian II had himself rowed to and fro across the strait throughout a whole night, wondering whether he dare land to face the nobles enraged by his treatment of their Swedish counterparts and relatives. Another treacherous monarch left a more permanent mark upon the place, for until as late as 1874 the little town was obliged to pay an annual fine which went by the curious name of 'Buggepengene'. It says little for the sense of history of the council of a town of several thousand people that they should have campaigned until they had the imposition removed, for the sum involved did not amount to one pound per year. Perhaps Middelfart was feeling financially insecure, but a fraction of a farthing levied on every ferry-load of people would have yielded much more and would have left the town with something that could no doubt have been developed into an attraction for visitors. For the Buggepengene concerned Middelfart alone.

That strange King Valdemar Atterdag (or Valdemar Mañana as we might call him today) had the familiar Danish trouble that he was at loggerheads with his Jutish nobles, who mistrusted him as much as he deceived them. Eventually he agreed to receive a delegation in order to thrash matters out, and he gave them a safe conduct to return to Jutland by the Melfar ferry. However, they never reached home. At Middelfart three of them were murdered. Not, of course, on any instructions from King Valdemar – if we may believe the oath which he so quickly swore when the news broke on a suspicious nation – but by men unknown and undetected. In court circles the assurance was hurriedly put about that it must have been fishermen who murdered the three men, down by the ferry landing. Of course it was an unfortunate coincidence that the victims happened to be leaders of the opposition to Valdemar himself, but then fishermen might murder anyone for the sake of robbing their pockets – was that not so? Certainly the Melfar councillors should protect visitors and travellers better than that.

In the absence of any actual culprit who could be brought to justice, Valdemar imposed a punishment upon the town of Middelfart itself. Perhaps he was careful to ensure that the load of injustice should not be too great, for the fine was little more than nominal. The levy was to be paid annually, and honour would be satisfied. Thus the Buggepengene was imposed, taking its name from Nils Bugge, one of the three murdered men.

Middelfart has a charming little harbour and the town itself is much more attractive than Fredericia, which faces across from Jutland toward the village of Strib, set in the nick by the lighthouse which marks the northern entrance to the narrows. Fredericia was built as a fortress, and as it was the scene of one of the greatest of Danish military humiliations it is perhaps best passed over. Besides, the town is dull, the railway junction is just like other railway junctions, and the harbour is overhung by the clouds of aroma drifting down from the cat-cracking operations close behind the tanker jetties. A glance at Fredericia through the glasses was enough to make us turn the other way to round the tip of Fyn, and leaving the beautiful strait behind us to head across the bay to Bogense.

Bogense is a typical town of Denmark. It has a very neat step-gabled church in a very neat churchyard, and of course the building is dedicated to St Nicholas, patron of sailors in Denmark just as he is the favourite of bargees throughout Europe. The town still has a number of pleasant burgher houses from former times. There are cottages in timber-frame, the woodwork black or green, the plaster vivid orange, blue, or crimson. Hollyhocks guard the doorways, window-boxes burst with colour as bright as the postman's red jacket. The windowsills have china dogs, relics brought home from voyages to England, and beside the parlour window there will be a two-faced mirror so that the supply of gossip within is continually fed by a view of what is happening without. There is a modest fish-curing establishment and of course a cattle-fodder warehouse for the black-and-white cows which seem to make so little impression on the acreage of buttercups. Cats stare at each other in the roadway, and just occasionally a motor-car or a bus will drive down the street and send them hurrying back to their windowsill perches. Somewhere a lorry is sure to be unloading Tuborg beer, or picking up empties of Carlsberg.

This description could apply as well to almost any small seaboard town in Denmark, and the curious fact is that such a place as Bogense is obviously prosperous in a modest way. Yet a visitor from the world outside can see no reason why it should be. Nothing seems to happen there now. Indeed, apart from raids by Swedes and perhaps some dark deed in medieval times, nothing has ever happened there. The town just exists as it has always done, neat and cheerful and spotlessly clean, a denial of all economic theory. And it is in this that the great charm of Denmark lies for any who go there from more planned and self-consciously integrated lands.

Any boatman who wishes to voyage around the coasts of Britain and France should first visit the Baltic. The confused sea which may be worked up after a gale in the Channel will perhaps seem formidable, but it cannot compare with the roughness which the Baltic is able to produce out of a hat without any warning at all. The only reliable sign seems to be that if the wind turns to blow from the north-west it is time to go below, pack down the china under the cushions, batten all the lockers, lay anything vulnerable on the floor, and mark down the nearest harbour on the chart in case one has to run for it. The wind may blow for two days, or for no more than ten minutes, and there is no means of knowing which is the more likely; but with the Baltic having many long and unsheltered stretches of very shallow water the waves – though much smaller than those on the ocean – swiftly build up to a steepness which never fails to surprise, and which makes Force 6 in the Channel appear as no more than the rocking of a pleasant lullaby. In Danish waters there may be days of Côte d'Azur calm, but there can also be others of the most obstinate curling waves which cannot be taken on the beam at all. The afternoon we ran the ship up the gentle Vejle fjord we were always within a few hundred yards of land and usually on both sides at once, yet the water leaped the bows, cleared the fore-deck and smacked us in the face about twelve times every minute for hour after hour. It was not dangerous, but it was very wet indeed, and the pitching made cooking extremely difficult.

Vejle has a fine extent of port, a single long basin running right into the town. Coasters and cargo-ships came and went all the while we were there, and one of the larger ships was a fine vessel bearing on her funnel the familiar Maltese Cross of the century-old

DFDS (the United Steamship Company), and thus proclaiming herself to be a cousin of the two splendid ferries which ran from Harwich to Esbjerg, the *England* and the *Winston Churchill*. I several times crossed the Western Sea (as the Danes call the North Sea) by this route to pick up the *Thames Commodore* in Kiel or Sønderborg, Middelfart or the Øresund, and by chance I had always found it was the *England* which awaited me, whether in Esbjerg or Harwich. I had come to have a real affection for that 8,000 tonner with its fine and powerful lines, the largest passenger and automobile carrier ever to be sent down a Danish slipway. Once my wife and I had a cabin in a wonderful make-believe part of the ship where children could build log-cabins, make a camp in a wigwam, retire like their stone-age ancestors into a cave, or stand on a miniature ship's bridge and steer the *England* herself into harbours of their imagination. I could happily have spent a day in the nursery myself.

The cousin vessel which came steaming into Vejle berthed opposite us. She came to collect the empty bottles and pile the quayside roof high with crates of full ones. Vejle would undoubtedly drink all that beer within the next day or two, I thought, for the very next morning the Crown Princess Margarethe was to marry her French Count Henri, who had already won the heart of the Danes. Or at least of most of them.

'The Count seems a nice fellow,' I remarked to a young fisherman as we stood watching the council workman put portable beds of purple petunias along the pavement where others had already erected poles for hundreds of Danish *Dannebrogs*.

'I wouldn't know,' he said briefly.

'I think it's a good match,' I persisted.

'Maybe. I couldn't say. I'm not marrying her.'

Vejle is a busy town and a modern one, its factories making everything from chewing-gum and toys to kitchen stoves. Its beauty lies entirely in the rare loveliness of its fjord shores, and if the town itself is not particularly interesting, the nearby village of Jelling more than makes up for any deficiency. We took the bus out to it, and as we pulled in to the village a farm lad with ginger hair who had just put on a bright orange suit and magenta shirt in which to court his beloved pointed to a steep green hill beside the road. 'You'll find the stones behind there,' he said.

I had read of the Jelling stones, but I found them very much more impressive than I expected, perhaps because of their extraordinary setting. They stand right by the church door, just in front of the porch where once the men would leave their weapons while they attended the service. For this church, so long and low and spotlessly white is a very old one and dates from the twelfth century – ancient indeed for Denmark – and it stands where there must have been an earlier wooden chapel built at the time when, only two hundred years earlier, Harald Bluetooth introduced Christianity to the palace of Jelling, the seat of the Danish kings at that time. Of this palace nothing is left but two immense tumuli tower so high above the church that it lies hidden in the dip between them.

The smaller of the two stones stands straight and square, its runes declaring that 'Gorm the king raised this memorial to Thyra his wife'. The other stone is much larger and is particularly famous because its one face shows the oldest carving of Christ in all Scandinavia. Surrounded by the coils of the tree of life he stands there, crucified but very Byzantine and no doubt reflecting the pictorial representations which Viking voyagers had seen on their long journeys into eastern Europe. The carving is very fine indeed, and so is that of the great Nordic serpent on the other side, the same serpent that peeps out of so much of the decoration on houses in northern Germany. 'Harald the king commanded this memorial to be made to Gorm, his father, and to Thyra, his mother, the Harald who conquered all Denmark and Norway and made the Danes Christians,' runs the runic inscription, placing the event squarely in history.

The hills which rise like grass-clad pyramids fore and aft of the church are giant burial mounds like those of the kings at Uppsala, and beneath one of them the great King Gorm and Queen Thyra were buried. Thyra outlived the king by some years, and the saga gives a dramatic account of the way his death was brought about. Gorm and Thyra had two sons, Harald (later Bluetooth) and Knud. Harald was a tough young man, a breaker of heads and drawer of the sword, whereas Knud was a gentle lad of charm and courtesy, a thinker and one of generous spirit. Anyone who is familiar with the way of the sagas will already be quite certain that Knud is going to come to a violent end, whereas Harald will survive with honour and glory; and so it was, for when the court at Jelling could stand Harald's bumptious violence no longer, Gorm sent the young man away to sea, telling him to go and work off his spleen on the Scots or the English. Unfortunately Harald's expedition ran into a party of ships belonging to his brother, and a quarrel sprang up. Swords were drawn, heads split, and Knud was felled to the deck.

Harald, formerly so jealous of the favourite of the family, now became seized with remorse and hurried back to the Vejle fjord and to Jelling, to tell his father what had happened. But when he and his companions arrived at the court they remembered that the proud king had been so devoted to the gentler son that he had sworn that whoever should report ill news of Knud should immediately die. None of Harald's party were anxious to offer themselves for this privilege, and even the redoubtable Harald himself was disinclined to risk the encounter. Not knowing what he should do, he broke the news to his mother Thyra and then asked her advice.

Thyra thought up an ingenious stratagem, which involved telling the tidings in the shape of a parable. Harald then went to his father and told him that once upon a time there were two hawks, the one white and graceful, pure and clean, the other a dark greyish bird of sinister mien, a dastardly and treacherous bird. One day these soaring creatures met in the air, he said, and fought. The white hawk was brave and skilful, but the grey one struck him so that he fell down from the sky, dead.

Harald stopped, and waited. Gorm was already beyond middle-age, and as he was also somewhat deaf the story did not make much impact upon him. Indeed he complained to Thyra that he could not make out what had come over young Harald, who was normally such a boisterous fellow but now seemed only to be obsessed with observing the habits of birds.

So Thyra had to work out another scheme. When Gorm had

shuffled away to his chamber she had the servants drape the dining-hall in black tapestry – of which plenty was presumably kept in store for occasions of mourning. She and her maids also dressed themselves entirely in black, and when Gorm came down to breakfast he found the company already seated and an ominous atmosphere of gloom overhanging all.

'It seems to me that some ill fate has befallen us,' he said as he came towards her.

'Why do you think that?' Thyra asked.

'Because it is not usually thus.' Gorm paused, thinking hard.

Nobody spoke, and the king looked round the hall. 'I know it now,' he concluded. 'This is the way in which you are telling me that which I have felt – that our dear son Knud is dead. Yes, that is it: Knud is dead.'

And as he muttered the words his own vow was implemented. He himself was the one who first told the terrible news, and with a fearful groan the mighty King Gorm staggered, fell back against the wall of the great dining-hall of Jelling, and collapsed dead at its foot. The throne was free for Harald, who later raised the splendid stone in memory of his parents.

The next inlet to the north is the Horsens fjord, not so strikingly beautiful as the densely wooded Vejle fjord but a pretty one just the same. At its inner end it runs into the town of Horsens, a place so exceedingly like Vejle that it is difficult to disentangle the memories of the two places. However, if Vejle has Harald Blue-tooth, Horsens has the pride of being the birthplace of Vitus Bering, as the murals reminded us when we had a dinner in a small and attractive *kro* in the town. Bering was in fact a Dane, although he sailed under the Russian command, being fired with enthusiasm by the shipbuilding exploits of Peter the Great.

It was in fact that Tsar who planned the enterprising voyages which Bering was to undertake, and after Peter's death the Empress Catherine proceeded to launch the expedition just as he had planned it. In fact her reign began with the order to Bering to proceed overland to the Sea of Okhotsk and then to sail the coasts and discover whether or not America and Asia were one continuous land mass. The journey across Siberia began in 1725, and it was two years before the party had assembled its stores on the Okhotsk shore and could build a craft sturdy enough to cross to the Kamchatka peninsula. The whole enterprise, complete with bears and peasants, fir-trees and snowy wastes is pleasantly set out in the picture-map of the inn, which conforms reasonably well with the facts of history.

Arrived in Kamchatka, Bering's party laid down another vessel on the lines of a Danish packet-boat, and in her they sailed up into the Bering Strait. As the land began to bear west, the commander rightly decided that there were two continents and not one, even if he had not traversed the gap between them. It was this that was to be the task of his next expedition, and after another terrible overland journey across the steppes and wastes of Siberia, he set out to sail over to America, and also to try to find the end of the North-East Passage so diligently sought by the English and Dutch sailors. One of Bering's last acts before he left St Petersburg was to draw up and sign a will by which, in case he should die, all his family property was to devolve upon the poor of his native town of Horsens, which he had not visited for thirty years.

On this expedition he discovered many of the Aleutian Islands, but now scurvy began to strike down his men. The voyage became slower, for the mere reason that so little sail could be hoisted because the crew was too weak to lower it quickly when a squall threatened. At last the ship was driven on a reef, lifted over it, and dropped in a smashed condition in the calmer water off the shore of a barren island. Half frozen and ridden with disease, some of his men died before they could be brought ashore. Others lingered on in a shelter improvised by roofing a gulley in the rocks with driftwood. The winter was bitter, and Bering himself was buried in sand up to his waist in a vain attempt to keep him from freezing to death. The only food for those still alive consisted in such dead whales and fish as were occasionally flung ashore by a gale, but at last the spring came, and the men managed to build a smaller boat from the timbers of their wreck. Putting out to sea they succeeded in making the Kamchatka shore, bringing the news that Bering himself was buried on the inhospitable island where his ship had been wrecked.

Jutland

The Horsens fjord is fronted by the islands of Hjarnø and Alrø, set in a sea so shallow that the steersman has to keep one eye on the echo-sounder and the other open for the sticks and brooms which mark the shoals. Add to this the need to watch for net-floats and the little flags on the lines of lobster-pots, and it is obvious that there may be a tendency to become fixed in a kind of squint when navigating these waters. Indeed, the whole of the Jutland coast south of the little lighthouse isle of Hjelm is beset with shallows and sands, but there are also such islands as Endelave and Tunø and Samsø beckoning to the boatman and calling to him to visit them. In fact we tried more than once to reach them, but always a stiff wind appeared as if from nowhere and contorted the water into such racing trains of extremely steep and unpleasant waves that we had to give up the attempt and aim for shelter.

Yet it was a fine and placid morning when we sailed out of Horsens, northward bound, and about lunch time we decided to put in to the small port of Norsminde to enjoy our midday meal. We had a new and up-to-date *Baltic Pilot* vol. I, and reading the directions we could easily see that Norsminde was a very suitable place for a midday break. 'Norsminde havn is a small harbour with a depth of 8 feet,' it told us. 'There is a wharf about 100 feet in length. Provisions, water, and a small quantity of coal can be obtained.'

With this assurance we chugged up the coast, skirting the sands about one mile off shore and avoiding the worst of the banks until we could eventually cut in to where the harbour lay. We scanned the coast for the masts of the trading schooners and fishing boats which would be lying there, but we could see none. However, the sharp little promontory immediately south of the place made it quite easy to identify the correct position, and with an eye on the flickering line of the echo-sounder we began the approach.

Lying off Norsminde was a rowboat some ten or twelve feet long, of a kind fishermen use for shrimps or tending their nets. There was nobody in it, and the craft was attached to a mooring buoy some two hundred yards out from the beach. One would not need to be an aquatic Sherlock Holmes to make the one simple deduction from this sight, but we failed to do so. Such is the aura of holy writ which surrounds a Pilot Book that it never occurred to us that if a boat drawing less than one foot of water was anchored in such an inconvenient position instead of lying in the harbour, that could only be because the port was not deep enough to accommodate her. We noticed that there were no harbour lights, but here again the enthusiasm of the Vice-Admiral who reigned in the Hydrographical Department of the Admiralty prevented us from considering why this should be so. Cautiously – in the absence of any approach buoys – we ran inward at dead slow, myself at the wheel and Bill standing on the bow to watch the shrimps and measure with a new pole I had acquired in Sønderborg the depth of the sea. He had just reported less than two feet of water at the bow when the *Thames Commodore*'s nose gently touched on the sand. We backed out, and thought awhile. If ships could put in here for coal there must at least be a channel, so we moved gingerly along the edge of the sandbar and made a second attempt, then a third. Each time we came to water so shallow that a seagull would hardly have wetted its knees if it had stood on the shoal.

I scanned the port with the binoculars, and so did Bill. There was no movement, no activity, not even an angler. The nearest sign of life was a child splashing in the edge of the sea a few hundred yards to the north. Puzzled, we picked our way out into rather deeper water and left Norsminde behind us.

It was nearly a week later that we mentioned this to the president of the Aarhus yacht club as we sat over a glass of the special beer produced in celebration of the wedding of the Crown Princess.

'Norsminde?' He was amazed. 'Norsminde? You didn't try to get in there, surely?'

We said that we had done just that, and I quoted the Admiralty dicta about the wharf, and provisions, the coaling facilities and the depth alongside.

He laughed. 'Norsminde has been closed for over twenty years,' he declared. 'I think it was in 1943 that it became too sanded to be used any longer.'

Frustrated from entering the make-believe port of Norsminde we cut across the Bight of Aarhus, to skirt the tip of the long and bulbous nose of the Helgenaes promontory, and make for Ebeltoft. Already the wind was rising to take up its favourite position for a good huff and puff, and so it seemed wise to take advantage of the only harbour for many miles ahead. Ebeltoft lay inside a deep bay and was sheltered from every direction, but as we bore down upon the entrance it seemed as though the port were entirely blocked by an immense ship of wood which had somehow been driven off its course for Ararat. This vast black hulk lay immediately inside the pierheads, a vessel so large that it occupied almost the whole of one side of the harbour. It had no masts, but a shallow pitched roof exactly like that usually attributed to Noah. I doubt if we should have been surprised if elephants and giraffes had peeped out of the many square windows along its sides, yet this extraordinary ship was not the Ark but the *Jylland* (or *Jutland*), one of the very last of the Danish men-of-war.

It is always difficult to know just what to do with ancient hulks, especially those for which people have some strong emotional regard. One can build a dry dock, as for the *Cutty Sark*, or turn the thing into a national shrine like the *Victory*, use it as a training ship like H.M.S. *Worcester* or the U.S.S. *Constitution* in Boston Harbor; or one can turn it out like an old pensioned cart-horse in a meadow of buttercups, and moor it in some place where it will not be too much in the way and where the water is so shallow that the poor old thing will only sink an inch or two if it should founder. Such was the fate chosen for this last of the Danish frigates.

The *Jylland* has a Society of Friends or supporters, whose aim is to restore her to her full glory, shipshape and fitted out as though ready to sail away and fire another broadside at the wicked Austrians – for however improbable it may seem, one of the battle squadrons which engaged her in the sea-fight off Heligoland in 1864 was of the Austrian navy. The *Jylland* was then almost brand new, and she was a very remarkable ship. A 2450-tonner with three masts, she also had a funnel just ahead of amidships, for her secret weapon was a wheezy and not very powerful steam-engine which turned a propeller shaft that could be lowered into the water and pulled up again to reduce the drag when she was proceeding only under sail. A few pieces of this strange machinery still remained on board when we went over her, but she was in such a state that I wondered whether the noble band of friends had not taken on a task of impossible magnitude if they really expected one day to fit her out again so that she resembled a ship.

Inside, the *Jylland* was strangely austere. There were no bulkheads and the crew of 430 men merely slung themselves in hammocks from the deck-head. Plumbing consisted of a pair of benches, one on either side of the bow-sprit, each with a row of holes which could accommodate five naval rumps. The bilge was filled with mountains of glacial boulders to act as ballast. Yet in her day she had been a fast ship, and King Christian IX had sailed in her to Iceland and to Russia – though it was of course the fact that she survived the battle against the Austrian and Prussian ships which secured her a permanent place in the hearts at least of those Danes who looked back nostalgically to the olden days of sail.

Ebeltoft is a holiday resort, a small, almost Devonshire village with an old town hall and post office so neat and small that one can hardly believe that they were built for any real purpose, unless perhaps as a stage-set. Scores of thousands come during the summer to see these curiosities and to explore the recesses of the old *Jylland* down in the harbour, where occasionally a small German tramp or a schooner will put in to load a curious material which

Ebeltoft

looks like pellets of horse manure and is apparently intended as cattle fodder.

On our arrival the only vacant space was beneath a loading chute down which these pills of dried grass compacted with molasses could be shot into the holds of ships. I do not like making fast beneath any kind of obstruction, but as the chute cleared our windshield by nearly four feet I was not worried – for of course there was no tide. However, I knew that the wind could play strange tricks with the water levels in Scandinavian harbours and on the second night of the prolonged blow I slept lightly, occasionally kneeling up in my bunk to check the height of the quay alongside.

In the small hours the wind increased, but the rocking of the swell must have made me doze more soundly. The first heavy blow upon the top of the ship had me out of bed and up on deck swiftly enough to push the ship out from the wall just before the next wave could throw her up again. The water had risen three feet in little more than an hour, and with the swell making her rise and fall the *Thames Commodore* had struck the loader violently with her windshield. This shield was made so that it could be dismantled, and that was just what the loading chute had done to it. But toughened glass can be very tough indeed, and the panes lay intact upon the deck, ready to be reassembled when the smith of Ebeltoft had straightened out the frames. There was no further damage, and after moving the ship to a berth alongside a coaster I returned to bed.

At last the wind dropped, as suddenly as it had come. The water receded, the gulls stopped their screaming, and on a summer sea we ran out of Ebeltoft and down its beautiful bay, the deck-hose sweeping its jet into every corner to wash overboard the cattlefood which lay in brownish musty drifts from bow to stern and filled the dinghy as though it were intended as a manger.

IX

Thames Commodore in the fog – Faaborg's bovine bronze – salute by cannon – Svendborg ferry – the bell of Nyborg – Omø and Nyord – the Falster smugglers – Vordingborg of the Valdemars – Femø harbour – the fate of the human male

FOR landbound holidays Jutland is one of the most attractive parts of Denmark. It has hills and forests, a sprinkling of castles and some pleasant lakes with an old steamer. Indeed the countryside might well be English, except that it lacks fly-overs and huge concrete road junctions sprawled over the valleys, and the best views are not always dissected by high tension cables. But the shore of the northern half of the peninsula is as bleak as that of East Anglia, a long line of low cliffs of boulder clay with plenty of scope for a holiday tent or hut, and none at all for the boatman. It cannot compare with the Danish isles as a part of the world where the boatman can lose all sense of time and urgency in the sheer delight of voyaging from one little harbour to another. When we put into Grenaa the news that a yacht had arrived in the port brought the reporter from the local paper to the harbour to ask why we had gone there at all. This was not an easy question to answer, for Grenaa was merely a small commercial port with car-ferries to Sjaelland and Sweden, lying some way out of the town, and even the town itself seemed to expect no visitors. So far as I could discover its only unusual feature was that no bloodthirsty royal tough had ever been murdered there by another.

We sailed from Grenaa with certain misgivings. Two hours further up the coast we examined the shore of Jutland on the chart, on a land map, in the pilot book, in a Danish sea-guide, and finally through the binoculars. There could be no doubt about it – Southern Jutland and the islands south of Fyn had much more to offer. So, to the surprise of the jellyfish and seagulls we put about and headed back the way we had come, calling only at Aarhus because it was so large and at Hov because it was so small.

It was nearly a month later that my wife and I arrived at Sønderborg again, fresh from another crossing to Esbjerg aboard the *England*. The *Thames Commodore* was sitting in the evening sun below Mrs Tingleff's balcony, waiting impatiently for us to come aboard and run up to Dyvig for a dinner of fried eels before setting off on a still morning of thick fog to round the tip of Als and cross to the southern side of Fyn, the most beautiful of all the larger islands of Denmark.

Fog on the water invariably gives me a sensation of floating in outer space, something having gone wrong with the rocket mechanism which was to return me to earth. It is not a frightening experience, though in the English Channel it can be disquieting because one knows the banks of vapour to contain a number of forty thousand tonners coursing through the Strait without a care in the world or even – to judge by the frequency of collisions between sea-giants – half an eye on the radar screen. No doubt many of the masters in fact navigate with care, reduce speed, and give the proper signals laid down in the *Regulations*, but others appear to put their feet up, push forward the engine-room telegraph to Full Speed Ahead, and reckon that any other ship will see them coming. The only safe thing is to make for water too shallow for these monsters, and wait. Sometimes this has curious consequences, too. On our way home from Denmark my wife and I found ourselves being pursued in a very thick fog by a two thousand tonner, the bows of which were just visible about twenty-five yards astern. Perhaps the skipper thought we knew the way, which we did. But the fog was dense enough for us not to be able to see as far back as his bridge, and as I did not like a ship continually to gain on us when so close astern I signed to the two look-outs lounging at the bows that their ship should slow down. One grinned, the other said something not very polite, so knowing that we had some shallows very close on the starboard side I turned that way to protect the *Thames Commodore*'s exposed rump. Almost at once I saw close ahead of her bow a buoy which marked the edge of a spit with depths falling to two feet of water. Watching the line on the depth sounder I ran over the boundary, and at the four foot mark I stopped. Miriam let go the anchor and I turned off the engines so that we could better appreciate the imprecations in Flemish which passed between the look-outs on the bow, the captain at the wheel, and the chief engineer – who seemed worried by the speed with which the engines were turning in the efforts to refloat the ship and pull her off the shoal. That, I thought, would teach them not to follow a yacht too close.

In the waters between Als and Fyn there was no possibility of being run down. There were few ships, and such as there were would be small tramps, schooners or fishing-boats with heavy chugging engines which would be heard in plenty of time. Much more probable was a grounding on one of the many shoals which lay scattered throughout the sea, well-marked with sticks and brooms when visibility was good but less obvious in the thick grey blanket of suspended droplets which now drifted over our deck. However, we decided that once we had found our way through the narrows to the exit of Dyvig's inlet there was no reason why we should not skirt the shore of Als until we had turned through half a circle, when it would be time to cut due east and aim for the land fifteen miles away across the Little Belt. I had no doubt that with echo-sounder, compass, stop-watch and common sense we could do this in perfect safety. The only obstacle would be the lines of net stakes protruding from the shore.

The fog proved to be patchy, so that sometimes the ship's own nose was hidden in mystery, at others we could make out the dim outline of the shore a hundred yards away on the starboard side. We met some ducks, exchanged a long sound on the hooter with two black-and-white cows, swerved sharply to avoid a row of stakes which stood up like telegraph poles set in the sea, and headed north. I had measured the distances carefully and knew that after fourteen minutes the land on our right should begin to cut away eastward towards the Nordborg lighthouse. Thirty-five minutes more, and the lighthouse should be on our flank, with the coast running east and west. It was as simple as that.

Every few minutes we had faint glimpses of the shore, but for some strange reason the coast of Als had decided on this particular day not to bear round to the right as usual. On we went, five, ten, twenty minutes, half an hour beyond the moment of change of direction and still the mainland was just visible close beside us while the compass showed that we were still heading due north. Three quarters of an hour up from the mouth of the bay we came in sight of a church. There was none marked on the chart, so I ran in to examine it from a position in only one fathom of water. It was not a church, I discovered. It was the Nordborg lighthouse, which looked very much as though it had been built by an unemployed ecclesiastical architect from the baroque of southern Germany. Our Danish chart had a little marginal sketch of it, and there was no doubt about its identity. I counted the windows and chimney pots to make quite sure, and if I wondered why they did not bother to turn on their foghorn I was still more surprised to see from the compass that the coast still ran north and south, and not east and west as it did on the chart.

We floated for a few minutes, rocking gently on our own wash as I tried to work out the meaning of this curious phenomenon. Then the curtain of fog dropped, and we were alone in a blackness of chilly cotton wool. An idea came to me, and putting the wheel over I put the ship to dead slow and described a complete tight circle. It was easy to know that we had done so when we came upon the bubbles of our own wake ahead of us. All the while I watched the compass. It strongly denied that we had turned a circle at all. Whichever way I turned the ship the instrument insisted that we were heading due north. And this, I felt, was unlikely.

We floated again, and Miriam brought up some coffee to help me think. It did not take long to guess what had happened. For some reason the needle had fallen off the underside of the compass card.

We had a small spare compass aboard which we had bought on the Rhine the year before, and I now fetched it up. Another slow circle showed that this second instrument allowed the ship to turn underneath it, and as we knew that we were just off the Nordborg lighthouse it was easy to set off again, clicking the stopwatch at the start of the voyage. I had already worked out that

after two hours and six minutes we should have the tall cliffs of
Lyø close on the port side; and sure enough, as punctual as a
Danish train, the yellowish bluffs arrived and we knew that the
channels through the banks to Faaborg were not far away.

It was on Lyø (or Lee Island) that Count Henry of Schwerin
managed to get even with King Valdemar the Victorious, whom
he had rightly suspected of having seduced the Countess, after he
had entrusted her to the monarch for safe and chaste keeping
while he went on a pilgrimage to the Holy Land. To challenge
Valdemar openly was out of the question, for Schwerin was an
insignificant petty province and the Danish king had more than
one thousand ships at his command. The only commodity in which
Valdemar was inferior to the Count of Schwerin was ingenuity.

Count Henry never let a word of reproach or even a frown
escape him. Instead, he courted and flattered the king until he
was accepted as a friend and invited to the hunts in which King
Valdemar delighted. Still he stayed his hand until the occasion
when the chase was on Lyø, and then after a day of hunting and
feasting and drinking the court retired to their tents to sleep
soundly. All except Count Henry and his trusted men, who
swiftly and silently bound and gagged the king and the crown
prince and hurried them to the shore. Pausing only to drill holes
in all the other boats they rowed out to where a ship was waiting
to carry the valuable cargo to the southern shore of the Baltic.

Count Henry was excommunicated for this treacherous act, but
he did not worry. For almost three years he kept his royal prisoners,
and when at length King Valdemar bought his freedom it was at
the expense of a large slice of his territories, a heavy sum in silver,
and the handing over of his own two sons as hostages for the bar-
gain. As for Lyø, it gained a spring which gushed out of the ground
in astonishment at what had happened during the night of the hunt,
and has remained ever since to supply the needs of the cows and
farmers of the island.

Faaborg was just as I remembered it, a bustling little market
town with a street of gay little cottages leading to the town belfry,
which is all that is left of the church of St Nicholas. As at Bogense,
hollyhocks stood straight as sentinels beside the doors, carefully

Horne church, near Faaborg

held back so that their leaves did not obstruct the view in the gossip-mirrors. It was a happy little street in bright colours, and I did not find it hard to imagine Hans Andersen striding through just such an alley as this, his student heart burning with love after his first sight of pretty Riborg Voigt. Yet there was something in the middle of the market place which I was sure could not have been there eleven years earlier, a huge bulk of bronze.

It is extremely difficult to take this massive sculpture seriously. Not that I have any particular objection to the frank representation of a certain part of the male anatomy which, to judge by the golden shine imparted by years of continual handling, is a great favourite with local children, and if the people of Faaborg were once dreadfully shocked, my own reaction was rather different. The mixed-up mass of arms, legs, cow's udders, tail and tongue did not make me think of the creation of the world so much as of some awful accident at the cattle market, when a particularly large cow fell out of a truck and crushed two nudists who happened to be passing at the moment.

The Ymerbrønden (or Well of Ymer) is supposed to show one stage in the legendary creation of the world and its inhabitants. In this northern version the giant Ymer was first formed by the drips of fog condensing on the walls of Ginnungegap, just as the sea-mist had dripped from our mast. The drops of water also gave rise to a cow, which licked and licked at the Niflheim glacier until she had licked out a whole man – or perhaps a deity, for he was to be a forefather of Odin.

Eventually Odin and his relatives made the world from the body of Ymer, whom they had murdered, using his cranium to make the firmament, his dispersed brain-matter for the clouds, and his eyebrows to enclose Midgaard – the abode of man. They manu-factured the nordic Adam and Eve (Ask and Embla) out of some driftwood which was washed up on the beach, and finished by devising the rainbow with its fiery arch to keep all the evil spirits away from their own Olympus. Faaborg's group shows Audhumble the cow suckling Ymer, and at least one can agree that Audhumble is a nice enough name for a cow, whatever one may think of the bronze.

We stopped at Faaborg to shop, and while we were there a thunderstorm came to break the fog and sweep the sky clean for an afternoon of warm sunshine. As soon as it had left port we followed in its wake, intending not to touch at Fyn again but to pass all the way along its southern shore and through the Svend-borgsund to turn northward and stop for the night at Lohals, on the northern tip of Langeland. Past Bjørnø and Avernakø, Svelmø and Drejø and Skarø we chugged ahead, wondering once again at the sheer beauty of these waters south of Fyn with their sixteen larger islands and the forty-two which even now are uninhabited except by the gulls and ducks, the swans and geese and waders which reign alone over the deserts of coarse grass and

brackish marsh or peat. Between the islands the wind may drive
the sea to such fury that it will even fling itself over the shores to
smash the windows of the houses and break down the little hedges
of the trim gardens of which Danish cottagers are so fond, but
more usually the water lies stiller, hardly betraying that it is
sweeping strongly through the Svendborg sound, eastward or
westward according to the direction of the last drive of the wind.

Our intention to run to Lohals without a halt was broken by a
most unusual interruption. Already we were coursing down
between the wooded shores of the Svendborgsund, when just as we
were passing the hamlet of Rantzausminde a cannon was fired
from the sloping land above the shore to our left. There was a loud
rolling report, and a cloud of smoke drifted away from the gun,
which stood on the lawn in front of a long, low house with a pinkish
roof, placed in just such a position as might be any retired boatman's dream, for it faced south across one of the most beautiful
sounds in the world.

The *Thames Commodore* at once hove to and turned inshore.
She was not being shot at but merely saluted by one of her
admirers. Captain Freddy Wessel had been watching over the
water with his telescope and he had seen her approaching. He had
hurried out, charged the cannon and fired it, and now he was
standing by his private jetty telling us through a loud-hailer to
pick up the yellow marker buoy, haul up the chain attached to it,
and make fast with a line. This done we rowed ashore to spend an
hour or two with this remarkable man who had flown (as a Dane)
in the Royal Flying Corps in the First World War and now lived
(as a Briton) on the shore of the Svendborgsund, furious that he
was not allowed as a foreigner to register his vote against the
socialist government which now ruled the land and – like other
similar governments – seemed bent on raising taxes and putting
up the cost of living.

Before we left, Captain Wessel presented us with a new silver
five-crown piece which had been struck to commemorate the
Royal Wedding. In return, I wrote in one of the books of the
Thames Commodore's travels which he had on his shelves, and
instead of putting the actual date I wrote *Momsdag*. There had

been notices in many of the shops exhorting people to buy everything from needles and thread to books and motorcars before
'Momsdag', the first Monday of July, and of course it was not
difficult to guess what the word meant. Under the influence of
sentiment and sales pressure the Americans had introduced
Fathers Day, and Scandinavia had followed suit with a Fadersdag
or Farsdag. It did not need much imagination to see that Momsdag
was the Danish for the Fête des Mères which we had met in other
summers in other lands. All the same, I was impressed at the way
in which children and husbands were apparently expected to buy
radio sets, pianos, cameras, even bottles of beer for the beloved
mama of the family.

Captain Wessel read the inscription. 'Momsdag!' he exclaimed.
'I'm afraid so.' And he added something pungent about those
confounded socialists making everything so much more expensive.
It was several days before I discovered just why he was so annoyed
to be permanently reminded of Momsdag. The Moms were not
mothers at all. Moms was a new socialist levy, exactly similar to
the Oms already instituted in Sweden. I am not certain just what
the letters actually stood for, but Moms was a decree which put up
the price of everything with a blind all-round increase of ten per
cent. Captain Wessel was not the only one to be annoyed with the
economists who had thought it up.

Beyond Rantzausminde the Svendborgsund was now crossed
by a great new bridge which had driven into retirement the ferries
which had long linked Fyn with the large island of Tåsinge
immediately opposite Svendborg. This was always an important
crossing, for traffic bound for the islands of Langeland and Aerø
used also to leapfrog over Tåsinge, and since at least the beginning
of the sixteenth century the business of ferrying was strictly
regulated and nobody but the ferryman at Vindeby might convey
vehicles or passengers across the sound. Much surreptitious rowing
and sailing must have been done by night to avoid paying the
charges, but officially the monopoly was vested in the owners of
Castle Valdemar which stands pleasantly shaded by its trees at the
entrance to the sound, but has nothing to do with any king,
whether Victorious or Atterdag. It just happened that a nobleman

named Valdemar Christians once owned it, or leased it, or perhaps built it.

The baron of Castle Valdemar let out the ferry to his tenants at the terminals on either shore, and it was not until 1926 that the local authorities bought out his rights. A century ago the carrying was let to the fiery Ferryman Løve on the Vindeby shore and Widow Schulz at the Svendborg end of the crossing, this worthy woman being given the task of summoning the ferry with a horn made from a conch shell whenever passengers wished to cross over to Tåsinge, where the ferry lay.

It happened one Sunday afternoon that some young cheerful lads (juvenile delinquents, they would now be disapprovingly called) got hold of her conch and tooted it, with the expected result that Ferryman Løve roused himself and set sail for Svendborg. When he arrived he found no passengers, and he promptly demanded from Widow Schulz the fares of the non-existent travellers. She naturally refused to pay him, and the dispute had to be referred to the authorities, who wisely decided that the good woman should take better care of her conch shell and that in future the ferryman was not to sail back at once to Vindeby after dropping passengers on the Svendborg side.

Another dispute occurred about the doctor, who was taken over one day to attend patients in the almshouses. It was a regulation that the doctor was to be carried free of charge when travelling on such business, and naturally the ferryman regarded this as something of an imposition. When on this occasion the doctor wished to return, Løve kept him waiting and then abused him. The quarrel became one for the courts; the ferryman stoutly maintaining that the medical man had taken the opportunity to visit some private patients while he was on Tåsinge – something not covered by the exemption. This the doctor denied, and the case went up to a higher court. As usual, the only ones to gain were the lawyers.

Through the bends of the sound and beyond Castle Valdemar our course led us out into the channel between Fyn and Langeland, and looking across to the shore of that elongated island we could make out some small brickworks down by the water and also the church of Egeløkke close by the manor where the youthful

Grundtvig had worked as a private tutor, long before his restless spirit had settled down to the business of becoming the creator of the first of the Danish People's High Schools, a bishop, a poet, the author of most of the Danish hymns, and an enthusiast for the nordic sagas – many of which he translated. All this was in the years after he had been sent by King Frederik IV to Oxford to calm down, for his early years had been marked by violent academic quarrels and even libel actions. These in turn had followed on a volcanic loving which had swept over him at Egeløkke, where he fell passionately in love with Constance Leth, the intelligent wife of his employer. It was when he was reading to her Psalm 50 that he was overcome with a sense of disgust at his own lack of self-control.

'What right have you to recite my statutes, or take my covenant upon your lips? For you hate discipline, and you cast my words behind you. You keep company with adulterers.' In fact Grundtvig was neither an adulterer nor a companion of adulterers, but smitten with remorse that such a thought had perhaps crossed his turbulent mind he was seized with a depression which ended in nervous collapse. Escorted from Langeland by friends he roused the alarmed occupants of the hotel at which the party was staying overnight by shrieking that the devil had coiled himself round his body in the shape of a huge and horrible snake.

Had the Baltic remained smooth for twenty-four hours on end we should have spent the night at the small harbour of Lohals and then turned the tip of Langeland to run all the way to Vordingborg, or further. But the wind decided to indulge in another bout of huffing and puffing, with the result that we ran up the lee of the eastern shore of Fyn as far as Nyborg, from where we could let the *Thames Commodore* take the waves on her rump to help her on her way. Nyborg is such a busy ferry terminal that always there are several of the large ships to be seen on their way across the Great Belt between there and Korsør, but behind the ferry berths there is a pleasant town and an excellent harbour for everything from cargo-ships to coxed fours. It was late evening when we swung alongside the quay by the pretty customs house, and as we did so a bell began to toll. This was not a mass (Denmark being almost exclusively Protestant) nor for a night-time funeral. It was not even the bell of some ancient curfew, revived as a tourist attraction. While I filled out the list of wine and beer which we happened to have aboard, the extremely handsome young customs officer explained that it was left over as a relic of rejoicing from one of the Swedish–Danish wars. (If I remember rightly there were no less than twelve of these conflicts before peace came finally and permanently, in the nineteenth century.)

Denmark's greatest danger always lay in a winter so severe that the Sound and Belts might be frozen over and their whole country laid wide open to attack. This is just what occurred in 1658, when the Swedish forces streamed over the thick midwinter ice from Jutland to attack Fyn from the western side. The great fortress of Nyborg which commanded the Great Belt was forced to surrender, and the Swedes were delighted to find four Danish warships frozen in the roads outside the town. But the Danish captain had the ice broken round the ships every night so that the Swedish soldiery could not safely assault them; and just in case the enemy should succeed in reaching them he had water thrown over the rails and decks so that the vessels were as slippery as a skating-rink. And so he preserved them until the thaw came and the ice broke, when he sailed the ships out of the roadstead and up to Copenhagen.

All the same, Nyborg had fallen, and the defences of the town were greatly strengthened before the time came when an army of Danes, Dutch, Poles and Austrians invaded Fyn to recapture it. They succeeded, and the two generals commanding the Swedish garrison were obliged to flee across the Great Belt to Korsør, where King Carl X of Sweden was awaiting them. General Stenbock – whose name could be translated as a species of ruminant – gave a long-winded explanation of how all the circumstances of the fight were unfortunately against them, but the king cut him short.

'The devil has taken the sheep,' he said, angrily. 'And he can take the goat too.'

Meanwhile, Nyborg was celebrating its relief. In the evening the Danes surged into the town, and the people received them with almost delirious delight after the year and a half in which they had been oppressed and obliged to work as forced labour for the Swedes. All day they had heard the gunfire drawing nearer until the Swedes had fled, and now their priest had run into the belfry and himself tolled the bell. Soldiers and townspeople streamed into Nyborg's church to sing a joyful and sincere *Te Deum Laudamus*.

It was a quarter to ten when the priest tolled the bell on that November night three centuries earlier, the customs officer explained. At a quarter to ten the same bell had been rung ever since, to celebrate the Danish victory. Apart from the Nyborgers few people knew why the bell was rung in the evening, and no doubt many took it to be for some service or other; but no, it was to recall the drubbing given to the Swedes, and only very rarely had the bell stayed silent. That was when there had been important visitors from Sweden and it had been thought a little lacking in courtesy to ring the bell to recall the day when their forces received a sound thrashing. After all, we were all good Europeans now, were we not?

When we set out from Nyborg very early the next morning, we laid a course for Omø. While we were at Rantzausminde I had mentioned to Captain Wessel that we hoped to put in there, and his natural question was why we wanted to go there at all.

'I thought it would be rather out of the way,' I said.

'Well, if you like places as out of the way as that, then go there,' he said. 'Nobody could say Omø is a much visited island.'

I think we were really more attracted by the detergent name of the island than by its isolation; besides, the crossing of the Great Belt gave us a reasonable length of run before breakfast. Soon we saw Omø's tall lighthouse lifting over the edge of the earth, and at last I could make out a tiny car ferry, berthed close to the harbour. The ship was larger than the *Thames Commodore* but was none the less a real midget among ferry-boats, and the fact that she was berthed on the outside of the mole should have made me realise something I discovered a few minutes later. Small though she was, she could hardly have squeezed through the entrance, and had she done so she could certainly not have turned round inside Omø's harbour.

Omø was crowded with small fishing craft and lesser sailing yachts which had put in because of the weather. The free space in the centre was enough for us to turn in, provided I kept the bow over two sleeping Germans and swung our dinghy above the cabin-top of a Dane. All these good people were unused to seeing a ship manoeuvre over their heads, and woken by anxious wives they tumbled out of their bunks to see what could be going on. Soon the whole harbour was awake, wondering what on earth could have possessed us to take such a vast ship into such a small hole.

'Because,' I assured our neighbours, 'I wanted to see Omø.'

I would like to be able to say that Omø is a beautiful islet, rich in legends and tales of mermaids, and adventurers, and kings and knights and rovers. So far as I know it is not. It is just a patch of land, half fields and half marsh, with a church and a few very ordinary houses dropped as though at random. Its pleasures would probably be exhausted in a day if not in an hour, but certainly it would be an admirable place for anyone content to sit on the jetty and dangle a line for fish, breathing an air which contains a healthy tang of rotting sea-grass. In Britain such places are nearly extinct, but Denmark still has plenty of island villages tucked away from the world around.

On our outward journey we left Omø at midday and ran to Vordingborg, then made Copenhagen next morning in a single run. On the return the weather had decided to oppose us as much as it could. It was only at the third attempt that we succeeded in leaving Copenhagen at all, for a westerly wind was throwing into heaving corrugations the broad Bight of Køge. Several of the following days brought gales – and this in mid-August – but the advantage was that we were obliged to progress towards the Kiel Canal by a sort of 'grandmother's steps'. I doubt if children now play such a simple game, but when I was small there was nothing excited me more than the sport of stealing up from the rear and being sent back to the start if the object of attack looked round and saw me moving. This was precisely what we had to do with the Westerlies, except that our visit to Nyord was merely to have breakfast.

Nyord is not a large island and its harbour is smaller even than
that of Omø. As we turned toward it I wondered whether the
Thames Commodore could actually squeeze through the entrance
at all. But she did, even if her presence would have prevented any
craft other than a rowboat from entering after her. The Danish
harbour guide stated clearly that there were three Dukes of Alva
in the port. And so there were. They proved not to be drowned
noblemen but piles set in the water for moorings. The same term
is used in French – *Duc d'Albe* – and in Dutch, and perhaps in
other languages also. Imagining that there must be some historical
reason for the name – similar perhaps to the origin of a 'sandwich'
– I had often asked harbourmasters why they called their mooring
piles by this curious aristocratic title, but invariably they looked
at me with a puzzled expression and said that they called them
Dukes of Alva because that was what they were. The Dutch had
certainly heard of the tyrant who had once perpetrated horrible
cruelties in their country, but they knew of no connection between
the Spanish governor and mooring piles. It was not until we were
in Germany again that Siegfried Engel, who had translated the
Commodore's Skagerrak voyage, discovered from a very learned
dictionary that these piles had formerly been known as *Dikdalben*
or *Deichdalben*, – dike piles, that is. Maybe the Dutch were the
first to transmute the term to a noble and infamous name, and by
the time the word had become anglicised the duke had been
dropped overboard and only the 'dolphin' remained.

Nyord's town of Nyord By is a slight scattering of cottages on the
slope near the harbour, a reminder to any boatman from England
that the *by*-laws or town-laws of his local council at least owe their
name to the nordic peoples. The customs officer must have plenty
of time to tend the begonias and dahlias, marigolds and roses and
hollyhocks in his gay garden, for a foreign vessel must be a great
rarity. Perhaps he had given up all hope, for he never came to visit
us. Or maybe this was because Nyord itself was in the midst of an
administrative upheaval.

Though only a mile or two from Sjaelland the island, as one of
the few inhabitants explained to us, was so isolated that for some
time past they had not been able to find a teacher for the school.

Even a pastor was unobtainable, but every second Sunday the
incumbent of Steege came over to conduct a service. The island
had two very small general stores, but otherwise nothing other than
the cottages and farms, and young people found the place so dull
that they tended to leave as soon as they could. There was no
employment for them on Nyord (except that the post of teacher
was still open) and as the youngsters soon tired of commuting by
boat to Steege, particularly in stormy weather, the depopulation
of Nyord had accelerated to a point where the government had
decided to do something about it. They were building a causeway
to link Nyord to the island of Møn, hoping that this would bring
Nyord's inhabitants to the threshold of the modern world so that
people might actually want to live there again.

Unfortunately the scheme had not reckoned with Nyord's
postman, who was accustomed to fetch and carry the mail between
Nyord and Steege every day by boat. The bridge and causeway
would mean the end of the mail packet, and as there was nothing
he liked so much as steering his little craft across the windswept
shallows the thought that he might have to have a motor-van was
more than he could stand. The postman had simply gone on strike
and refused to collect or deliver the mail at all. If they were going
to deprive him of his mail-boat in the future he was not going to
help them now. Nyord's mails lay uncollected, the storewoman
explained to us as soon as we had pushed our letters and cards
through the letter-box slit. They might remain there for years.

These waters south of Sjaelland are as good a sea for exploring
in small boats as are those below Fyn. And the boats must be
modest, particularly if they are sailing-craft, for a six foot keel is
likely to run on the bottom even in the dredged navigation channel
of the Bøgestrøm which twists between the small islands and the
Sjaelland coast. One can stand on the bow and watch the fish
darting to either side as the stem approaches, fleeing to hide in the
green grassy weed which grows so thickly that from the air the
area looks like one vast meadow and not water at all. Strangely, the
half-salt of the Baltic is favourable not just to herring and eels but
to pike, and as we ran under the great bridge which leaps from
Sjaelland to Møn an angler rocking in his skiff beside one of the

G

pillars was reeling in a heavy one, lithe and powerful and vicious-looking. Vordingborg's fish market also had crates of pike as well as eels and the plaice which the fishermen were deftly skinning and filleting for their customers. The pike were being beheaded and gutted, these remnants filling barrels for the mink farmers and the flesh presumably going to make that excellent delicacy pike sausage.

Before we turned to Vordingborg I decided to touch on the large island of Falster, so we headed across the sands to round Bogø and enter the beautiful Grønsund – rightly named, for the fields and woods ripple down to its shores in waves of green. Our land map of the sound had a note that 'in the days of sailing ships scores of vessels would often be found at anchor off Stubbekøbing, waiting for fair weather in the Baltic', so at least we had the satisfaction of knowing that our own dose of recurring wind was nothing unusual. The run over the sands was in water so shallow that I was not altogether surprised to discover that when the Swedes had taken Bogø in 1659 they actually waded across the sea to attack Møn. Nowadays one may occasionally see a farmer drive his horses or his tractor across to the isle of Farø without sinking more than knee or axle deep, and this same extraordinary shallowness explains why the sea is covered with thousands of swans – for they have only to dip their necks to snabble the juicy weed from the sea floor.

Stubbekøbing is just one of those Danish towns with butchers and bakers, post office and brick town hall, a harbour for tramps and fishing-craft and grain barges, a pair of silos and a sausage stall. It also has a customs house, but as the local officer was on holiday we were visited by the travelling relief man who toured from port to port in his car, towing a caravan which served as customs post, excise office and all. It was provided with shelves of forms, rubber stamps, string and seals, and a table on which stood a photograph of the wife and family he had so nobly left behind when stern duty or the annual leave of others tore him away to roam Falster and enforce the laws of the crown.

I thought at first that the Danish habit of installing customs officers on each headland and up every creek was merely an ingenious way of reducing unemployment, but at Stubbekøbing we learned the terrible truth about this dangerous profession. After the travelling officer had accepted a glass of something tasty from the chandlers on the Kiel Canal he looked anxiously at his watch.

'There is yet time,' he said ominously. 'But before dusk I must drive to the coast south of the sound.' He looked inside his holster to check that his revolver was still there. 'Yes, it is a dangerous business.'

'Dangerous? Why? Not smugglers, surely.'

'Yes, smugglers. Plenty, plenty. Tonight is new moon. We have word there are five fast ships lying in Stralsund, ready to slip out. Probably they are now on the way. The Zone government, you know, would not stop them. They do not interfere. Perhaps they like it if smugglers upset our economy.'

The officer sipped his glass of whisky. 'Yes, they will try to land tonight,' he went on, tightening his belt. 'There is much coastline to watch. We think they will land where the woods are. We must be ready for them. And of course these are men who will stick at nothing.'

'What are they bringing? Political agents?'

'No, nothing so harmless.'

'Liquor, I suppose. Vodka and . . .'

'No, no. The boats are loaded with cigarette papers.'

Cigarette papers! Surely it was not worth having fast ships and being prepared to mount a gun battle just to smuggle cigarette papers, I thought. It sounded most unlikely.

The officer then explained that it was very worthwhile indeed. It seemed that the Danish government had a tobacco monopoly, or maybe it only levied the tax on complete cigarettes. That was why cigarettes were so expensive in Denmark. The financial security of the country was threatened by Danes who were crafty and unpatriotic enough to roll their own, and it was to stop such a wicked habit that the government had put an excise duty on cigarette papers – at the rate of about one halfpenny, not on every packet but on each individual slip of thin paper.

'So a packet is worth plenty money, you see. In his pockets a man can have thousands. In a speedboat, millions!' He shook his head. 'Bad men will risk the sea, a fight, anything to bring cigarette papers to Denmark. There are fifteen of us who will try to catch them tonight. Perhaps we catch one, but I think not. They are too clever. And watching the coast like this costs much money for a small country, but there is no other way. There is no other way to stop men smuggling the cigarette papers.'

'I know how you could do it,' I said, to cheer him up. 'Suppose the government took the tax off the cigarette papers, what then? There wouldn't be any point in smuggling them any more. You could all go home and fish instead of prowling about the woods like something from a wild west film.'

He considered. 'Perhaps, yes. But it will not happen. Politicians, you understand. . . .'

We gave him another tot to stiffen his resolve for the dreadful night-time encounter, and he took his leave. I hope he survived, and did not risk his life and love for the sake of anything quite so foolish as preventing people rolling a cigarette if they wished to.

Vordingborg, with its memories of the Valdemar kings, is a pleasant place. Unfortunately the great castle was sold as a brick-and-stone quarry in the eighteenth century and only the tall 'goose-tower' remains, topped with the golden goose which seems to scream defiance against the Wends and the Hansa merchants. The palace had declined ever since Prince Jørgen (or George) had gone off to England to be the husband of Princess Anne. He was a dull and heavy man, a good dancer but not imaginative in his remarks, and it is said that whenever news of a fresh disaster to the fortunes of James II was reported he could only exclaim in very proper court French, '*Est-il possible?*' At last he himself decided that the revolution would sweep away the Stuarts, and he disappeared to join William of Orange. The news of his defection was brought to the king. 'So, is est-il possible also gone?' he exclaimed. 'I only mind him as connected with my dearest child. Otherwise, the loss of a stout trooper would have been a greater one.'

The goose-tower was probably used for torture, and certainly as a dump in which unwanted opponents could be dropped through a hole in the floor to linger perhaps for a few years in damp and dark and their own excrement until they mercifully died. Today it is a tower where young couples can scamper up the stairs from their tents in the camping site at its foot, to watch the sunset in the happiness of each other's company and without a thought of those who died because the Valdemars did not like them.

One who narrowly escaped an even more horrible death was a Holsteiner named Klaas Lembeke. A wealthy widow in Holstein rightly suspected that Valdemar Atterdag would covet her possessions, so to protect herself she married as second husband the redoubtable Lembeke, a minor nobleman who had the familiar Jutish characteristic of preferring his own will to that of the Danish king. Valdemar was suspicious of Lembeke, and when the opportunity came he called the knight to step out before him and swear allegiance.

Lembeke looked around and saw that he was amongst men he knew and trusted. 'If the king wishes an oath I will give it,' he declared. 'And here it is. I will never be his vassal.'

The king passed it off as a joke, but as time passed he resolved to be even with the man who had humiliated him in front of his own court. He invited the knight to visit him at Vordingborg to patch up their differences. However, Klaas Lembeke knew enough of the king's reputation to pay no heed to the promise of safe conduct, and instead of taking a land route and being murdered he sailed to Vordingborg in his own ship.

It happened that among the royal servants there was a lad to whom Lembeke had often been generous – for he was a kindly man by nature – and when this boy saw the Holsteiner disembark and start up the path toward the castle with his companions he ran to the battlements and sang a song.

Das Wasser steht beim Feuer und siedet schon
Die Eber mögen nur kommen.

This blunt musical message that the pot was on the fire and there only lacked the boars for the boiling was not lost on Lembeke. He turned and hurried back on board, sailing out of the inlet just in time. And it later turned out that the boy had not exaggerated, for on his deathbed Valdemar groaned that he wished only that he could have boiled Klaas Lembeke alive when the cauldron was already seething on the fire in readiness.

If Valdemar failed to trap Lembeke, the Holsteiner paid him out dearly for the attempt. Knowing that one of the Danish bishops had the reputation of betraying confidences he waited for an opportunity to reveal the sins of his soul to this holy man in the confessional. He confessed that he was party to the fearful secret that a great many had sworn together that they would not rest until they had poisoned the king. Just as he had expected, the bishop at once hurried off to the palace and blurted out what he had heard in the confidence of confession, and from that moment Valdemar could neither eat nor drink without imagining that the victuals had been poisoned. The trick finally so worked upon the royal nerves that the king left Denmark and resided for some time in Bohemia, where he thought himself safer.

We lay a whole day in Vordingborg while the wind sent waves racing under the two mile length of the Storstrøm bridge. When we thought the sea west of the strait looked reasonable enough for the forty-mile run to one of Langeland's harbours we set out again, but within a quarter of an hour we had changed our opinion. As soon as I was sure of six feet of water across the sands lying off Falster we cut over into the lee of the group of islands which lie north of Lolland, and so came to three little harbours which we would otherwise never have thought of visiting. The first was on Femø.

Femø is a dream island, a rolling land of low hills and valleys without streams. It has two townships, North Town and South Town, each consisting of a few farms or cottages scattered over the north or south of the island without any obvious centre of gravity. We walked to the island's only shop (in North Town) to buy some bread and milk; but as the dairy proved to be two miles away in South Town the girl in the shop insisted on taking us there in the van, telling us all about the island on the way as she drove. She was as proud of Femø as a queen might have been of her own land, but she had sometimes been away from it. High School meant a journey to Sjaelland, where she now had a job awaiting her. And in hard winters the sea could freeze and then one might skate across the water to Fejø.

The harbour was at neither hamlet, but all on its own as the centre of trade with the great world outside Femø. The imports came in a sixty-ton barge with its own derrick, and the skipper swung the bags of fertiliser and other goods ashore to a small wooden warehouse from which the consignees could fetch them in their own good time. Before entering the harbour he would stop to put down an eel-net, for these shallow waters had an endless population of rather small eels. On the previous night his net had trapped six pounds, which he regarded as an average haul. Even in Denmark a daily quota of six pounds of eels must be worth having – and selling.

As soon as the unloading was finished the farm carts began to arrive with loads of cases of apples, which the skipper neatly swung aboard with his derrick and winch. Meanwhile another commodity of Femø's export trade was arriving in a succession of wooden wains pulled by farm tractors. These carts were piled high with bright yellowish-green gherkins, which were speedily shovelled into a pair of red motor-trucks which would carry them over the motor ferry on the first stage of their journey to a pickle factory somewhere in Lolland. Always there was something happening at Femø's little port, even if it were only the barge-skipper skinning an eel.

Femø's church lies impartially, neither in North Town nor South Town, but hidden at the back of one of the apple orchards. It is very simple, very beautiful and Danish in its spotless white-wash. Models of ships of departed Femø captains hang from the rafters, and I hoped that one day a model of the bluff sixty-ton apple-barge might join them, but probably it would be thought too humble a vessel to hang with the splendid craft already there. Over the chancel arch is a medieval painting which must have struck terror into young hearts across the ages, especially those of the boys. It is a last judgment scene. An angel leans excitedly out of a top floor window to watch the saved rise nude and golden-haired from the churchyard and stream through the door below. The angel has a long balloon protruding from his mouth like a character in a comic strip, with an explanation half Latin, half Danish, of what is going on. But the elect are, without a single exception, women. The men and boys have a very different fate, for a grey batman-devil with a fork is shovelling them into the mouth of an ochre dragon as though they were gherkins loading for the ferry on their way to become pickle.

On Fejø

X

Fejø, isle of onions – Onsevig – Holmegaard's glassworks –
Copenhagen harbour – the mermaid of Langelinie – Malmö
– the church of St Ibb – Grimhild and Hvenhild – Ranke's
revenge – Hven, the unchanging island

BY mid-afternoon the wind decided to take a siesta, and we
stole another step on our way westward by running to the next
island, Fejø. To distinguish it from its neighbour and to avoid all
possible confusion Fejø does not have North Town and South
Town, but East Town and West Town instead, and Østerby or
East Town is a real village with a long street of one-storey houses,
their timber frames painted bright green, or blue, or red, and the
roofs snugly thatched with reeds.

As we walked towards Østerby we sniffed the air and decided
that somebody was frying onions for supper. The odour increased,
as though all Fejø, both East and West, was celebrating some special
occasion with a communal feast of fried onions, and if the scent
had not drifted across the sea to reach us at Femø that same
morning this must only have been because the wind was a little
too northerly. Normally Fejø must be detectable by its scent over

a long distance for – as we soon discovered – East Town has a flourishing factory for fried and frizzled onions.

These Fejø onions are real king onions, tennis-ball sized, and they grow over the island from one end to the other. Muddy and squelching they were being dumped in heaps in the yard of the works, where a man shovelled them into a rotary sander which scraped and scrubbed them to a presentable cleanliness. The headman of the industry – at least, I took him to be so because he wore a white surgeon's overall – popped the washed onions one at a time into the mouth of a shredding machine which in a moment would dissect the whole bulb into hundreds or thousands of flakes. A girl shovelled flour over a heap of shreds, shook them up, then transferred them to large wire baskets which were dropped into a long trough of simmering oil to be watched over by an old man and a pair of brawny women strong enough to lift the trays. Fizzle and spit, frizzle and shrivel and fry, soon it was time to draw out another basket and pour its contents on newspapers spread over a table. Quickly drained and drying, the brown curly fragments were sent to climb up the stairway of a conveyor belt past two women who deftly snatched out any pieces of leaves or skin or coagulated onion before the mass toppled over a precipice to a shaking and weighing chute. An empty carton, a tread on the pedal, a shower of onion chips, and the woman at the machine handed the filled container to a very pale girl who put on the lid and stacked the cartons of Fejø's product in larger boxes. She never smiled. I thought she had anaemia, but perhaps it was just the effect of eating fried onion every minute of the day – for I noticed she was always taking a pinch or two from the belt.

The headman gave us each a carton of the product, and very delicious it was. Later I recognised the blue lids in stores all over Denmark, in Germany, and even in London. Fejø, it seemed, had the measure of the fried onion market, and a handful of villagers could supply the world.

As at Femø, so at Fejø the church seemed anxious to keep away from the villages. We walked to it through fields of onions waiting their turn to be fried, and we had just climbed up to the belfry to look out across the water toward Lolland when a man in blue overalls entered the bell-chamber. He did not even glance at us but took hold of a rope attached to a lever on the headstock, and walking over to one of the windows he stood there, smoking a pipe and looking out over the wide flatness of Fejø's pasture and marsh and onion beds, pulling rhythmically on the rope behind his back all the while. Thus he tolled the evening bell, though for what purpose we did not discover, for there was no service. Perhaps like the bell of Nyborg it recalled some local victory over the Swedes, or perhaps the Wends.

The sexton pulled the bell until it was swinging through a wide amplitude. Then he let go the rope, and the heavy bell continued to toll while he stood with his hands on his hips, looking down at the churchyard and blowing a wisp of blue smoke out of the sounding hole in the wall. Suddenly he spun round, ducked his head and rushed in under the edge of the bell to grab the clapper with one hand and drag on the rim with the other to slow the swinging. It was very neatly done, and since I myself could hardly lift the spare clapper which lay in the corner of the tower I wondered whether he had had many bruised or broken finger joints before he perfected the trick. Finally he gave three sets of three smart blows with the clapper, stuffed his pipe in his pocket, and left us.

Next morning we set off early from Fejø while the wind was still abed, but we had only been gone two hours before it awoke to find that we had tricked it, so in anger it began to drive steep seas across the shoals and shallows off Lolland. We could already see Langeland clearly ahead, but I decided to turn down for Onsevig and let the breeze blow itself out – which it did, in the course of a few hours.

Onsevig serves a few local fishermen, but I doubt if other ships often put in. There is hardly a hamlet, though curiously enough there is a hotel tucked away in the edge of the woods and presumably frequented by those who want a very quiet holiday indeed, where no business associates can find them. A mile and a half away down the road I came upon a small general store, one of the two which constitute the whole of Onsevig's shopping centre. The proprietor was evidently an old sea-dog.

'You English, yes? You know London? I been in London, many times. In Surrey.'

'In Surrey?'

'Yes, Surrey. Here Wapping, here Surrey.' He drew with his finger on the counter.

'Surrey Docks,' I said. 'So you were with a timber ship.'

'Yes, Swedish timber to Surrey. Evening I go whoosh – so!' He made a diving motion as though he were going to plunge into the cupboard where he kept the detergents. 'Whoosh, under Thames, see? Charley Brown's, aha!' He chuckled at his memories. 'Sometime I go whoosh, Dirty Dick's. Always whoosh in the bus.'

He counted out the eggs and weighed the slice of cheese I had selected. 'I tell you, Cap'n,' he said sagely. 'More doing in Charley Brown's than in Onsevig.'

Which I think may well have been true.

Only two weeks earlier, my wife and I had been aboard the *Aylesbury Golden-Eye*, a narrow canal cruiser on which Fred and Lisa Doerflinger were making an enterprising voyage which began at Market Harboro' and led them through the area of the Pytchley hunt to burrow underground in one tunnel after another and arrive in Cheshire. Poised at the top of the Anderton lift, the only canal lift in Britain, they waited for us to find them – just as in previous years they had often found their way to the most unlikely places on the continent to coincide with the *Commodore*'s arrival.

The watery cage of the Anderton lift dropped slowly down from the level of the Trent and Mersey canal to the ground floor of the River Weaver Navigation, a waterway which would lead us to the Manchester Ship Canal. Once or twice as a boy I had been halted at a bridge over the Weaver because it had been swung open to let some dirty little coaster pass up to the Imperial Chemical Industries plant at Northwich, but I had never seen anything so startling as the ship which on this July morning suddenly appeared round a wooded bend in the river below Saltersford lock. She was a huge vessel, a real *Mannigfual* by the standards of the waterways of Britain, and bold as brass she was chugging her way through the Cheshire countryside and astonishing the bankside cows with her sheer bulk. Of all surprising ensigns it was the Danish flag which flew from her staff, and as we see-sawed over her wash we looked up at her high stern and saw her name: *Holger Andreassen, København.*

What this giant could be doing, threading her course between the wooded hills of red sandstone, I could not then imagine, but now by a curious coincidence we came upon the other end of her trail and discovered that she ran regularly to the Weaver, loaded soda from the I.C.I. works just opposite the Anderton lift, and chugged away again to reach the Mersey and pass round the north of Scotland and the Skaw. Down the Great Belt she voyaged, and turning past Omø she would thrust her bows through the fishing village of Karrebaeksminde and throb gently up the canal to Naestved, where she would unload direct into the supply silos of the Kastrup-Holmegaard company. On the Scandinavian voyage of the old *Commodore* many years earlier we had run up that same canal without knowing that it had an intimate connection with the glass trade, for it was in fact cut by the energetic Count Christian Conrad Danneskiold Samsøe, so that the timber from his nearby forests could be exported. And it was the same Count Christian who founded the famous Holmegaard glassworks.

We heard about the *Holger Andreassen* when the *Thames Commodore* was sheltering in Køge from another bout of Aeolian exuberance and we had been invited to spend the day at Holme-gaard itself. As we watched the men deftly twirling the glowing lumps of glass on their blow-pipes we realised that it was North-wich soda from the River Weaver which combined with Belgian sand and Danish limestone to make the frit which simmered in the furnaces.

Perhaps it is partly the result of childhood memories, but I still think there is no factory quite as impressive as a glassworks. Much of the romance has now vanished from flat-glass making and a long, smooth, enclosed tank of steel tended by white-coated engineers or even by a god-like computer has taken the place of the streams and rivers of orange-red molten material which once would be poured from gigantic ladles, its surface throwing out a heat that parched the skin and frizzled the hair of anyone bold enough to dare to look at it. Yet there is still something marvellous about the way the flames play and swirl over the mixture of sand and soda-ash and limestone to convert it into a substance so unlikely and so beautiful as the crystal-clear and shining glass which emerges hot and panting from the end of the annealing chambers. And at Holmegaard more romance remains than at most factories, because so much of the manufacture is individual, the work of craftsmen. Besides, even the machine presses are spectacular.

Many factories bar their gates and shut people out from the holy of holies. Not so Holmegaard, which welcomes the public and lets people wander in to roam around and see the mysteries for themselves. Many thousands do so every year, and I suspect that when they have once been to Holmegaard they can never again pass the window of a glass-shop and see the little trade-mark of the crowned swan without remembering that fantastic scene in the blowing hall. If I say that Holmegaard's hall is just as one might imagine hell to be this is not meant as a reflection on the firm's industrial conditions or social responsibility, both of which are exceptional. It is just that there are so many caverns with white heat streaming visibly out of their doors, and dozens of little imps running hither and thither with devils toast-forks, some of them bearing between the prongs a soft and dull-red object – the soul, no doubt, of some wicked fellow left over from medieval theology.

Holmegaard glass is famous, both for its form and colour. And much of it is still a product of the 'off-hand' blower, who just dips his pipe in the furnace, pulls out a lump of glowing, treacly glass – and blows it by eye. It all looks very simple; and no doubt it is, to the man who can do it. But glass-blowing is not just a matter of strong cheek muscles. The hot metal has to be twirled, heated, blown, perhaps swung and blown again, until there appears as if by magic a glass bulb of exactly the right size and shape. Up comes a lad, hot and sweating from the devil's cauldron, who adds to the bulb a soft and wobbling sausage of glass on the end of a metal rod. Another twirl, a light pull, and there is the stem of the wine-glass. The gaffer who blew the bulb deftly removes his own pipe, and the lad hurries away with the object to put it on the conveyor for annealing. The ends will later be trimmed and cracked off by a machine which works tirelessly to cut the glasses round. A whirr, a ping as the sliced top falls, a tinkle as the remnants rattle down into a bin of cullet to go back to the furnace, and every second or two the machine delivers another glass, its edge fire-softened in a flame so that there will be no cut lips at dinner parties. Watching the blowers and the trimmers at work I could only wonder that so many glasses could be absorbed into the world at all.

One of the neatest inventions of a Holmegaard worker is the particular kind of low bowl with a turned-in edge which is blown – but not by mouth. The master receives a lump brought to him from the furnace, spins it swiftly to form a disc, and while he rolls the rod to and fro on the iron arms of his chair he bends down and scoops a cupful of water from a pail to pour it over a board lying on the floor. He places his glass disc gently on the wet wood, the water beneath the hot metal boils, the steam blows the glass upward and outward, and as the rod spins and the master bobs the soft disc up and down he fashions in only a few seconds a steam-blown bowl of a dull fading red which soon will cool to an azure blue or perhaps a deep green or archiepiscopal violet.

Much of the output of Holmegaard is automatic, but a machine process is not necessarily a dull one. It all depends on the mechanism and its inventor. One might perhaps expect a bottle machine to be a mundane sort of device, but it is not. The Kastrup-Holmegaard company in its three factories makes, I believe, nearly every bottle and jar used in all Scandinavia, whether for beer, aquavit, nail varnish, pills, sauce, ink, squash, cola, coffee, jam or scent; and as most bottles in the world are throw-aways the battery of bottle machines must work fast and tirelessly to keep pace with the sheer consumption of beer, aquavit, nail varnish, pills and the rest.

From an overhead furnace a bright red sausage which glass-makers call a 'gob' helterskelters down a chute into one of a batch of moulds, and while that is being blown out in a mould another gob is on its way into a second mould. And so on. The machines drip with hot oil and hiss with the steam of the mixture of oil and water which lubricates the chutes, and as each mould flies open the fingers of a blind but very intelligent robot snatch up the bottle and without so much as hesitating dump it exactly beside the last one on a conveyor which all the while is flowing slowly past. This, of course, is not so difficult an operation to plan. No sophisticated computer is needed. A batch of gear wheels and a few elliptical drives and one is home. But to see one of these machines work as fast as it can and never make a mistake is curiously fascinating. One has a feeling that one should speak in a hushed voice in the presence of any being so extremely accomplished.

Holmegaard is not in an industrial area, because Denmark has no Tyneside or Lancashire and is a blessed enough country to have escaped conurbations and planned trading estates. The name means 'Islet Farm', and the manor house of the farm is still there, standing on what was once an island in a marshy moor where oak and beech, birch and myrtle grew among the peat. Early in the nineteenth century a Holstein glassworks had found that peat was an excellent material for bottle-making, as it provided the heat for the furnace and the ash for the mixture, leaving only the sand and limestone to be brought from outside. Count Christian, the same ingenious man who had cut the 'Danneskioldske Kanal' to export his timber from Naestved, realised that the great acreage of peat bog around his mansion of Holmegaard could be put to good use. There was plenty of sand and limestone to be had near at hand in Sjaelland, and the sand was good enough for early nineteenth century bottles – even if better and purer sand from Belgium is now imported for the high quality modern glass.

Count Christian sent to Norway for a *bouteillemager*, who was to superintend the building of a furnace at Holmegaard, but while the work was in hand the Count himself died. However, the Countess Henriette carried on the scheme with great energy and in November 1825, two years after her husband's death, manufacture began and the first bottles were produced.

It was curious – but extremely practical – that the wages of the Holmegaard glassmakers were originally paid very largely in kind, the men receiving grain, wool, grazing rights and farm produce on an agreed scale. This meant that the home farm had to be developed, and soon other farms were bought and added to the works. The glassworkers originally lived on the farms, but as production increased the family built houses for them. In fact the Danneskiold Samsøes owned Holmegaard for more than a century as a private family business. It is their heraldic swan, proudly wearing a coronet on its head and a jewelled band around its neck which looks so confidently aristocratic upon the red or blue labels of the Holmegaard decanters.

The *Thames Commodore* was rewarded on her northward voyage by one of the motionless days which can make the Baltic so pleasant for the boatman, and she carried us from Vordingborg to Copenhagen lock without drawing breath. Most people know Copenhagen for its museums and its spires, and of course the Tivoli Gardens, but I doubt if anything in the city is as striking as the beauty of its ochre warehouses and russet hoist-gables which spread right through the town, parting here and there to give vistas up the city canals which now serve only as moorings for hydrofoils, small private cruisers, or a rare tramp delivering at an unfrequented quayside. The waterway is as busy as the Thames at Greenwich, and it has two famous features near its northern end – the great crane with its stone tower and a jib of heavy wooden beams, and on the other side of the channel the plaintive little mermaid who sits so small and exposed upon a rock in the shallows of Langelinie. Like the graceful figure on Temple Island at the end of Henley Reach she could not hope to escape for ever the hands of those who feel a curious but irresistible impulse to destroy a thing of such beauty. Just as Cromwell's men in England and the Revolutionaries in France blindly wrought their senseless fury upon statues or stained glass, so one night the little mermaid lost her head to the hacksaw of some fool who just hated and hated her because she was simple and beautiful. Only a year or two before, a deck-hand from a ship in Copenhagen's harbour had been so moved to see her on a freezing day of winter, cold and sad upon her rock amid the snow, that he had waded through the shallows, torn off his own jacket, and wrapped it round her slight form. He was a true boatman, that lad, and I think a true Dane also. Yet it seems that the people themselves had realised that she would be hated by a few as much as she was loved by many, and they already had a spare head waiting. It was merely a matter of brazing it in position and tidying up the joint of her neck.

I had always wanted to see Malmö if only because the jibs of its

Copenhagen

cranes were visible from the Danish coast south of Copenhagen.
I did not know anything of the place itself except that it was one of
Sweden's larger cities and had of course once been Danish. It lay
immediately across the Øresund from Copenhagen, so we dipped
our ensign to the brave little mermaid, ran out between Copenhagen's moles, and turned right – for between ourselves and the
Swedish shore lay the large, flat and apparently quite uninhabited
expanse of Saltholm, a few square miles of island which must
always have been little more than a quagmire if it has remained
undeveloped at the very gates of the capital. As we skirted its off-

lying sands we could see that not a single tree grew on it and there were no houses at all. It was a wilderness, set round with lighthouses and buoys to prevent the ships from running it down.

From the Copenhagen roads we could see Malmö, or at least the hair of its head, its blocks and silos and cranes standing erect over the edge of the curving and watery earth. But the circuit of Saltholm made our voyage across the sound a longer one than crossing the English Channel, and it was more than two hours and a half before we were off the entrance, running up our Swedish courtesy flag and wondering whether it would bring Jehovah's Witnesses down to the ship as it had done in other Swedish ports years before.

Although Malmö is Sweden's third largest port and bustles with cargo vessels and hydrofoils and train-carriers one may sail straight into the town and make fast at the end of the main basin where the medieval ring of canals connects with the sea. All is quiet and sheltered, except when once every quarter of an hour some giant ferry such as the *Gripen* or the *Øresund* churns the harbour into a seething hiss of water as it swings round to the ferry berth. There were fifty-nine sailings on this short sea route the day we put in to Malmö harbour.

Visually, the port is the best part of Malmö. The rest of the town is a collection of large blocks mixed with nineteenth century, and hardly a building survives from more modest days. The town hall was rebuilt in the 1860s to look like what an architect of the 1860s assumed that the earlier builders would have done if only they had known how – and I suspect they knew very well how but had the sense not to do it, preferring the pleasant but very noble form of the neighbouring Governor's Residence, where the three Scandinavian monarchs met in August 1914 to discuss what to do about the First World War, and very wisely decided not to become involved in it.

The Governor who once resided in this noble little palace was Danish, and he governed the province of Skåne or Scandia, from which the whole of Scandinavia takes its name. Skåne held the key to the Baltic by way of the Øresund – or at least one of the keys,

the real master-key being further north and on the Danish side
at Elsinore. So Malmö had a moated fortress, the Malmöhus, but
as it was almost entirely burned to the ground not very long ago the
modest remains of the gatehouse have been converted to a museum
of art and the rest cleared away. Only the tall rampart banks
remain, so the first impression the visitor has is that he has come
upon the town reservoir.

Malmö is not a beautiful city, but it is a port, and there is something curiously intimate about a port of the Baltic and its approaches, even when it is as busy a ferry terminal as Malmö, with
the *Absalon* and *Øresund* and the other big ships which come and
go between the two shores of the Sound. It was some time before
I realised just why the harbours of the Eastern Sea have that
character of crowding down to the quayside to welcome an
approaching ship, but of course it is the tidelessness which gives
Malmö and Hälsingborg and a score of other ports this friendly
appearance. The water lies a mere four or five feet below the
quaysides, and as even the severest gale is unlikely to drive the sea
to rise over the roadway the houses can be built right to the water's
edge. There is no foreshore, no horrid expanse of sludge and
bicycle frames to be revealed by the ebb and mercifully covered
by the succeeding flow, no soft glutinous mud-slope on which
the small craft will lie atilt like stranded porpoises. The sea just
sits in port, as constant as the Serpentine and almost as motionless
– except that in Malmö the churning and turning of the large
ferries is enough to send the water skirling round the basin,
sweeping the debris out to sea.

Malmö, as I have hinted, is not a very enthralling city. It has
supermarkets, and trams, and being Swedish it has excellent
bookshops – for the Swedes buy nearly ten times as many books
per head as do the British. In its centre is a cemetery which now
serves as a park, so that one may take a calm and somewhat
melancholy walk by the side of a disused canal and ponder
mortality and immortality, the fear of being and non-being, and
the way that modern theology has removed the notion of a last
judgment so beloved of medieval church artists, who obviously
enjoyed being commissioned to visit some such place as Femø to

paint the devils stoking a fiery, furnace-faced and four-footed monster with an endless supply of naked dead.

I have never been able to resist Swedish glass. Later, on her same northern voyage the *Thames Commodore*'s lockers came to hold a considerable quantity of Holmegaard from Køge and other Danish towns, but at Malmö the Swedish products lured me as much as they had ever done. Perhaps here again it was partly a matter of sentiment, for thirty years earlier my wife – or fiancée, as she then was – went with me to Liverpool, where we searched the shops to find the first object we would buy together for our future home. Suddenly we saw something in the window of a shop down Bold Street. It was the loveliest thing imaginable, and it was an Orefors piece, half bowl, half dish, somewhere between blue and green, and glistening with a flame-smoothed surface from the furnace. We bought it, and we still have it.

The second time we acquired some Orefors was actually at Hälsingborg, when the old *Commodore* was outward bound for the Göta Canal. It was so heavy a piece that the stout handle of the suitcase in which I carried it home from the boat broke. However, the bowl had already survived a rough channel crossing, and even now I can never see it without recalling that voyage through the beautiful skerries of the north. As we were again in a Swedish port I walked again and again past the windows of the glass shops to see if I could find anything as good. There were many superb pieces, as there always are, and I would have liked to fill the *Thames Commodore* to capacity. But there must be moderation, and when I had acquired as much as I thought I could safely carry home to England in the ferry-boat I returned to the harbour.

If we stayed at Malmö longer than was strictly necessary to buy glass and books, and visit the Tycho Brahe exhibition at the public library, this was for the familiar reason that the Baltic was up to its tricks again, trying every sleight of hand and isobar to detain us. First came a wind strong enough to send waves to rock us at the far end of the harbour, then there arrived a fog which set the diaphones going on every mole and lighthouse within all the miles of hearing. To cross from Als to Faaborg in a fog was one thing, but to sail out blindly into the Øresund amid all its great ships was quite another, so the *Thames Commodore* preferred to wait until she could see her companion ships, and all the beauty of a ruffled Baltic too.

The fog only lay in a line offshore and in banks across the Sound, so we could still look out over the basin as easily as before, and watching the people disembark from the Copenhagen steamers we noticed that two young Swedish girls with motor-scooters appeared to be waiting for friends, for one or other of them would enquire of the driver of a car as it came down the ramp from the ferry. They did not approach every motorist, but only one car in every two or three. The others they evidently decided would not be able to help them in their search.

Through the binoculars we could see that the girls were identical twins, blonde and with that strangely unreal straw-coloured Swedish hair curling out from under their white motor-cycle helmets. They were dressed identically in red trousers and blue jackets, and their scooters were also identical twins, specially selected to match their clothes.

After a while one of the girls went off to the café across the road and returned with two bottles of pop. Then they took up their posts of devotion again, hopefully asking one driver after another if he had any news of their beloveds, who were coming over from Denmark. Always the answer seemed to be negative, though we could see that some of the drivers thought the girls very handsome and perhaps wished that it was they who were so diligently sought. The ferries came, the cars drove ashore, but never was there a sign of the lost lovers. One of the girls went off on her scooter for lunch and came back an hour later to relieve her twin, but for the rest of the afternoon they both stayed at the quay, doggedly approaching the latest arrivals by ferry. In the brief intervals between ships they would talk with the customs men, but they never lost hope. It was nearly seven o'clock when they decided to give up, and scootered away.

Next morning we were surprised to see the girls there again, fresh and immaculate in their red and blue suits and shining white helmets. Evidently they had mistaken the day their true loves were to arrive, we concluded. Miriam began to be concerned and sad for them, and about noon she persuaded me to walk round the end of the basin and ask if we could help in any way.

'Poor things,' she said from the kindness of her heart. 'They've been there a day and a half already. It says something for the girls that they don't pack up and go home. You could suggest that they leave a message at the pier, or with us.'

So I made my way round the end of the harbour and approached the ferry quay. The twins were there, very fair, very fresh, and showing no signs of sadness or depression. But I did not offer them our help, for just in time I noticed that each wore on her jacket a neat little badge of one of the larger petrol companies. Their job was to welcome foreign motorists to Sweden and tell them anything they wanted to know. As for the lost lovers, these existed only in our imaginations.

Both shores of the Øresund are dotted with harbours for fishing craft and yachts, and during the next few days we put into several of them. Yet delightful though some of these little Scandin-avian Riviera villages may be, none of them put such a spell upon us as the isle of Hven (or Ven). This very beautiful island lies in the middle of the Øresund, and now that I have described it as very beautiful I must at least try to justify my praise. In a way there is nothing to Hven but a patchwork of fields and meadows covering a clifftop area three miles long and two miles wide, a tract of sea-girt land with a scatter of cottages and lighthouses, and only one building of any great antiquity apart from a few ruins. These ruins are underground and covered over with copper-bound lids, so that they do not strike the imagination by coming suddenly into view round a corner. In fact they are not easily seen at all unless the sun happens to shine down the apertures, and they are not very extensive remnants at that. But to a boatman who knows anything of the history of science these mute remains are more romantic and moving than many a battered castle keep with its tales of tortured prisoners and defenestrated maidens, for they are all that is left of the Uraniborg and the Stjerneborg, where Tycho Brahe first accurately plotted the heavens.

It was Tycho's discovery of the new 'star' (a *nova*, that is) in Cassiopeia that finally persuaded the young man that he would devote his life to astronomy, but the climate of thought in sixteenth-century Denmark was not favourable for a man of science and Tycho resolved to leave his own country and settle in Basle. In the nick of time King Frederik II heard of his intent and sent a messenger, who found the young man in bed and bade him get up and attend at once upon the king. To his astonishment this enlightened monarch offered Tycho the isle of Hven as a site for his observatory and laboratory, and enough endowments to relieve him of all financial worry.

So began the great days of Hven. But they were not to last, for King Frederik's successor reversed the policy of patronage. He stopped the grants, and Tycho was forced to leave his beloved country. Had Tycho not been so shamefully treated after the death of his protector and patron Hven and nearby Copenhagen might have become the scientific centre of the world. That was not to be, and the great astronomer sadly left for Prague, carrying away those of his instruments which could be dismantled. Some of them could not, for they were built into underground chambers to prevent the accuracy of the measurements being disturbed by the slightest movement caused by the wind. For then, as now, there must have been plenty of wind on Hven.

The outline of the Uraniborg, destroyed to make way for the house of a royal trollop, is visible only as a series of curiously curving banks behind the new church in the centre of the island, and a visitor who knew nothing of Brahe might be pardoned for taking them to be some hill-fort of the Vikings. At their extremity stands a fine bronze of the astronomer, his robes falling straight to the ground and his arms hanging limply. But his chin is thrust out and his face turned eagerly toward the sun or the stars above him, whilst below his feet and far away the chimneys of the copper works at the edge of Hälsingborg send long plumes of feathery technological smoke to drift across the Swedish countryside.

As for the one building of antiquity, that is the old church of St Ibb, whitewashed and with a roof of bright orange, but without spire or tower. Locally it is said that the tower was blown up by the Russians when they laid waste the whole island, burning all the other houses, cutting down every tree and leaving untouched little but the simple rock-drawings from the bronze age which can still be discovered among the shore boulders half-way between St Ibb's old church and the site of Tycho's vanished paper-mill where, after lamenting in a Latin poem the current price of paper, he manufactured his own. There is little evidence that the Russians ever came to Hven, and if the church once had a tower it probably just collapsed; but the church itself is part of the charm of Hven, and the way the squat building stands stolidly on its hill above the cottages of the fishermen so fascinated somebody in the Admiralty that the *Baltic Pilot Vol. I* is provided with a little sketch of it as seen from offshore. The detail in the drawing suggests that the officer drew it because he loved the place, and hints that if the Lords of the Admiralty were not so renowned for their prudishness he would sketch the lovely form of the Langelinie mermaid also and not confine himself to drawing so elegantly all the spires of the city of Copenhagen.

St Ibb has very much the name of a Cornish or Breton saint, but probably he was merely St James (or Jakobi), whose church was conveniently abbreviated to St Jb's and so became St Ibb's. Certainly the church dates from the eleventh and twelfth centuries, and some of the islanders say that there was at that time a certain man named Ib Skjalmson, who lived near Landskrona on the Swedish shore of the Øresund. This young man had heard the imperial call – which perhaps did not really apply to him as he lived outside the Holy Roman Empire – to join a crusade and teach the Saracens a lesson or two, and so he hurried off to join the German Knights. However, somewhere in Germany he fell sick of an epidemic and an old monk named Jacobus tended him until he was eventually fit enough to return home to Skåne – for either he was too sick to go to the Holy Land or more probably the crusade had already left without him.

Jacobus the monk made him promise to build a church in thanksgiving for his recovery, and this Ib Skjalmson undertook to do. Yet once he was safely home he somehow neglected to put the building in hand. A few years afterwards he was sailing across to Sjaelland when, like many a more modern small-boat sailor, he was overtaken by a storm. His boat was overset, but his plight was fortunately seen by some fishermen on Hven who bravely put out in a dangerous sea and saved him. That same night Ib was awoken by a voice which called him sternly.

'Ib Skjalmson, remember your vow. It is I, Jacobus, who recall you to your promise.'

And this time Ib did as he should have done before. He built the white church on the cliff at what is now Kyrkbacken (or Church Cliff) and at his own wish it was dedicated to St Jacobus. But the farmers and fishermen of Hven knew nothing of St James. They were more familiar with the man who had become their benefactor and had built them a church at his own expense; and whatever the ecclesiastical authorities might call the building, to them it would always be St Ib's.

So, one way or other, the church is St Ibb's, and it already stood there long before the Brahes took possession of the island. When Tycho and his family came to occupy the front seats he had the family arms carved on the ends of their two pews. Seeing them, I wondered whether Tycho did this as a matter of course because he was lord of the manor, or whether perhaps he wanted to assert publicly that he was of noble birth – as indeed he was, even if in the better circles of Copenhagen he was looked down upon because of his beloved Kirstine, a mere common girl, whom he had taken to him because a top-class wedding was not possible for any man with a false nose, even if that ersatz organ were of silver and gold, as his was. His own he had lost in a duel fought in Rostock about the rights and wrongs of an abstruse mathematical calculation.

The isle of Hven itself is confidently said by some to have been formed when a giantess who lived in Skåne had acquired the habit of wading over the Øresund to fill her apron with earth from Sjaelland and return with it to build up and remould the Scanian countryside in a better shape. On one of these trips her apron unfortunately parted under the strain, and down went the whole load of boulder clay into the Sound to form the island. The name of this giantess was Hvenhild, so the island's name of Hven is merely an abbreviation of 'Hvenhild's apron-load' or something of the kind. But in an old Danish saga Hvenhild was not a giantess at all. She was a serving maid, and her role was very different.

It is said that Hven once had four castles at its corners – and not all that long ago, for they are actually shown on a map drawn in the fifteenth century. Not a stone of any one of them survives, but at least the name of the North Castle is preserved in the tiny fishing harbour of Norreborg's *hamn*. Another stood on the cliff not far from the Hakens lighthouse on the point above the harbour of Bäckviken (Brook Cove) into which my wife steered the *Thames Commodore* as we approached the island from the Swedish mainland. Each of these two castles in turn is involved in the saga of the days long ago, a tale rich in the violence which was the life-blood of the north.

The island – the story tells – once belonged to Grimhild, a woman whose very name is forbidding enough, and who invited to a feast at Norreborg her two brothers Folker and Helled who lived in Sjaelland. The brothers were on bad terms with their domineering sister and no doubt they were surprised to receive her invitation. Trusting – which was particularly foolish of them in those Viking times of treachery – they found a boatman to take them across to the island, which was not as yet called Hven. The skipper tried to dissuade them, and so did a charming young mermaid who popped up like a tunnyfish and said that Grimhild was perfidy personified. Yet for some inscrutable reason the brothers persisted, and at length they landed at Norreborg. If any suspicions had entered their thick and honest heads these were quickly dispelled when their sister greeted them with every show of affection, feasted them well, and sent them off to beds which were each provided with a beautiful maiden under the blankets, as was often the custom in Scandinavia.

Next morning the climate of hospitality seemed to have changed, for Grimhild's two mightiest fighters were sent to wake the young men and challenge them each to a duel. The brothers agreed, and Grimhild somehow managed to extort from the simple Helled a promise that if he stumbled he would accept defeat and not rise to continue the match. Because her brothers were such honoured visitors Grimhild had had the floor of the hall covered with skins, and under them she had secretly strewn quantities of dried peas. The worthy Helled was also given a strong draught of mead to stiffen his courage, and when he strode in with flashing sword and stout shield to attack his opponent he staggered and fell. Recalling his promise he gallantly lay there, and one of his sister's men struck off his head. A similar fate quickly overtook his brother Folker, and it is difficult to read this ancient saga of the Danes without thinking that such a pair of simpletons richly deserved their fate.

Nine months later a boy was born on the island. He was named Ranke, and he had been born to Hvenhild, the maiden who had been placed in Helled's bed – the same girl whose name is perpetuated in that of the island itself. As Ranke began to grow toward adolescence he came to hear about his father, and how Aunt Grimhild had ingeniously wrought his death. Far from admiring his aunt he decided to revenge the father who had died so shortly after his own conception, and he succeeded in luring Grimhild into the eastern castle to show her the very costly treasures which were stored in the cellar. As soon as she had entered the chamber he darted out, slammed the door and locked it on her. Then he went to the edge of the cliff and flung the key into the Øresund.

No doubt Ranke thought that his aunt Grimhild would die a lingering death in the treasure-room, but as the key sank in the water below the cliff there came a mighty rumbling and crashing, and the whole of the mighty castle disintegrated and vanished. Perhaps this was why we ourselves could find no trace of it, but the Hveners say that when three fatherless boys are born on Hven on the same day, each bearing the name of whoever was in fact his own father, then the castle will appear again in all its glory and the key will return from the sea to unlock the door – and presumably to reveal the grim old aunt also. But considering the very small population this contingency seems unlikely indeed, unless the men of Hven are more unprincipled than they appear to be.

Yet an old church, a disgraced astronomer and a bloodthirsty legend are not enough to make an island beautiful. And Hven is, I think, probably the most truly enchanting island south of the

Swedish skerries. It owes this to the sun which highlights the cornflower among the blue-green wheat, and reflects as a golden sheen from the fields of mustard over which the wind sends waves as clearly defined as those of the sea below the cliffs.

Besides, it is not an island overrun by cars. Eleven years earlier there had been only one car on Hven, and it belonged to the doctor. As we made over the Sound towards the moles of Bäckviken harbour I wondered if we should find a car ferry taking caravans by the dozen to an island laid out with white-lined parking lots like cemeteries. But Hven had not changed. The motor traffic had increased fourfold, but there was room enough on the island for four cars. The supply boat from Landskrona was idling at the mole, and the villagers were boarding her to go to market on the mainland. At the end of the jetty the sturdy horses stood patiently at either side of the shaft of the rubber-tyred cart which served as the island bus. Three flaxen haired little boys with eyes as blue as the Øresund were fishing for shrimps and fry where the wavelets lapped the inner end of the harbour. The scent of corn dropped to the sea over the edge of the cliff, and the gulls sat on the ridge of the small general store, waiting for a day with wind enough to lift them effortlessly far above the island top. No, Hven was just as I remembered it, and I hoped it would long keep its own rare peace.

Hven, the Bäckviken bus

The battlements of Elsinore

XI

*Hälsingborg – the Sound ferries – young Sweden – Råå
harbour – the Kronborg – Rosencrantz and Guildenstern –*
Thames Commodore *turns southward*

ACROSS the strait north of Hven, Helsingør and Hälsingborg
face each other in a proud flutter of flags, red with a white
cross on the one shore, blue with a yellow cross on the other. Once
both towns were both Danish, next they were fortresses in rival
lands, each watching over the Sound – and in the Danish case
levying dues upon all ships which used the fairway. So well
established did this prerogative become that at last the maritime
nations had to club together and buy out the toll for a huge sum of
money. Choosing first the Swedish side, we ran in between the
stout bullnoses of the harbour of Hälsingborg and came to rest
in the North Basin, as we had done eleven years before.

'Didn't we pass you on the Thames?' It was an unshaven and
piratical-looking Scottish deck-hand who called to us, leaning
over the rail of a rusty old Panamanian which was berthed ahead

of us at the quay. I could not remember the ship – we had met so many on the way from Limehouse to the Øresund – but I thought he would probably be right.

'Ay,' I yelled. 'Up near Greenwich.'

'That's it, man,' he shouted back. And then, 'How's George? Seen him lately?'

'Not lately,' I answered. 'But last time I did he looked fine.'

I had no idea who George was, but that did not matter. We were often greeted in this casual and genial way by ships which had seen us before, though more usually it was just with a short toot on the ship's siren as we passed, a signal too brief to be taken for any important message such as that the vessel was turning to starboard.

I noticed across the basin a paragraph ship that we had seen loading in Hven's western harbour of Kyrkbacken. During the day other trading schooners came into Hälsingborg, all of them seeking shelter from a storm raging in the Kattegat. They were known as paragraph ships because they kept just within each paragraph of the law, which laid down tonnage limits for a given size of crew – which was usually man, wife, and a boy – in the same way as many of the inland barges of the German waterways were designed so that their tonnage was 999, because at 1000 tons another hand had to be carried. If the paragraphs needed to shelter we also should be in Hälsingborg for a day or two, I thought. And the idea did not appeal to me, because the year we visited Hälsingborg aboard the *Commodore* I did not like the place, and the things I had wished to say about it were so uncomplimentary that in the end I thought it kinder to cut from the proof the page which dealt with the town in detail.

On that occasion I would perhaps have agreed with the people of the Swedish province of Småland, who used to say that the peculiarities of the inhabitants of Skåne were easily explained by the fact that they were created by the devil when the Almighty happened to be busy shaping the beautiful Småland countryside and its virtuous inhabitants. The Scanians on the other hand related that one day the Lord God and St Peter were wandering together in the woods when they heard a fearful din. St Peter was sent to see what might be happening, and when he came back he reported that he had found Satan and a Smålander engaged in a fight with no holds barred. He had tried in vain to separate them, but they would not heed his entreaties. He thereupon lost his temper and drew his sword – as he had done on a more biblical occasion – and with a mighty swing he had sliced off both their heads with a single blow.

The Almighty commended him for his prompt action, but being very much against such slaughter he told St Peter to go back and put their heads on again, just as they had been before. If he then touched the necks with his sword the wounds would be healed and the antagonists would be restored to life. Peter hurried off to do as he was told, but in his enthusiasm he changed over the heads. Since when, according to the Scanians, the Smålanders have always had something of the devil about them, whereas those who have met the devil will all agree that he is in many respects hard to distinguish from a Smålander.

On this second visit it was only half past five in the morning when we ran in to Hälsingborg, and beyond the basin nobody was astir except the men who worked in the ceaseless ferry traffic and the driver of the municipal road-sweeping vehicle, a giant orange contraption which sprayed and swept and sucked to make Hälsingborg clean and tidy for a new day. I walked the streets behind the harbour until the first bakery opened, and I wondered why I had disliked the town so heartily on that earlier visit.

Hälsingborg is not beautiful. It does not pretend to be so. Almost all its older features have been swept away and replaced by modern blocks of no particular merit. The town hall, somewhat in the style of Calais but on a reduced scale, is a red and ugly building and the skyline of the town is spoiled by day with enormous lattices and framework structures of illuminated advertising such as one might find in the United States. Yet the place has a real character of its own, and if the fierce north-westerly wind was to keep us there for three days we eventually became grateful for the chance to make a closer acquaintance with this large Swedish port on the Sound.

The harbour is an important one, with deep-freezers and container traffic, and direct services to Hull and Manchester, East

Africa and the Levant, The Great Lakes, the Gulf of Mexico and even the Pacific, but first and foremost Hälsingborg is a ferry port from which stream so many craft that the charts of the Øresund have a red-printed caution to masters of ships to be careful that they are not run down. This warning is reasonable, for there is plenty of opportunity for collision. Almost the entire traffic of Copenhagen and Stockholm sweeps past the castles of the narrows whilst the ferries run on a course at right angles, following each other so frequently that at no time of day are there less than six on the way from one side or the other.

From breakfast to midnight and after, Hälsingborg bustles with all the colour of the comings and goings of these ships which carry the traffic on the shortest crossing to Denmark. A century and a half earlier there was only a single small jetty for fishing-craft and schooners, but modern Hälsingborg throbs to the sound of the giant ferries which come and go at such short intervals that there are in fact more ships than berths. On a summer's day four thousand cars are whisked across the water by the *Primula*, the *Kärnan*, and their sisters. Trains, waterborne in sections, hover-craft and hydrofoils buzz and roar over the water, and besides these are the swift passenger-ships which streak down to Trave-münde in Germany, the Sound Buses to Sletten and Hven, and the dear old craft which once was Charlie Chaplin's pleasure yacht and now makes leisurely runs to the smaller harbours along the shores, a stately vessel surviving from an age that is gone, a sort of relict fauna of the seas.

If the ferries carry their share of the motor traffic between Denmark and Sweden, the ships are also thronged with Danes spending a day in Sweden and Swedes out for a visit to Denmark, the youngsters in bright trousers and multi-coloured shirts, girls in the gayest that the synthetic dye industry has yet evolved, families with picnic bags and almost everything they will need. Not quite everything, however, for one of the specialities of the ferries is a swift duty-free trade during the brief twenty-minute crossing. One morning we crossed to Helsingør, and the instant that the hawsers were let go the windows of six serving hatches were opened to sell spirits and tobacco, coffee and chocolate and

H

whatever might be dutiable in the country only a bare two-and-a-half miles distant. And as the crowds of travellers are such that no customs system could hope to deal with one shipload before the next was at the quayside, all formalities are abandoned and a packet or two of coffee and a box of cigars 'at Sound prices' is considered just one of the little extras which any benevolent government might wish its citizens to enjoy when crossing the Øresund on a visit to the neighbours.

By day Hälsingborg is a bustle of coming and going. Then, in the evening, it changes its whole nature. The families disappear, but the ferries work hard to clear the long lines of freight-wagons and heavy trucks. Carl Milles' fine bronze on the pillar above the harbour square is floodlit, an angel of dull gold looking out over the dock-basins where the ocean ships are lying. The portly General Magnus Stenbock, defender of Hälsingborg in one of the fights with the Danes, stands out green and pigeon-spotted in the glare of the lights in the square before the town hall. A few tired hitch-hikers are still enquiring for rooms, but otherwise the waterfront is almost deserted. The grown-ups are at home with the telly or in bed, and Hälsingborg belongs to the young.

If all the flaxen tresses of all the girls behind the cattle-fodder silo on the North Harbour were twisted end to end they would make a considerable fathomage of hawser, I thought. And beautiful rope too, as fine as perlon and not altogether unlike it. Most of these youngsters had grown it to reach down to their waists, hiding all but their arms and whatever they may have been wearing at the upper end, and giving them an appearance curiously reminiscent of trolls – though I doubt if even the best of trolls were so beautiful as these young things. There must have been many hundreds of girls, blue-eyed and mauve-lipsticked, and every one of them in trousers, either white or of some brilliant combination of orange, magenta and green. Though they were trying very hard to look grown-up their height alone gave them away for the juveniles they were, the thirteens and overs, with an upper limit of no more than sixteen. They were assembled behind the fodder silo because inside the fence by the railway track there was a rock-palace from which filtered the strains of the dance. One had to pay to go in, so the more economically-minded young things all stayed outside, ogling the long-haired boys and just enjoying the sheer gregariousness of it all. Four policemen in breeches and forage caps stood embarrassed by their cars as though not quite certain what it all meant, and because they were perhaps ten years older they were so out of keeping with the youngsters that they might as well have been Martians.

When one is in the grandfather class one may look on these youngsters or at their rather older counterparts in Britain and other lands with scorn, or contempt, or even alarm. But I doubt if any of these sentiments were mine as I walked through the crowd of little men and little women on my way back to the dockside. After all, they were very ordinary young people, and with the cocksureness we all have when rather young they had revolted against the world of their parents and were determined to have nothing to do with it. The girls let their hair flow because older people couldn't. The boys grew theirs long to emphasise the difference between their youth and the balding patches of the greying forties and fifties. No grown woman could hope to put on the tights these girls were wearing, without looking ridiculous and displaying a certain breadth of beam; no father could adopt skin-fitting jeans and a vermilion shirt without appearing a clown. It was the old story of the rejection by the young of two generations which had allowed all the follies from Verdun to Belsen and beyond, and no doubt these boys and girls were right to reject such things – unaware that their own parents and grandparents might once have been quite as appalled as they.

Yet there was more to it than mere revolt. It was a despairing gesture of eat drink and be sexy, for tomorrow we die. Not die in a literal sense, but merely the awful knowledge that the world would go dead upon them. Not one in a hundred of these kids had any future but that of deadly routine in unskilled factory work or at best in an air-conditioned centrally-heated prison of an office where once every half-year a mechanic would call to service the machines which did all the brainwork. Until then every hour was precious, life had to be lived to the full, not the seventy soulless years of its hygienic span of welfare planning but the brief

time of freedom between puberty and the cage of modern employment. These few months, or perhaps three years at the most,
would hold all to which the boys and girls could ever look forward
– or so they thought, unaware in their pupation from childhood
of the deeper joys which might still lie ahead.

That our civilisation had done this to them made me sad, and
if I had a tendency to anger it was not with the youngsters but
with the world that could offer them nothing but the gay strutting
of pullets in the fleeting time before they became battery hens fit
to work regulation hours for a regulated number of years before
being quietly killed off with a pension. The lads and lasses of
Hälsingborg knew this as well as I, and all I could hope was that
the earth would go off its axis or undergo some other remarkable
and unpredictable change which would upset the schemes of even
the most enlightened, socially-planned community. This would
perhaps give us compass trouble on the *Thames Commodore* or
even cause the Øresund to freeze solid in mid-summer, but I still
thought it would be worth any such inconveniences.

We needed to lay up the ship for a few weeks while we returned
to England by ferry, and I had thought Hälsingborg might be a
suitable place. The harbour master was kind and helpful, but there
was so much traffic coming and going in the port that he could only
offer us a berth at a quay which would be somewhat pounded by
the swell if a gale should blow from the south-west. He studied
his plans and maps, and then he had an idea.

'Go to Råå,' he said. 'It is much more sheltered. I will telephone
and say you are coming.'

Råå was a few miles south of Hälsingborg, and almost opposite
Hven, but it was under the rule of the Port of Hälsingborg. Once
it was a great centre of shipbuilding, and before Hälsingborg existed
as more than a very small harbour Råå was a haven bustling with
sailing vessels which ranged the seven seas. It was a river port,
built on both banks of the stream (the Råå å in fact) which made a
convenient double bend just before it reached the sea, and so it
was sheltered in every direction. The fact that the river brought a
slow flow of fresh water was a particular attraction to us, for I
thought this would kill off the green weed and Baltic barnacles

which were making their summer home on the *Thames Commodore*'s bottom and would thrive if she lay motionless for weeks in salt water.

Scandinavia has many places which are quietly attractive and yet have no very special feature. Råå is one of these, and if it is a delight aboard a boat I think a landsman would probably find it just as pleasant – except that he would not so easily make the acquaintance of the ship-grocer and the harbour employee whose job it is to wheel up a barrow-load of hosepipe to any ship needing fresh water in her tanks. There is no need to own a boat if one wants to fish. Several times a day all through the summer a large schooner chugs throatily out of the harbour, loaded with anglers from the camping site a mile out of the village, and there is never any lack of fishermen willing to pay a few shillings to anchor for an hour or two over the deep-water shoal north of Hven, where the supply of fish seems inexhaustible. It was a cheap way of feeding the family, I thought as I watched the fishermen return, each angler carrying as many fish as the children could be made to eat or the wife to cook without causing a mutiny. And there must be something very satisfying for an angler when he goes off amid the scarcely concealed scorn of an unbelieving family and can return with fish not only caught but sizeable and edible.

The harbour of Råå is a business-like piece of river with a timber wharf, a slipway for tramps, a long, curving quayside with plenty of space for yachts, and a number of small wooden fishing craft, blue and white and green. It has an unusual industry and one which some people might find rather smelly, particularly if they should moor as we did above the pipe leading down from the floor of the small factory building beside the wharf.

Every morning there arrived a succession of trucks piled high with bales of fish backbones, heads and tails, guts, or whole fish which either had been condemned or were surplus to market needs. Compressed and frozen stiff as timber, the fish-meat steamed – or rather, its coldness made miniature clouds form in the air in contact with it, baby cumulus which fell over the side of the truck and vanished. A fork-lift whisked up the bales, which were then broken in pieces while a man in bright yellow rubber boots played a hose

over the fishy mass to thaw it and soften it so that it became a soft
heap of slippery pinkish grey. Other men with broad-tined beet
forks and shovels pushed or ladled the agglomeration up to a
conveyor, which lifted it to pour down a stainless steel chute into
a high speed mincer. Cod heads, herring ripe for phosphorescence,
filleted flatfish skeletons, surplus mackerel, fishes trampled underfoot in the market, all were reduced by the swift snicking blades to
a pulp which was stored in a silo, ready for the big bowser lorries
which came every day to fetch it away. *Minkfoder*, they declared
in bold letters along their gleaming sides. And mink fodder it was,
ready to be rumbled away along the cobbles of the wharf and taken
to the farms where the hungry, sharp-eyed and biting little
creatures would fall upon it greedily, building up their lustrous
coats until the time when they would be summoned to be skinned
and their rich furs would be cured, cleaned, and converted into as
fine a fish-fed mink coat as any girl could wish.

Råå

The village of Råå smells not just of mink fodder, but of the sea. Captain Street, Sailor Street, Ship Street, Helmsman Street, Skipper Street – each alley between the houses of the fishermen and sailors has its own straightforward and maritime name. There is a shipping museum too, one which disregards even nearby Hälsingborg's achievements and is filled with pictures of Råå skippers and Råå ships, and the insignia of Råå aldermen. An old Råå fisherman was in charge when we entered, his net spread over the floor as he swiftly knotted another row while waiting for the next visitor.

Altogether Råå proved just such a place as the *Thames Commodore* loved, and within a day she had made such friends with the grocer and the chandler, the harbourmaster and the mink-meat-thawer that she might have known them for years. She was quite content to sleep there for six weeks under the green canvas bedjacket she carried with her, folded away behind the saloon settee. Then at last we returned, dressed her, noted that the fresh water of the Råå å had stripped her completely of marine growths, and with handshakes all round the harbour we turned her nose toward the entrance, and steered straight for Elsinore, her furthest north.

> *Let us think of them that sleep,*
> *Full many a fathom deep,*
> *By thy wild and stormy steep,*
> *Elsinore!*

The trouble with poets is that they will often become emotional about places they have never even seen. Thomas Campbell's 'Battle of the Baltic' makes two definite statements about the Øresund strait, and one of them at least is wrong. The water may be 'full many a fathom deep', if one considers a depth of seven to eighteen fathoms to be full many, but there is no wild cliff or bluff at Elsinore, which in fact is a flat and exceedingly sheltered place well covered by the sands of the Lappegrund to the north. Yet Elsinore is very, very impressive, for its castle stands right out on the Kronborg point, dividing the view of the town into two and even obliging the place to have two separate harbours, one on

either side of the moated and mounded Kronborg itself. From the
deck of a ferry or the *Thames Commodore* the sight is one never
forgotten, the Kronborg standing very square and elegant like the
court of a Cambridge college except that it is topped with such
copper-oxide pinnacles of green as only Denmark provides, one
of them now containing a ten-sector light which can be seen
thirty-four miles away and which proudly announces itself once
every ten seconds with a double flash that seems royally to declare 'Kron . . . . borg'. And again, 'Kron . . . . borg'. In foggy
weather a moan more terrible than any groan of the ghost of
Hamlet's father issues from the castle to remind ships that the
Kronborg is still there, unseen, and they had better not run it
down.

It is natural that Elsinore should live on Hamlet as well as on its
shipbuilding, but the Kronborg has not become trashy. This may
be because, like Windsor Castle, it is still used by the crown and
has its sentries standing in striped candy-boxes, not quite sure
what they should do if all these busloads of escorted tourists should
suddenly turn berserk. There is naturally a plaque of Shakespeare
on the back of the rampart, and patient and motherly guides explain to their flocks of Greeks and Italians, Americans and Turks
and Spaniards that Hamlet was a real prince though unfortunately
he lived in Jutland and poor old Shakespeare probably set the
scene in the Kronborg because it was the only castle he had
heard of.

There is a curious coincidence about the *dramatis personae* of
Hamlet which I have never seen recorded, and which was mentioned
to me by a professor in Leiden. Everybody has heard of Rosencrantz
and Guildenstern, but these are almost the only characters in
Hamlet to have genuine Danish names and one might wonder how
Shakespeare came to choose them. Some literary experts believe
that a certain blank patch in Shakespeare's life was occupied by
his acting in a company travelling the Netherlands, and that the
company visited Leiden. If that is so, then one might guess that
Shakespeare's eye was caught by one of the acquisitions of the
library of the newly founded university, a copy of Tycho Brahe's
Astronomiae instauratae mechanica, which was printed at Hven,

on paper specially made in Tycho's own paper mill, and dedicated to the Emperor Rudolf II in Prague. This book carried a supplement with the precise locations of a thousand stars as calculated at the Hven observatories, and it was of course designed by Tycho as a bait to draw the Emperor to employ him, now that he was forced to leave his own homeland. The work succeeded, and Tycho was at once installed under imperial patronage.

The astronomer was somewhat sneered at in Denmark on account of his attachment to the simple Kirstine, and as he realised very well how necessary it was for the future to stress his own connections with the nobility, the end-papers of this vital book with which he was to sell himself as a court astronomer were emblazoned with the arms of two noble families with which he had some connection. And there they are – on the one side Rosencrantz, on the other Guildenstern.

The 'daily cast of brazen cannon' remarked upon by Marcellus may long ago have been given up, but the 'impress of shipwrights, whose sore task does not divide the Sunday from the week' is still characteristic of Elsinore, for in the South Harbour is one of Denmark's largest shipyards. It is this combination of industry and history that makes the place what it is, for the great castle standing on the Kronborg point stands against a backcloth of tall and moving jibs, and perhaps the new-painted funnel of some giant merchant vessel will peer over the ramparts like some Francisco or Bernardo stolid at his post. Elsinore is very, very impressive, and it is not a blood-stained ruin but a bustling port set around a castle which would have been just as splendid if Shakespeare had never known of its existence.

Yet inevitably the great fortress of the Sound has had its adventures, as in the seventeenth century when the Swedes – the continual villains of Danish history, just as the Danes were the perpetual disturbers of the righteous designs of the Swedes – invaded northern Sjaelland and actually captured the Kronborg, where they found immense booty of various kinds. Since the days of Gustavus Adolphus they had been inclined to pillage works of art to give a foundation of culture to their own land – Drottningholm and Uppsala are both well supplied with treasures from

Prague and Bavaria – and so they laded whatever they could of the Kronborg's riches and put them aboard a ship for Stockholm.

The Swedish command had, however, made one error of judgment. It was their practice to deport some of the population, and on this occasion there were some Danish peasants among the cargo. But there was also on board a young Danish naval man who had been captured years earlier, and who had carefully cultivated the Swedish Admiral Wrangel and won his confidence. This youngster managed to whisper to the peasants that when he judged enough of the crew to have gone below he would give a signal and they were at once to close the hatches.

Carefully watching his moment, Dannefaer gave the sign, and immediately turned on the captain and ordered him to surrender. The officer resisted, so the Dane killed him. Then, standing behind the mate with a drawn sword he ordered him to steer for Copenhagen. The peasants had meanwhile dropped the hatches and the few Swedish sailors on deck prudently made no attempt to interfere. The ship sailed into Copenhagen and unloaded the booty, which was eventually restored to the Kronborg.

It was to Copenhagen that we also were bound as we ran out of the fishing harbour early in the morning. We had hoped that the Baltic weather might at last become calmer and more settled, so that the *Thames Commodore* could forge her way up to the Skagerrak and explore the Telemark Canal in Norway. As she turned away from the quay I had to make the decision – left or right. It was fortunate that I chose right and headed southward, for the strong winds which were to follow us for weeks would have made the Skagerrak very inhospitable for a boat which, however brave and determined, was really a river and canal craft. Norway, I decided, must wait for another year. We would run instead for Lauenburg and there enter a waterway which, in its original form, was the oldest watershed canal in Europe, the Stecknitz Canal of the fourteenth century.

The Kronborg lay at first on the starboard bow, but soon on the beam and then astern, its roof glinting in the early sun which rose to flood it with a gleam of gold from the hills behind Hälsingborg

across the Sound. Hven lay faintly in the haze. Hidden in the
distance but only a few hours away was Copenhagen, and the route
which we should follow southward between the soft shores and
peaceful sounds of Denmark's pleasant isles.

INDEX OF NAMES

*(For ease of reference people and legendary creatures or beings are
listed in italics)*

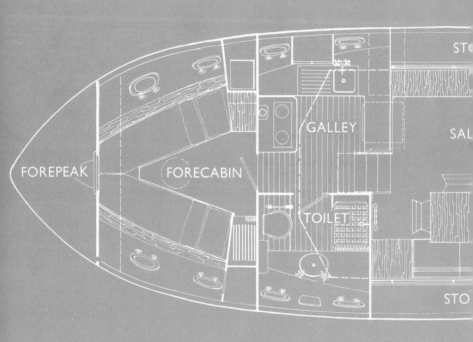